Essential Skills for Youth Work Practice

Essential Skills for Youth Work Practice

Kate Sapin

Los Angeles • London • New Delhi • Singapore • Washington DC

© Kate Sapin 2009

SAGE Publications Ltd
1 Oliver's Yard
55 City Road
London EC1Y 1SP

SAGE Publications Inc.
2455 Teller Road
Thousand Oaks, California 91320

SAGE Publications India Pvt Ltd
B 1/I 1 Mohan Cooperative Industrial Area
Mathura Road
New Delhi 110 044

SAGE Publications Asia-Pacific Pte Ltd
33 Pekin Street #02-01
Far East Square
Singapore 048763

Library of Congress Control Number: 2008924998

British Library Cataloguing in Publication data

A catalogue record for this book is available from the British Library

ISBN 978-1-4129-3092-5
ISBN 978-1-4129-3093-2 (pbk)

Typeset by Keyword Group Ltd
Printed in Great Britain by The Cromwell Press Ltd, Trowbridge, Wiltshire
Printed on paper from sustainable resources

Thanks

Thank you to the young people and colleagues I have met through youth work practice. Thanks also to past and present course participants, tutors, assessors and supervisors, employers and other colleagues I have worked with on the University of Manchester's community and youth work learning programmes. Your examples and insights have formed this book.

Thanks to those who read drafts and made suggestions: Barbara Sapin, Alison Healicon, Joanna Connor, Marcella Walsh, Tania de St Croix, Dorothy Cantwell, Graham Griffiths, Joseph Morris-Doherty, Amelia Lee, Leigh Cook, Gill Potts, Gill Clarke, Baljeet Gill, Abby Escreet, Mary Kenny, Dan Moxton, Richard Davis and Hannah Thomas.

Love to family and friends and thanks for your encouragement and support.

Contents

List of figures

List of tables

About this book

Essential Skills for Youth Work Practice attempts to bring together a relevant body of knowledge that can be applied to practice in different youth work settings and roles. The book presents a range of examples that address the core values and the purpose of youth work and that are grounded in participatory and anti-oppressive practice. This is not to say that all youth work conforms to the definitions and principles presented. The intention is that the analysis provided might assist the readers to become involved in continued debate and reflection to develop their practice and their organisations.

Youth workers and their analysis of practice have defined the structure, content and approach of *Essential Skills*. The book is based on *praxis*, or reflection on action, which has taken place through joint work, evaluations and discussions with experienced youth workers, community workers, activists and informal educators for well over twenty years at the University of Manchester. The process of developing relationships with young people and enabling their participation reflects youth workers' actual experiences. The practice examples and suggestions from youth workers are rooted in real events and projects. Some are single instances; some are typical examples drawn from frequently occurring experiences. Discussions of genuine professional dilemmas have established the values, principles and key issues explored in the text.

Essential Skills for Youth Work Practice attempts to reflect the wide range of experience that has contributed to this book. Discussions included paid and unpaid youth workers working with children and young people, young adults and mixed generational groups. Whilst the majority of those participating have been based in England, individuals involved in similar work in other countries and on exchange programmes with countries around the world have also played their part. The practitioners, as well as the young people and the communities they work with, included individuals who have self-defined or come together as white or black British, Bangladeshi, African, African-Caribbean, Jewish, Indian, Pakistani, Chinese, Vietnamese, Travellers, refugees, young parents, disabled people, lesbian, gay, bi-sexual, transgender, women, tenants and residents, and more. Many have been based in local government departments and other services relevant to young people, whilst others have worked in "third sector" organisations, such as non-government organisations and charitable trusts. The projects, groups, organisations, networks, multi-agency structures and communities in which they work have been defined by geographic area, housing development, community of interest or specific need, issue or activity. Both similarities and differences are explored.

Essential Skills for Youth Work Practice takes the reader through the process of youth work practice, from initial contacts with young people to their participation in the management of projects. The introduction provides a definition of youth work, an explanation of the practice-based approach of the profession and the underlying values and principles for practice. Part A establishes some of the ways in which youth workers bring their understanding of the values and principles of youth work to practice in different settings, make contact with young people and build appropriate and voluntary relationships. Part B looks at the skills of forming groups, bringing young people together to have fun, learn and deal with the ups and downs of working together. Part C looks at how youth work can make an impact through enabling young people to participate in developing and managing research and other projects. The final chapter examines how youth workers maintain a professional focus to their practice by using and providing supervision.

Whilst the main emphasis is on examples of practice, *Essential Skills* also provides some signposting to key texts, definitions and theories. Each chapter begins with a summary of the content. The headings within the chapter highlight some relevant essential skills, which are then listed at the end with some recommendations for further reading. Practice examples, quotes from key theorists, suggestions and figures are in numbered boxes to enable easy access. Lists of figures and tables appear after the contents page. Practice examples in shaded boxes are provided for illustration rather than as prescriptions for practice. Except where indicated otherwise, the practice examples in italics are the voices of youth workers. Sources and all of the recommended reading references are listed at end of the book. Definitions for youth work terms and phrases are provided in an appendix as guidance for practice rather than to be pedantic. For example, the distinctions drawn between policies and procedures or principles and values, are only suggestions.

Introduction

'Youth work', as used in this book, identifies a specific approach to professional practice with young people based on certain core values and principles defined in this introduction. Youth work can have a positive impact on young people and their communities through a process of developing enjoyable activities, appropriate services and relevant learning based on young people's expressed needs and interests. The starting point of this process involves careful listening to young people about their understanding of themselves and their situations. Youth workers endeavour to establish a voluntary and equal relationship with the young people with whom they work. The practice enables young people to make choices about becoming involved, take responsibility and work together to address change in their lives.

Youth workers usually work with young people aged between six and eighteen years old. Although abilities, rates of maturation and circumstances vary widely amongst individuals, in general, children below the lower end of the spectrum usually require more supervision of activities and adult intervention than is typically provided by youth workers. Younger children are often less ready to undertake responsibility for social interactions outside of their family or structured environment such as school. Individuals above the upper age range are usually more interested in and ready for adult responsibilities, activities and services. Young people between these two groups can benefit most from the independent social opportunities provided by youth work.

The period of transition to maturity that young people experience is a process of development involving a series of changes and choices. Most individuals undergo major physical, mental, social, emotional, sexual, domestic and psychological changes and development. Youth work is one of the ways in which adults can work with young people to provide positive, creative and challenging experiences to support these transitions. Opportunities are developed for young people to build and act upon to further their understanding of the personal, moral, spiritual, social, economic and political aspects of their lives. Through participation in youth work, young people develop confidence. The skills, knowledge and awareness acquired can assist them to make informed choices for themselves and for anyone for whom they are or become responsible. The process is at their pace, on their terms and based in their realities.

Although youth work often provides a positive, therapeutic and preventative function for young people and society, youth work practice aims to be liberational as defined by Nyerere (1976, see Box 1) rather than prescriptive. The primary purpose of the youth work practice outlined in *Essential Skills* is to involve young people in decisions about issues that affect them. Learning from participation and from each other, young people gain control over decisions relating to their lives.

Box 1: A definition of education for liberation

'The personal and physical aspects of development cannot be separated. It is in the process of deciding for himself what is development, and deciding in what direction it should take his society, and in implementing those decisions, that Man develops himself. For man does not develop himself in a vacuum, in isolation from his society and his environment; and he certainly cannot be developed by others. Man's consciousness is developed in the process of thinking, and deciding and of acting. His capacity is developed in the process of doing things.

But doing things means co-operating with others, for in isolation Man is virtually helpless physically, and stultified mentally. Education for liberation is therefore also education for co-operation among men, because it is in co-operation with others that Man liberates himself from the constraints of nature, and also those imposed upon him by his fellow men. Education is thus intensely personal. In the sense that it has to be a personal experience – no one can have his consciousness developed by proxy. But it is also an activity of great social significance, because the man whom education liberates is a man in society, and his society will be affected by the change which education creates in him.

There is another aspect to this. A Man learns because he wants to do something. And once he has started along this road of developing his capacity he also learns because he wants to be; to be a more conscious and under-standing person. Learning has not liberated a man if all he learns to want is a certificate on his wall, and the reputation of being a 'learned person' – a possessor of knowledge. For such a desire is merely another aspect of the disease of the acquisitive society – the accumulation of goods for the sake of accumulating them. The accumulation of knowledge or, worse still, the accumulation of pieces of paper which represent a kind of legal tender for such knowledge, has nothing to do with development.' (Nyerere, 1976: 27)

Rather than defining youth work simply as a type of social service providing information, advice and activities, *Essential Skills* explores a process of working with young people in voluntary relationships to design and implement activities, projects and services based on their own concerns and interests, rather than those that are exclusively societal. Youth work practice promotes change and development through a commitment to relationships based on respect for young people, listening to them and mutual learning. This definition relates to community work as defined by the *Federation of Community Development Learning* (see Box 2). This practice-based approach to youth work requires a focus on *praxis*, or action based on reflection, and on the relationship between youth workers and young people.

Box 2: A definition of community work

'Community work is about the active involvement of people in the issues that affect their lives and focuses on the relation between individuals and groups and the institutions which shape their everyday experience. It is a developmental process that is both a collective and individual experience … . The key purpose is to work with communities experiencing disadvantage, to enable them collectively to identify needs and rights, clarify objectives and take action to meet these within a democratic framework which respects the needs and rights of others.' … (*Federation of Community Development Learning* website)

Recognising the core values

Youth work practice has a clear relationship with values and principles (see the figure in Box 3). The values provide the foundation

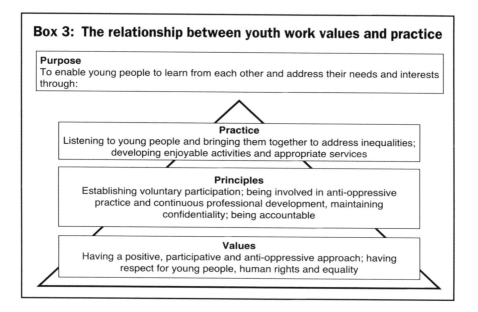

Box 3: The relationship between youth work values and practice

Purpose
To enable young people to learn from each other and address their needs and interests through:

Practice
Listening to young people and bringing them together to address inequalities; developing enjoyable activities and appropriate services

Principles
Establishing voluntary participation; being involved in anti-oppressive practice and continuous professional development, maintaining confidentiality; being accountable

Values
Having a positive, participative and anti-oppressive approach; having respect for young people, human rights and equality

for a profession that starts 'where young people are' with a positive, participative approach to young people and their human rights. The principles apply the values more directly to youth work practice and define the essential activities of enabling young people's voluntary participation and actively seeking accountability to them and their communities. To carry out ethical youth work, youth workers need to be involved in continuous professional development to clarify any boundaries and barriers to their role. These values and principles lead to the approach to youth work practice that is outlined in *Essential Skills*.

Applying values to practice

Positive practice means that youth work should be enjoyable, pro-active and make a difference. Taking a *positive approach* allows a youth worker to appreciate the need for fun, warmth and nurture as well as change and development. Youth work needs to be fun for young people to encourage their participation in voluntary activities and to counter the effects of oppression. Rather than seeing young people as problems, victims or needing help, youth workers welcome young people to participate in activities that they enjoy and/or benefit from because they want to be involved. Youth work is also about learning and taking action to address their concerns.

The *participative nature* of youth work recognises young peoples' rights to choose and to be involved in decisions over issues that affect them. Recognising, valuing and building on participants' contributions and experiences puts young people 'at the centre' of youth work practice. Young people make decisions, take responsibility and develop greater control over their lives while learning new skills and finding out about new opportunities. Participative practice brings groups of young people together so that they gain support and learn from each other and encourages them to 'keep it real' by exploring genuine and realistic options. Rather than simply providing a service, youth work encourages young people to find their own solutions to problems and develop their own plans and organisations to address issues affecting them.

The *anti-oppressive approach* acknowledges and addresses young people's all too frequent exclusion from these decisions as well as the neglect, rejection and denial of opportunities experienced by some individuals and groups more than others. Societal attitudes and practices can mean that many young people are denied access to a range of opportunities available to a privileged minority. Racism, sexism, heterosexism, class and disabilism can exclude certain individuals and groups from equal access to education, employment, housing, health and leisure activities. Other individuals, due to birth or upbringing, are denied safety, security or love. Youth work can go some way to address these issues through assisting young people to make sense of their circumstances and broaden their understanding of ways to move forward. Youth workers raise awareness of issues, develop strategies to address inequalities and are pro-active in carrying them out. The pervasiveness of oppressive influences on attitudes and behaviour requires an active and positive approach to individuals and groups that are oppressed.

The approach used in *Essential Skills* is that youth work needs to be linked in with communities. Communities are the context and environment for young people's lives; knowing about their communities assists mutual understanding and can provide support for practice. Networking and interactions with parents, neighbours, local shopkeepers and other relevant agencies and societal structures can enhance anti-oppressive practice and enable young people to participate more fully in those arenas. Youth workers observe and intervene in community and institutional processes and tasks to enable young people's participation. Youth workers who are restricted through targets or duties to working only with young people may find that their perspective and activities are limited. Youth workers who are able to allocate time to outreach work and participation in local committees and forums will be able to promote youth work values and practice, research and identify relevant issues and involve other members of the community as volunteers and activists.

Applying the principles to practice

The values and principles of youth work enable youth workers to address the effects of inequalities in society, through their practice of encouraging individuals from a variety of experiences to communicate, share perspectives and come together to enjoy themselves. The table in Box 4 outlines same examples of how youth work principles relate to practice.

Box 4: Youth work principles and their relationship to practice

Principle	Practice
Respect for young people	<ul><li>Listen to young people</li><li>Engage in dialogue</li><li>Learn from them</li><li>Value young people's points of view</li><li>Recognise that young people may have a different perspective from other age groups</li><li>Respect individuality; reject negative labels</li><li>Recognise young people's rights to liberty and equality and to be treated with dignity</li><li>Promote positive images of and opportunities for young people</li><li>Challenge negative stereotypes of young people</li><li>Be open and honest with young people.</li></ul>

Continued

Box 4 - *Cont'd*

Voluntary participation	• Allow young people to choose to participate • Create welcoming and accessible environments and enjoyable activities • Facilitate activities based on expressed needs and interests • Keep young people informed about opportunities and resources • Provide opportunities for young people to take responsibility and make choices in relation to youth work and in their lives • Encourage and enable young people to have a voice, participate in decision-making and address issues that affect them.
Accountability	• Work with young people and other members of the community to involve them in youth work activities, opportunities and decisions • Ensure that resources are allocated according to clear criteria • Seek out feedback and ideas from diverse groups and individuals • Recognise that responsibilities to young people may be in conflict with others • Prioritise work that benefits young people • Monitor and evaluate practice, respond to feedback and accept responsibility for own shortcomings.
Anti-oppressive	• Recognise that youth work is for the benefit of all young people and particularly those whose human rights are at risk • See youth work as an agency for change and challenge for the status quo • Take positive steps to address oppression and the effects of oppression • Respect differences and build bridges between different groups and individuals • Identify and promote positive role models, images and participation by individuals and groups often excluded from participation or facing societal oppression • Identify and address barriers to participation, challenge negative discrimination and provide access to appropriate resources and services • Avoid stereotyping, negative discrimination, particularly in relation to 'race', gender, class, sexual orientation, nationality, age and other identity issues • Educate self and others about barriers and enablers to participation and the causes and effects of oppression • Explore the implications and application of anti-oppressive perspectives, such as feminism, a black perspective, a social model of disability • Inform others about oppressive language, attitudes, practices and structures • Continuously re-assess practice in relation to negative discrimination through consultation and evaluation • Take responsibility for own actions and education.

Box 4 - *Cont'd*

Confidentiality	• Recognise that young people may disclose information to youth workers that they are not ready to tell others
	• Be aware that information about individuals should not be recorded or passed on to others except in exceptional circumstances related to safety
	• Preferably prior to disclosure, inform young people of any boundaries to confidentiality, especially any situations that could require further action or intervention.
Ethical practice	• Seek out information and other perspectives on practice
	• Be involved in continuous professional development and supervision
	• Develop clarity about the role of a youth worker, use of self and professional boundaries
	• Be reliable and trustworthy
	• Maintain youth work values and principles as above.

Further reading about youth work values and principles

Hope and Timmel (1995); Banks (1999); (The) National Youth Agency (2004)

PART A   Building bridges

The first part of *Essential Skills for Youth Work Practice* focuses on the skills required for building bridges to establish appropriate relationships with young people. Chapter 1 establishes the primary concerns of youth work practice, namely to keep in mind who youth work is for and to promote the voluntary nature of youth work. Chapter 2 looks at the varied settings for youth work practice and the role of a youth worker in developing positive, participative and anti-oppressive practice within them. Chapter 3 looks at the first stages of the process of youth work, which starts with reaching out to young people to make contact and get to know them. The nature of the autonomous and voluntary relationships that are the foundation for youth work practice is examined in Chapter 4.

CHAPTER 1: Youth work practice

This chapter introduces the role, responsibilities and duties of a youth worker in relation to the core values and principles for practice.

A youth worker's role in addressing the purpose of youth work as outlined in the introduction to this book is to promote social, educational and political change at various levels. Youth workers provide information and other support to effect changes in attitudes and practice within young people, services, communities and society as a whole in order to enable young people to have a say in the issues that affect them. Some organisations or youth workers may focus more on individual or personal change than organisational or societal development. These distinctions are sometimes reflected in the terms used as job titles.

Many organisations and professionals working with young people see their role as primarily educative or protective. Providing support for young people to become responsible adults, particularly when more standard provision seems to be ineffective, is compatible with youth work. Use of the term 'youth development worker' can indicate this focus on young people's positive transitions to adulthood. PAULO (see Box 1.1) also emphasise the developmental and educational functions of youth work for young people.

Involving communities and having a community perspective provides a wider perspective on the role of a youth worker. According to Youth Work Central (on their website) 'youth workers help to shape the lives of the young people they work with. These young people in turn, will shape the futures of their own communities'. The title 'youth and community worker' may be used in recognition of the value of involving members of the community or of working with young people within the context of their communities. The Development Education Association's more political definition of global youth work highlights the need for action to develop change (see Box 1.2). This approach implies a connection with developing a community's capacity for sustainability often associated with the title of 'community development worker'. The FreeChild Project advocates 'social change led by and with young people around the world, particularly those who have been historically denied the right to participate' (on their website), which further celebrates anti-oppressive practice.

Box 1.1: A definition of the purpose of youth work

'To work with young people to facilitate their personal, social and educational development, and enable them to gain a voice, influence and place in society in a period of their transitions from dependence to independence ... .
Informed by Youth Work values, the role of the youth worker is therefore to work with young people in ways that are educative, participative, empowering and promote equality of opportunity and social inclusion.' (PAULO, 2002)

Other terms used to describe the role of a youth worker reflect different emphases in relation to role. The terms 'enabler,' 'facilitator' or 'emancipator' focus on the process of developing young people's understanding of their own and others' power and control. 'Animators' or 'informal educators' work with young people to develop their self-expression through art, drama, poetry or music and may also be known as 'arts development workers'. A focus on particular activities used 'as a vehicle' for informal education may also be highlighted, e.g. a 'sports development worker' or 'health development worker'.

Box 1.2: A definition of Global Youth Work

'Global Youth Work ...
1. starts from young people's experiences and encourages their personal, social and political development
2. works to informal education principles and offers opportunities that are educational, participative, empowering and designed to promote equality of opportunity
3. is based on an agenda that has been negotiated with young people
4. engages young people in critical analysis of local and global influences on their own lives and communities
5. encourages an understanding of the world based on the historical process of globalisation
6. recognises that the relationships between, and within, the North and South are characterised by inequalities caused by globalisation
7. promotes the values of justice and equity in personal, local and global relationships
8. encourages an understanding of, and appreciation for, diversity – locally and globally
9. sees the people and organisations of both the North and South as equal partners for change in a shared and interdependent world
10. encourages action that builds alliances to bring about change.'

The Development Education Association website

Checking practice for youth work values and principles

As youth workers carry out their practice in different settings and organisational structures, often with other professionals and workers from other occupations, the following checklist (Box 1.3) based primarily on Bernard Davies' (2005) *Manifesto for Youth Work* can be used to identify whether the practice clearly relates to the principles of youth work. An essential skill is to be able to apply this checklist to practice even when working within an organisation that may have a very different approach to working with young people.

Box 1.3: A checklist for youth work practice

Davies (2005) asks:
- 'Do the young people choose to become involved? Is their engagement voluntary?
- Is the practice seeking to tip the balance of power to young people?
- Are the young people viewed and welcomed as young people? Are their contributions respected and valued?
- Is the practice starting where young people are? Is the expectation that they will be able to relax, meet friends and have fun?
- Is the practice focused on young people as individuals?
- Is the practice respectful of young people's peer networks and actively responsive to them?
- Is the practice respectful of young people's wider community and cultural identities and actively responsive to them?
- Where young people choose, is the practice seeking to help young people strengthen their community and cultural identities?
- Is the practice seeking to go beyond where young people start? Is it encouraging them to be outward looking, critical and creative in their responses to their experience and the world around them?
- Is the practice concerned with how young people feel as well as with what they know and can do?' (Davies, 2005:7)

To enhance the participative approach to youth work, the following questions could be added:
- Are young people benefiting from participation
- Is the practice bringing young people together so that they can learn from each other and work together for collective action and change?
- Is the youth worker engaged in continuous professional development through reflection on learning from the young people, supervision, networking, training and research?

Being clear about who youth work is for

The primary focus of youth work is on young people rather than exclusively on the provision of a service for the community or society as a whole. When called upon to address issues of concern to local, regional or national government institutions, political bodies, the media or religious organisations, youth workers attempt to ensure that their work is also compatible and relevant to the needs and interests of young people. Youth workers need to maintain clarity about the purpose of their work and pay attention to practice when others make demands. Youth work can all too easily become diverted into providing services for others even when these interests conflict with those of the young people. If the needs of society, local communities, the youth workers, the funders and the youth work organisations are all compatible with what young people want, then youth work can flourish. If others' interests have priority, then youth work principles can be compromised.

Understanding power in youth work

Young people's voluntary choice to participate has a significant effect on a youth worker's role and methods. Power, control and autonomy are key issues. Young people control the degree and manner of their engagement. Youth workers work on the basis of equality with young people as described by Holt, 1983 (see Box 1.4) and with the expectation of learning from them as described by Gandhi, 1931 (see Box 1.5). The practice requires dialogue and sharing of information and power. This communication facilitates two-way learning as well as a participative approach to decision-making. Youth workers who practice in settings where young people are required to attend need to be aware of the implications. Most importantly, efforts will need to be made to introduce elements of choice.

Box 1.4: A definition of working on the basis of equality

'If I had to make a general rule for living and working with children, it might be this: be wary of saying or doing anything to a child that you would not do to another adult whose good opinion and affection you valued.' (Holt, 1983 as quoted on The FreeChild Project website)

Youth workers use their own power judiciously to provide young people with opportunities to develop a better understanding of power relationships in society and therefore their abilities to exercise control over decisions. For example, rather than simply providing young people with solutions to problems, a youth worker will involve young people in identifying their own problem solving methods. In this way, youth workers do not just provide services to a passive clientele or assert social control.

Box 1.5: Gandhi (1931) on learning from young people

'And believe me, from my experience of hundreds, I was going to say thousands, of children, I know that they have perhaps a finer sense of honour than you and I have. The greatest lessons in life, if we would but stop and humble ourselves, we would learn not from grown-up learned men, but from the so-called ignorant children.' (Gandhi, 1931: 361)

Enabling participation; not just providing a service

Youth work programmes and activities have to be flexible, attractive and accessible while addressing young people's needs and interests as they rely on voluntary participation. Youth work responds to the expressed needs and interests of the young people, focussing on their issues of concern rather than others' agendas. Issues such as physical and mental health, healthy living, safety, protection from harm or neglect, the environment and employment are approached through projects owned and organised by the young people rather than through a set curriculum. Organisational aims and objectives may need to take second place.

Youth workers often become involved in providing services to young people, their parents or other professionals. Youth workers are well placed to offer advice and support for the design, provision and management of a range of services related to young people, such as education, health and leisure. Through listening and working closely with young people, youth workers can become quite knowledgeable about young people's interests, issues and needs, can appreciate how to provide appropriate services and understand how to access well developed networks of existing support and information.

Offering information and suggestions on ways to tackle specific issues related to young people's lives can take over from a youth work role. 'Sign-posting' young people to relevant support services and passing on condoms, pool cues, footballs, spare furniture or education may provide useful services in some instances. However, these activities are not what youth work practice is about. Youth workers are interested in providing more than 'quick-fix' solutions. When youth workers do become involved in services, such as the examples in the table in Box 1.6, the services should be offered within an interactive process in response to the expressed interests of young people themselves.

Box 1.6: Services and facilities for young people

Type of service	Possible relevant activities
Educational	Alternative education, outdoor pursuits, sports and social skills, mentoring
Information and advice	Sexual health, drugs, counselling, careers, housing, signposting to relevant services and support
Caring	Holiday play schemes, camps and after school clubs, crèches, playgroups
Support	Young mothers/parents/fathers groups, young carers groups, mental health groups, identity specific groups
Housing	Refuges, sheltered accommodation, emergency housing
Environmental	Gardening and clean up projects, park and playground design, murals
Media	Internet cafés, radio stations, DJ facilities, local newsletters, texting services
Leisure	Cafés, youth centres, sports activities, indoor games
Health	Counselling services, multi-agency health clinics, health promotion, condoms, needle exchanges, keep fit classes, healthy eating groups
Social control	Diversionary or preventative activities, surveillance and supervision

A youth worker is not a 'helping professional' who defines the problems and controls the solutions. To conform to the voluntary principle of youth work, youth workers offer services to young people rather than deliver them to unwilling or passive recipients. Avoiding patronising and over-directive support, a youth worker allows young people to a have a genuine say in whether to accept any help that is offered. When youth workers offer specific assistance to someone who is experiencing difficulties or blocks to progress and that assistance is accepted as a genuinely useful resource, this enhances mutual respect. Services that call into question an individual's independence or ability to make her or his own choices can be humiliating and disempowering (Best, 2000). The difference is not only in the help that is being offered, but the ways in which it is offered.

Whilst youth workers may provide or contribute to services specialising in or addressing the needs of young people as defined by others, the goals should be to involve young people in facilitating or managing the activities and to promote their ownership and control of any plans or strategies. (See the practice example in Box 1.7.) Youth work carries a more profound purpose than to provide leisure and recreation-based activities, care or diversionary services. The facilitation of diversionary and preventative activities related to young people's experimentation with risky activities or anti-social behaviour can only be described as youth work if the activities build on young people's interests and stated needs and they have a say in how the programme is designed and carried out. The presentation of interesting activities for young people, such as sports, crafts and music can form part of youth work in many settings within schools, youth centres, churches, enterprises and so forth – but the service needs to be designed, evaluated and developed through dialogue with the young people. Otherwise the 'service' is merely an exercise in social control.

Box 1.7: Practice example: A youth service becomes participative

An after school club provided a service for young people and their carers: the young people were looked after whilst their carers were at work, busy elsewhere or simply needing respite. The youth workers aims were to develop self-esteem and confidence amongst the children and young people accessing the club. The young people were asked how the club could be improved. The members started by stating which activities they preferred. Soon they were designing the programme and publicity. Before long, they became involved in the management of the club and arranged for a partial merger with a disabled young people's project. The members realised that the young disabled people had few opportunities to socialise with other young people in the neighbourhood and that if the After School Club was going to service the whole community, issues such as access, integration and independence needed to be tackled. The young people challenged the notion that the club was a service for parents and carers to demand a service for all of the young people in the area.

Recognising role conflict

Leadership and supportive roles carried out with young people, such as helping young people towards certain educational or social goals, is often described as 'youth work'. Unless the young people are able to influence decisions about what goes on in the educational or diversionary activities carried out with a youth leader, mentor, instructor, counsellor or youth tutor, these job titles or roles could be more accurately described as work with young people. Clarity about the distinction can minimise role conflict.

Youth workers may be called upon by communities, other professionals, the government or other funders to engage in those activities that control young people rather than those activities that enable their self-expression and autonomy. (See Box 1.8 for an example of youth work as crime prevention.) Youth workers need to be able to recognise the differences in various roles so that they can decide when to 'take a stand' and define and defend their professional boundaries and when flexibility and co-operation can work for the benefit of young people. The values and principles of the profession assist youth workers in deciding whether certain activities are part of their role or whether they are compatible or in conflict with that role.

Box 1.8: Practice example: Diversion as crime prevention

A football project was funded as a 'diversion from crime' initiative. The youth workers involved the team members in managing the project. The young people developed the funding application, recruited and inducted new members, handled the finance, trained volunteers and organised the travel arrangements, tournament participation and sponsorship deals. They also set up a support group for volunteers amongst previous members, parents/carers and local members of the community who became coaches and referees. Using youth work methods, the football project developed from being a 'take care of our badly behaved young people' service for the community into a community-based initiative where the young people took a leading role.

Increased bureaucratisation or efforts to control individuals or groups can lead to needless monitoring and oppressive surveillance of young people's activities. Through partnership work with other agencies or funding that becomes available for particular projects, some workers have been drawn into a surveillance role without questioning or necessarily recognising the changes and their implications for youth work practice. Records of contacts, hard outcomes and working to a pre-planned programme are procedures often expected and required by funders. Detailed record-keeping, particularly when information can be accessed by others, does not usually comply with youth work principles of accountability and confidentiality. For example, assessed alternative education, prevention training and probation services can demand a lot of record-keeping and judgements that have far-reaching effects, such as failure, withdrawal from a programme and imprisonment. When recording and maintaining detailed records turns into judging young people's behaviour or a punitive intervention, most youth workers would no longer describe the practice as youth work. Youth workers aim to identify and address discrimination and injustice rather than contribute to further oppression. Attempting to encourage socially acceptable behaviour or respect for others with young people who are being treated unacceptably and disrespectfully could be seen as collusion with oppression.

Youth workers may be asked to work on a one-to-one basis with young people and to target 'interventions' with named individuals or a caseload of 'clients'. Individuals may be identified as in need of intervention to promote their involvement in education, training or employment with 'youth workers' acting as learning mentors or personal advisors. Action programmes may be devised and implemented to address these aims with little involvement of the young people. Programmes are then assessed on whether these named individuals return to learning or enter employment rather than on any contribution made to the quality of community life, personal flourishing or social relationships that may arise out of the process.

Such intervention work is an example of one of the many ways in which adults retain and demonstrate care, protection and control of young people as they move from childhood needs for protection to undertaking adult responsibilities. A youth work approach would be to provide young people with the opportunity to make considered and informed decisions based on a better understanding of situations and consequences. While most young people progress towards adulthood taking on new or different responsibilities for financial, economic, social, careers and domestic matters, some experience more difficulties in making these transitions than others, sometimes due to their particular circumstances or make-up. Youth workers need to be aware that undertaking a protective rather than an interactive relationship can lead to role conflict.

Undertaking youth work tasks and duties

Youth workers undertake a range of tasks and duties including face-to-face work, linking with other organisations, taking responsibility for managing other staff or volunteers and looking after venues, budgets and resources (see the table Box 1.9 for some examples).

Box 1.9: Youth work tasks and duties

Face-to-face work
- Establish contact with young people in different settings
- Build relationships with young people individually and in groups
- Bring young people together in groups and shared activities
- Involve young people in assessment of needs defined by area and/or target group
- Enable the participation of young people in planning, monitoring and developing as well as participating themselves in relevant activities, projects or services

Box 1.9 - *Cont'd*

- Facilitate discussions, arts-based activities, community/environmental projects, residential activities, outdoor education and sports activities
- Raise topics related to personal and social education (for example, health, fitness, smoking, drugs, relationships, bullying)
- Address issues related to anti-oppressive practice, such as racism, sexism, heterosexism, disabilism, class, age-ism
- Act as an advocate for young people's interests, for example, environmental issues, involving young people in decisions, improvements in resources and services for young people.

Building links, networking and partnerships
- Find out about community issues, influences and interests
- Work with other agencies to develop services and facilities across communities
- Work with parents and other community groups to address issues and improve services and facilities
- Work with others as a member or leader of a staff team.

Management responsibilities
- Recruit, induct, supervise and train paid and unpaid staff and volunteers
- Involve young people and other members of the community in the management of projects and the organisation
- Develop and implement policies, codes of practice and ways of working
- Manage and administer youth and community projects and resources
- Deal with administrative and office tasks; maintain records of finance, budget control
- Manage resources, such as buildings, equipment
- Identify and pursue sources of funding for projects
- Draw up business plans, write reports and make formal presentations to funding bodies.

Service oriented work
- Advise and guide to young people, their parents and other professionals and service providers working with young people
- Provide personal and social education, mentoring or support
- Instruction in sports, outdoor activities, keeping fit, martial arts, drama, art.

Identifying unacceptable youth worker behaviour

As youth workers hold privileged positions in the lives of young people, clarity about professional boundaries and respecting young people's rights are important factors in youth work relationships. Youth workers have a high level of responsibility for the care and safety of young people, particularly when working with younger age groups or in residential settings. Young people could be vulnerable or at risk from violent, exploitative or otherwise inappropriate relationships or behaviour. The values and principles of youth work define good practice and are intended to protect young people from physical or verbal abuse, being unfairly blamed or 'scape-goated' and from receiving inaccurate or inappropriate information and advice (see Box 1.10 for some examples of unacceptable youth worker behaviour).

Box 1.10: Examples of unacceptable youth worker behaviour

Most organisations would find the following activities unacceptable for a youth worker:

- Wilful, knowing or negligent failure to comply with relevant legislation or organisational policy
- Exercising undue influence on young people or other members of the community for personal or financial gain
- Using the position for financial gain
- Carrying out youth work activities whilst under the influence of drugs or alcohol.

Some organisations would also find evidence of 'moral unfitness' outside of working hours unacceptable, for example:

- Any sexual activity with a legally defined 'minor'
- Involvement in illegal activities.

Specific definitions or expectations of acceptable professional behaviour can vary in different situations and organisations. Recognition of an individual's suitability for youth work usually depends on standards that could include legal, moral or political views. Many organisations will not use volunteers or employ individuals with a history of drug use or violence. Legislation may dictate whether individuals with particular histories, such as sexual exploitation or violence, are allowed to be in the company of young people, much less work with them. Evidence of certain illegal or risky behaviour, specific judicial sentences or particular mental health diagnoses will preclude involvement in some youth work organisations or in some countries.

Youth work organisations and youth workers need to take serious and sensible precautions to ensure the safety of young people in their care whilst at the same time involving youth workers who have a lot to offer. Youth workers often draw on past experiences of family upbringing, backgrounds or lives to inform their youth work practice, particularly in relation to some of the more challenging issues that young people face. Some individuals who have past experiences of 'anti-social' activities and have been able to change their lives can provide valuable insights for young people. A criminal record does not necessarily preclude involvement in youth work. First-hand experiences of the criminal justice system can provide a deep awareness of some of the implications and consequences of certain life-choices and circumstances, which can inform youth work practice. Appropriate policies about employing ex-offenders should take into account factors such as the nature of the offence, how long ago it was committed and evidence of learning from the experience.

Individuals applying to work with young people on a paid or unpaid basis should expect potential employers to check criminal records. Whilst record systems vary in relation to accuracy, relevance and ease of access, many employers will be required by law or organisational policy to check the criminal records of anyone applying to work with children and young people whether on a paid or voluntary basis. Others will insist on doing so. Applicants need to be prepared to discuss their past experiences with potential employers.

Understanding legal constraints

Youth workers need to be aware of relevant legislation and legal boundaries to inform their own choices about actions and any advice for young people. While most people are clear about what constitutes theft or assault, road traffic violations and illegal substances, additional knowledge of the law is useful to youth workers even in these areas. Knowledge of child protection, employment and health and safety matters can be particularly important. Many youth work organisations require youth workers to have specific training in issues related to physical restraint and sexual harassment prior to any physical contact with young people.

The values and principles of youth work are not always compatible with changing legal requirements or organisational policy and practice. Like other 'people-oriented' occupations and professions, youth work requires individual and flexible responses to situations that depend on individuals rather than stock responses. To maintain clarity of purpose and awareness of possible conflicts, youth workers need to be involved in continuous professional development to keep up-to-date with legal constraints on practice as well as political and moral issues that may affect the information and views that they hold and sometimes pass on to young people. The identification of appropriate responses requires discussion with young people and colleagues in relation to ethical and professional values and evaluation and planning through supervision.

Being clear about own motivation

Motivations for becoming involved in youth work vary, ranging from the desire to right wrongs and resolve social and political problems to ensuring that others do not experience the same difficulties. Youth workers sometimes have a clear or specific motivation for work with young people, which can form part of a 'mission' to improve the world and/or the people living in it. (See Box 1.11 for some examples of youth work as a mission.) Associations based on philanthropy or a religious, spiritual or emotional belief or a political cause may use youth workers or a youth work approach to make contact and build relationships with young people in order to spread the word and reach the next generation of disciples. Youth work motivated by strong ideological beliefs can provide interesting options for young people; beliefs in the superiority of particular groups or life choices and the imposition of belief systems onto young people are incompatible with the values and principles of youth work.

Box 1.11: Practice examples: Youth work as a mission

- A religious community that provides opportunities for the young people to form relationships with others sharing their language or beliefs to preserve a culture or faith
- A political party that has a youth wing to support the development of future leaders
- A campaigning organisation that recruits young people to projects aiming to improve awareness and practice in relation to relevant issue
- Some of the uniformed organisations,' aims are related to values, such as the Scouts and Guides who aim to create a better world, the Air and Sea Cadets who aim to foster good citizenship

---

Recruiting or converting young people to a cause through example and information can be distinguished from indoctrination. While youth work has an educative function, participative learning is appropriate and should be linked to action (see the table in Box 1.12). Youth work associations with a strong underlying belief system can carry out participative youth work without running counter to youth work values. An organisation may have a focus on non-violence or community spirit, concerns which are clearly compatible with young people's well-being and interests. A youth work organisation should not be involved in the coercion or exploitation of young people or involve them in destructive or exclusive groups. Young people would need to be made aware of the mission-related role models, structures, options, being provided and have the choice to opt out.

Recognising and using support

Having appropriate support can help a youth worker to promote best practice and handle role conflicts. Availability of such direction will vary

Box 1.12: Identifying appropriate learning methods

Appropriate learning methods	
Active and experiential learning	Learning from experience and reflection on experience to put into practice (Kolb and Fry 1975)
Learning from each other	Participative learning that recognises and values experience (Sapin and Watters, 1990)
Passing on information	Offering, handing over or transferring information
Illuminating	Clarifying or constructing a new or different perspective or vision
Methods to use with care	
Instructing	Teaching or directing authoritatively
Converting	Changing opinions or beliefs
Inappropriate methods for youth work	
Indoctrinating	*Thorough and systematic teaching that discourages independent or alternative thoughts*
Inculcating	*Using frequent and forceful repetition to fix in someone's mind*
Brainwashing	*Destroying prior beliefs and imposing a new set through coercion or conditioning.*

greatly depending on individuals, their employment arrangements and their organisational setting. An organisational culture and approach may clearly comply with professional youth work practice or could conflict. Attempting to change attitudes and practices within an organisation to address youth work values and practice requires support, a strategy and a will to engage in challenging activities. Some youth workers have prescriptive job descriptions, policies, procedures and codes of practice, which at least provide clarity about parameters for change. An unpaid activist working to self-defined styles and methodologies outside of an organisation would neither be supported nor constrained and may therefore be vulnerable or ineffective in the face of challenge. Many youth workers need to seek additional support with external supervision (see Chapter 12) and networking with other agencies to ensure that professional values and principles are upheld in practice.

Essential skills for youth work practice

- Understanding the role of a youth worker
- Checking practice for youth work values and principles

- Being clear about who youth work is for
- Understanding power in youth work
- Enabling participation; not just providing a service
- Recognising role conflict
- Undertaking the responsibilities of a youth worker
- Identifying unacceptable behaviour for a youth worker
- Understanding legal constraints
- Being clear about own motivation
- Recognising and using support.

Further reading about youth work practice

Davies (2005); Development Education Association website; (The) National Youth Agency (2004); Smith (1988).

CHAPTER 2: Working in different settings

This chapter looks at how the environment, organisational structure or culture in which youth work takes place can affect practice and young people's participation. This chapter explores the effects of youth work settings on provision and practice in relation to some of the opportunities and constraints.

Some of the responsibilities of a youth worker are closely related to the setting in which the youth work takes place, such as the geographical area, organisation or facility. Whilst the values, principles and process of the work with young people should remain consistent, the levels of access to resources and responsibilities for them can vary considerably. For example, a centre-based youth worker may be responsible for the workers and activities within and around the centre as well as maintenance and upkeep. A youth warden may have responsibilities for the environment within a garden, playground or sports facility. An area youth worker would probably cover a wider geographical area and may have managerial responsibilities for youth work activities and workers in more than one project or centre. Whereas a street-based or detached youth worker who develops activities outdoors would probably have very few responsibilities for resources other than those which could be easily carried.

In some situations, the physical environment, organisational aims or funding streams may conflict with young people's needs or interests. Adherence to the core values and principles of youth work may require youth workers to use considerable ingenuity to change or challenge prevailing policies or practices. A youth worker needs to adapt to work in varying settings, conditions and circumstances. Specific interests and needs may be accommodated in locations ranging from purpose-built facilities to natural open spaces. Activities may take place in small rooms that fit only a tiny number of targeted young people or in large, publicly accessible venues where anyone can drop in. Youth work may involve travel to new places or environments through excursions, camping, exchanges or other overnight residentials. Some settings have been designed for specific use and activities whilst others, such as unused shops, street corners or churches had anticipated a completely different purpose and may require adaptation.

The match between a setting for youth work and the demands of practice is not always ideal (see Box 2.1 for an example of a mis-match). Location and organisational settings can affect take-up and activities. Some may be more accessible for specific groups or individual young people, more suitable for certain activities or suit a particular youth worker's own skills and interests. Clearly a range of venues would be ideal for involving young people in different situations and with different interests.

Box 2.1: Practice example: Choosing the wrong location

Another youth worker and I had thought that we had recognised a good opportunity for starting a group. We had been talking with a few young men who we met in different outdoor locations and who seemed to share similar situations. They all seemed to be of a similar age and vaguely interested in doing something different with their lives. None of them were involved in actively pursuing employment or education, but it seemed like they might be ready to do so. It seemed to us that they would really benefit from getting together. So we booked a room in the local health centre and encouraged them to come along to discuss what we could do together. Although they said they would come, no one showed up. Later I found out that young people in the area thought that using the health centre gave them a negative reputation. Anyone who went there was assumed to have a STD (sexually transmitted disease) and was ostracised. I also should have known that being comfortable talking with us individually in passing was different from having a 'meeting' or discussing their issues with peers that they didn't already know. A few months later when we booked a session in the gym, several of them came along and began talking to each other.

Finding suitable locations for particular activities, groups or individual young people not only requires knowledge of the area, but attention to the young people's understanding of their boundaries or territories. Finding out where young people will go and which settings will provide suitable opportunities for full participation are clear priorities. Some limits may be externally imposed. For example, an area may be associated with an unfriendly group. Other 'comfort zones' may be self-defined. For example, a young person may simply have a preference for a known and familiar environment. Considering the make-up of a group and their interactions with all aspects of their environment can assist a youth worker to predict and prepare for certain eventualities, whilst discussions with the young people themselves will inform practice in different settings.

Working out of doors

The range of outdoor locations for youth work includes public access parks or open countryside as well as private or limited access outdoor facilities, such as funfairs, boats or adventure playgrounds. Outdoor education, sporting activities or physical exercise can be organised in a local setting or accessed through excursions and overnight residentials. If a location is easily accessible, appreciation and use can be developed beyond the youth workers' involvement. (See Box 2.2 for some examples of outdoor youth work in outdoor locations.)

Box 2.2: Locations for outdoor youth work

Natural outdoor public locations
- Excursions to the open countryside, beaches, rivers and lakes, mountains, moors, woods, rock faces and caves can be organised to experience a new environment and develop young people's knowledge or understanding of outdoor issues with environmental projects and enjoyment of the outdoors.

Outdoor public sporting facilities
- Activity-based youth work using bike paths, nature trails, basketball courts, football fields, skateboard ramps, swimming pools, golf courses and tennis courts can provide opportunities for outdoor sports, games and play to enhance young people's use of these usually accessible sites.

Other outdoor public 'built' areas
- Youth work in public parks and gardens, streets and street corners, canals, reservoirs, fountains, bus shelters, parking spaces and spare or waste ground, particularly around other facilities, such as train stations or shopping centres, is often detached work with young people in their own space. Campaigns as well as environmental and public art projects may also utilise these spaces. Examples might include work to address a specific issue related to young people in the outdoors, such as homelessness, drug use, sexual health or community relations.

Outdoor centres and other purpose built or organised facilities
- Playgrounds, outdoor education centres, field centres, water adventure centres, adventure holidays summer camps and other residential facilities, camping grounds, sea kayaking, white water rafting or canoeing and gorge walking are often used to develop a group's cohesion through outings away from a usual setting.

Other limited access (private or ticket only) facilities
- Farms, gardens, canal barges, boats, funfairs, amusement parks, stately homes, campgrounds, a roped-off area in a park, coach excursions to outdoor locations and open spaces attached to a centre (such as a field, playground, tennis/basketball courts) could be used to hold large and public events that link with other organisations, such as competitive sports and tournaments, or to promote, conclude or celebrate work with one-off outdoor events that are visible to the public.

The use of outdoor locations can require extra attention to preparation and planning or policies and procedures, particularly health and safety. Outdoor sites are less predictable or easily controlled than indoor ones even when access can be limited to certain age groups, numbers or individuals. In open or public settings, the observations, comments or interference from passers-by may affect young people and youth workers so it is not only changes in the weather that can upset plans. Unexpected visitors, whether young people, adults, professionals or animals may make their presence known. Young people are less 'contained' so that they may be free to roam, get lost and move out of earshot. Some youth workers respond to these potential situations by increasing the structure and supervision of the activities through strictly refereed sports or well planned and equipped projects. Others have a more flexible approach and can adapt the activities to suit the environment.

Carrying out detached youth work

Detached youth work involves making contact with young people in their own settings by going out to meet them where they naturally congregate, usually in outdoor settings. Through detached work, a youth worker can learn from direct experience about the context of young people's lives and any geographical, cultural or other territorial boundaries that they may use to organise themselves. Youth workers can also develop their knowledge of the communities they work with and the issues arising for young people and their neighbours. Detached youth work provides the opportunity to reach out to young people who cannot or choose not to become involved in other youth work settings and often engages groups that may not feel welcome in other settings. Sometimes the young people themselves may be referred to as 'detached' or 'hard to reach' as they may not engage with other social structures or agencies. A detached group could include individuals whose experiences of problematic relationships with schools, families, the criminal justice system or other professionals may have taught them to be wary of social systems or authorities.

A detached youth worker works outside of any youth work venues and becomes a 'visitor' in the young people's environment (see Box 2.3 for some examples of areas in which detached work might take place). An important part of a youth worker's approach is to recognise and acknowledge that the balance of power is clearly distinct from most other situations where adults tend to have more control over interactions with young people. Unlike discussions with parents, carers or adult professionals, young people in detached settings establish their own rules over conversations and activities and can also decide whether or not to allow a youth worker to become involved. In a detached setting, the young people's participation is clearly voluntary in that they can simply move away if they do not wish to engage.

Box 2.3: Areas for detached work

- A bench, bus shelter or crossroads where young people congregate to socialise
- A natural shelter, such as a cluster of trees or rocks, that provides some protection from the weather
- A section of a multi-storey car park or abandoned waste ground where homeless young people come together for mutual support or survival
- A street corner group which meets to gossip and have a laugh or conduct business, such as drugs or crime
- A section of the park or street which just happens to be a natural mid-way meeting point for different members
- Areas where young people are waiting for other provision or services, such as outside schools, court rooms or health clinics
- A bike or skateboard ramp, football field or basketball court in a public park: young people may join in or simply be involved as spectators, supporters or commentators.

Whilst a prescriptive approach to any youth work will always find exceptions that work perfectly well, most youth workers wait until they have developed a positive relationship with individuals before passing comments on minor or common misbehaviour carried out in their presence, particularly in an outdoor, detached setting. Some workers ignore language, attitudes or behaviour that they would more readily challenge in a centre-based setting. Moving on to another location or group would be preferable to colluding with or seeming to approve of any misdemeanours. Inside a youth centre, rules about dangerous or 'risky' behaviour, such as drinking, smoking, fighting, carrying out sexual or criminal activity are generally established practice. Youth workers in a youth centre would strive to limit or curtail such activities through discussions of the issues and consequences of 'bad behaviour.'

Working indoors

Youth workers need to be aware of issues that may be defined or influenced by a venue, for example, those related to access, opportunities and behavioural expectations. Although some indoor locations provide specific facilities that may be otherwise unavailable, certain venues may have regulations and established traditions which restrict youth work activities. Outreach work in premises owned and managed by other organisations may not suit young people, particularly if used by other groups or for alternative purposes. Short-term excursions and residentials to various public or private venues can provide rich and rewarding new experiences for young people, but can also require considerable organisation and preparation.

Centre-based work could take place within a youth work organisation's own venue. A youth club, drop-in advice service or football group in a purpose-built youth centre can provide a space for young people to take ownership and control. Similar services may be offered by a community association within a general purpose community centre, although attention will need to be paid to other users. Mobile provision in converted buses or caravans can be driven to particular localities. While temporary shelters for small groups, such as 'pods' or self-contained portable cabins, can be relocated into new areas as the need arises.

A centre that is owned and used exclusively by a youth work organisation should be able to provide a safe and warm environment. Ideally a youth centre should be easily accessible within a locality and become a focal meeting point for different age, friendship or culture groups within a community. In this setting, the various groups can get to know each other and the youth workers well and can develop the confidence to communicate their interests and needs, raise issues of concern and become involved in developing the provision and programmes. A youth centre may provide open access sessions in addition to providing certain sessions targeting groups and individuals with particular interests and needs. Some centres may be able to offer access to relevant information, services and advice as well as facilities and equipment for artistic, sporting and educational activities. These facilities may provide dark rooms, gyms and exercise apparatus or sports facilities, music equipment, kitchens or cafés, computer suites, car/cycle/motorbike repair garages and tools, and crèche or nursery facilities. A youth work organisation promoting young people's participation can also involve the young people in the management of the building.

Youth work within venues owned by others could include short-term satellite projects as well as longer-term outreach programmes. Youth work may be offered in a village hall or library, an empty shop or a church to suit a particular group or when other facilities are unavailable or under-used. Lunchtime and after-school provision within a school setting has the advantage of proximity for a large number of young people, which can increase levels of participation. A youth worker may take a detached group to a clinic or university to increase young people's understanding of health or educational options or go to a recreational or leisure centre to widen their experiences. Excursions to museums, galleries and restaurants can provide learning and cultural opportunities. A youth worker may also go out to other agencies working with young people, such as care homes, juvenile detention centres or prisons to make contact with a particular target group. Intervention programmes may take place in young people's homes, for example, remedial education, intensive supervision or transition mentoring with particularly vulnerable young people. Flexibility is required to build bridges with paticularly vulnerable young people who are having difficulties at school or attending school, with the criminal justice system or drug use.

The level of partnership with a host facility is dependent on a number of factors and stages. In some instances, a youth worker is invited in to address a particular need. Youth work may be facilitated in other organisational settings to make good use of existing facilities or to enhance the available provision. During a visit to an area or site, a youth worker may identify suitable locations for outreach services. Sharing facilities can be particularly useful, especially in rural areas. A village may have only one publicly accessible facility, such as a church, a room above a shop or a school building. Identifying potential indoor spaces may require some positive and creative thinking and negotiation skills.

Working within a closed system

Some youth workers are located within a 'closed system,' such as a school or prison, which generally have different, often conflicting aims and approaches to those of youth work. Although a closed system may restrict certain ways of working, opportunities may be provided for accessing young people who may not have taken part in youth work activities. For example, a young person faced with the prospect of a forced marriage may find that a youth worker based in a school is an accessible resource. Having the opportunity to discuss or disclose fears about a family holiday which they suspect is a cover for an unwanted wedding without having to make an outside appointment could be very welcome. Other youth work within a school or college could include working with students or pupils who are excluded temporarily from classes, providing a link between schools and communities, mentoring, facilitating taught sessions such as Personal, Health or Social Education classes, such as drugs awareness or sexual health and providing youth work sessions during breaks.

Youth workers attempting to work within an organisation or venue that is set up for reasons other than enjoyable leisure activities usually find that their practice is limited. Although some young people may appreciate the different approach of youth workers as compared with other professionals within an organisation, a youth worker's role in an enclosed environment is not always recognised. The youth worker may find that the young people and staff expect the provision to work on similar methods as the organisation in relation to formal address, records, policies and procedures, such as required attendance.

Finding different ways to offer opportunities and choices can alleviate the constraints of the organisation. For example, youth work in prisons can be limited by the constraints and purpose of the organisation, which may be to punish or isolate, redeem or rehabilitate. Since youth work practice is based on assisting young people to develop their awareness of their rights and to create opportunities for them to be involved in decision making, youth workers may make little headway within the controlled and controlling environment of a prison (see, for example, Box 2.4).

Box 2.4: Practice example: Youth work or surveillance?

I'm involved in an intensive supervision project with young people who have come out of prison. As a youth worker, I am ideally placed to work with these young men. I know them. I've been there. I know what they are going through. There are only three guys that I meet regularly for about three months to keep track of them. It's like I'm their big brother. They come out of prison and there's nothing else for them. They've lost their families and homes. There's no-one there. Next time they're arrested, it will be for real serious crimes and adult prison. They need someone to set them on the right path. This is their last chance. I know it's not the same as youth work, but I've got all of the right skills to work with these guys. They can't pull the wool over my eyes. So when we talk about options and what happens after they do something, they know that meeting me is part of what they have to do. So it's their choice. They come and see me or they go back to prison. In that way, I try and keep it as much like youth work as possible. When they come to see me, they choose what they talk about and whether to join in. Unfortunately, I have no control over what happens to the paperwork. But that sometimes is helpful. I tell the guys, look, if you don't come to the sessions, it goes down in this paper and you'll be going back to prison. It gives them some structure and they know what's going on and that I will be fair with them.

Organising excursions and expeditions

Going out together to a new environment can bring together young people from different backgrounds and provide a variety of new experiences and opportunities. For enjoyable activities to remain so, positive youth work practice implies change, development and learning, which are easily addressed through excursions and expeditions, whether to a local facility or a different country. Outings such as a cross community activity or an international exchange can involve hosting as well as visiting. Through exposure to new environments or cultures, young people can learn new ways of looking at issues and widen their understanding of the world. Taking time out from usual routines also provides adventure, generally shared by the youth workers, who may find themselves joining in activities that they too had never expected to enjoy (see Box 2.5 for an example of unexpected learning from a residential).

Box 2.5: Practice example: Benefits of residentials

The residential was invaluable. It brought the young people together as a group and helped build stronger relationships with the youth workers. The work that we had to do on our peer education project would have been less focused and more time consuming if we'd had to fit it in during normal sessions. The social elements helped the group to bond and acted as a reward. One of the best outcomes was unintended. The youth workers had been working for some time on challenging the overt homophobia of some members of the group, which they felt had improved gradually over many discussions. In the evening, the group started talking with another youth group staying at the centre which included some openly gay members. The groups sat up talking together until the small hours. The next day, one of the young men came up to the youth worker and said, 'You won't believe this – I've made friends with a gay guy – he's safe!'

Youth workers usually attempt to involve potential participants in planning and organising outings. Young people can contribute their perspectives at the same time as they learn about organising, budgeting and addressing parental or carer concerns, which can be significant factors in facilitating a successful project. Maintaining safety in outdoor settings usually means involving young people in considering the risk and safety issues (see Box 2.6). Basic training in health and safety and first aid is usually required and can be undertaken by young people and youth workers together. If an activity or project has limited or restricted access, a fair and open application or selection procedures and criteria will need to be devised. Attention to these matters should enhance young people's full contribution and cooperation (see also Chapter 10 on managing a project).

Box 2.6: Practice examples: Planning for water-based activities

- A group of young people expressing interest in extreme sports contacted various water sports centres to ask about costs and preparation requirements for a range of activities including sea kayaking, body boarding, sub aqua diving and kite surfing. Their involvement in the research generated a lot of excitement as well as an understanding about the need for fund-raising, swimming proficiency and detailed instructions from qualified staff.

- Young people who were planning a day-trip to the beach reviewed their own previous excursions where behaviour within the group had raised issues related to safety and consideration for others. They developed their own codes of conduct to restrict dangerous behaviour, discussed time-keeping and developed 'buddy systems' to ensure that members looked after each other.
- A sub-group of the young people's summer programme planning committee organised a visit to look around a lakeside facility and decided to book some one-off sessions in sailing, canoeing or kayaking as 'tasters' to see if members' interests were genuine and committed prior to booking a full course.
- Two youth workers who were working with a group planning a water-based activity carried out their own research amongst others working with young people to learn from their experience. The research enabled them to identify which facilities were unsuitable, some potential dangers or issues arising from such activities as well as some handy tips on ways to address them. The youth workers were able to pass on this information to the young people.

Working in different organisational settings

The organisational settings for youth work, whether in the public, private or 'third' sectors or in a partnership between sectors, can also affect the degree to which youth work values and principles can be maintained. Youth work practice may require challenging one's own organisation to adhere to principles of participation, positive action and anti-oppressive practice. In those organisations where youth work is one service among many being provided or where priorities are different, an approach focused on youth work may require continuous attention or development. Even within a youth work organisation that has a coherent and compatible set of underlying aims to provide support for practice, youth workers may find themselves in the position of promoting a youth work approach amongst colleagues with less commitment. (See Box 2.7 for some examples of youth work in different organisational sectors.)

Box 2.7: Youth work in different organisational sectors

Public sector youth work
- National, regional (such as state or county) or local (city or town) governments may offer a youth service or employ youth workers within other departments or services, which may be subject to bureaucratic and hierarchical systems.
- Some political authorities may be required to provide certain levels of statutory services for young people or their communities due to statute or legislative action that could require particular attention to specific targets or outcomes.
- Some youth work organisations, facilities and services may rely heavily on government support, which vacillate depending on current political agendas.

Box 2.7 - *Cont'd*

Private sector youth work
- Self-employed or freelance individuals or companies may be contracted to provide mentoring, training or other youth work related facilities, which would need to generate an income.
- Youth work may take place in profit-making companies, such as holiday camps or outdoor facilities. Fees are generally charged, which would restrict access.

Third sector youth work
- Community and 'grass roots' associations may focus on work with young people or include youth work in their mission or brief.
- International, national or local charitable bodies may fund or run youth work in relation to their concerns.
- Non-government organisations (NGOs) and other 'not-for-profit' groups may provide or be contracted to provide certain youth work related activities.

The practice and funding constraints associated with the different sectors can seriously affect youth work. Flexbility or impact can be affected by whether projects are fixed and short term, longer term or on-going. In some settings, youth work can be curtailed by tight time-scales, targets and requirements for data entry. Organisational practice can turn youth workers into instruments of surveillance or social control, which is incompatible with youth work principles. Professional judgement can be limited through laid down procedures which can get in the way of the youth workers' being able to approach young people as individuals, an essential part of youth work. (See Box 2.8 for an example of the changes that funding can make to a community group.)

Box 2.8: Practice example: Volunteers become employers

We spent fifteen years organising summer playschemes for young people in our area on the streets with no funding and no support. But we all had a great time; loads of kids came and really, it changed people's lives. I don't know what would have happened to some of those kids if they hadn't had something to do – and something to eat! We did street hockey, football, treasure hunts, parachute games, the lot. Sometimes we had a hundred kids of different ages all playing together on the spare ground. Finally we got a grant from a charity to employ someone so we could have someone spend some time just organising us better – and what happened? The funders said we had to advertise the post. They wouldn't let us just give it to the woman who had been doing the job for years. We had to ask for paper qualifications instead of looking for someone with experience. We had to write out a job description, person specification, hold interviews... It took loads of time. And then we ended up appointing someone from outside the area who didn't know the kids, or the local amenities ... it was a real eye-opener and caused a load of trouble. In the end it worked out great because the new worker supported what we were trying to do. But it took a long time to get things worked out. And the woman who had been a volunteer for years doing the job before? She's back working with us again now.

Working in multi-agencies and partnerships

Youth workers may work in conjunction with other organisations that are already serving young people or the community in interagency groupings, multi-agency partnerships or other cooperative arrangements (see Box 2.9). A partnership may involve representative participation in the management of projects or programmes or joint agency working at all levels of service provision. A youth work organisation may link up, whether formally or informally, on an individual or organisational level with the police, housing associations, schools, social services and district councils through community safety initiatives. This inter-agency work can involve certain areas of expertise, signposting to specific services, shared good practice, such as those related to drugs, crime and sexual health. Other agencies often value the close link which youth workers have with young people and use their expertise within their services to support initiatives such as youth consultation arrangements.

Box 2.9: Practice examples of partnerships

- A subgroup of a youth forum agreed to put together some training materials on a young peoples' perspective for some public sector agencies working with young people.

- A multi-agency group co-ordinating public sector services for children and young people within a politically defined area involves co-ordination of education, probation, health and social services as well as youth workers.

- A group of young people agrees to undertake a section of the recruitment procedures for a new member of paid staff.

- A partnership between the public sector education services and a third sector organisation uses teachers and youth workers to provide educational activities within a community-based setting for young people 'excluded' from school.

Box 2.9 - *Cont'd*

- A local church provides a venue for youth workers employed by a public sector organisation to facilitate diversionary activities for young people in the area.

- A national network gathers representatives from a range of organisations facilitating youth work to establish good practice guidelines in relation to a particular issue.

If youth workers are to retain their professional identity or more importantly, their values and principles, clarity about their role in different settings is essential, particularly in partnerships and multi-agency formats. In working together to benefit the community, youth workers need to be clear about their role in establishing voluntary relationships with young people that are developed over time and have a purpose to enable their participation. If young people can only participate through being consulted or using a sevice, then this is not really youth work. If a youth worker passes on information to other agencies, their relationships with young people can be damaged. Youth workers need to use their communication skills and understanding of their role to assert their values and principles and develop working relationships with other professionals that do not compromise their practice with young people.

Essential skills for youth work in different settings

- Working in different locations
- Working out of doors
- Carrying out detached youth work
- Working indoors
- Carrying out work in a closed system
- Organising excursions and expeditions
- Working in different organisational settings
- Working in multi-agency forums and partnerships

Further reading about youth work in different settings

Arnold *et al.* (1981); Benetello (1996); Crimmens *et al.* (2004); (The) Federation for Detached Youth Work website: http://www.detached youthwork.info.

CHAPTER 3: Reaching out

A youth worker establishes contact with young people by reaching out to a wide range of groups and individuals, listening to what they say and engaging in conversation. Youth workers also make contact with young people's families and communities, colleagues and other professionals to learn about the context of young people's lives and be able to signpost groups and individuals to appropriate services. This chapter looks at different methods of outreach and self-presentation.

Going out to where young people are

Youth work is an active process where youth workers take the initiative to locate and meet young people often on their terms or in their 'territory'. This process requires communication skills, flexibility and a willingness to learn. Venturing out to the streets, parks, schools, prisons or homes to find certain individual or groups of young people may take some youth workers to previously unexplored areas. A mental 'journey' may be required 'to put oneself in other's shoes' to understand or identify a young person's position or feelings. Emotional, cultural and spiritual journeys come about through changing feelings and experiences of fresh perspectives. New communication skills may be required, including the need to identify and use a wide range of creative methods to reach different young people. Developing confidence in negotiating the area and interacting with young people are key resources for safe practice.

The process of reaching out starts with networking in the catchment area. Some workers prefer to walk or cycle around a neighbourhood in order to see more of what is going on, have better contact with the community and feel less like a detached observer. Others find that an initial drive around allows them to develop an overview. Such outings will indicate where young people 'hang out' in unsupervised or detached groups and the location of the shopping areas, cafés or streets where young people socialise or find entertainment. Close observation can identify how major roads, housing projects or school boundaries define or split particular communities, which can be a major cause of territorial behaviour. Noticing the housing can also reveal a lot about an area and its population. For example, household sizes, patterns of housing and state of upkeep and repair can indicate income and economic status. (Box 3.1 has some examples of ways to find out about an area; Chapter 10 also outlines more in-depth research.)

Box 3.1: Examples of background research

Observation
- Look around: walk or cycle around the area
- Look at maps of the area
- Identify any public or open spaces
- Go into shops and markets to get a feel for the area
- Drive around at different times
- Notice where young people congregate

Literature search
- Check out plans for development and regeneration
- Browse information about local organisations in public posters and leaflets
- Look at listings in telephone books and libraries
- Read local papers and internet searches for information about the local politics and events
- Look at reports, newsletters and bulletins from own and others' organisations

Networking
- Ask young people what they think about their area and its amenities
- Listen to young people's stories
- Ask other residents about the neighbourhood and community relations
- Visit relevant organisations to identify potential resources and contacts
- Attend local meetings to find out about local issues

Locating the young people

Over a period of time, a youth worker uses different outreach methods to get to know young people and their communities (see Box 3.2). Going out at varying times of the day to explore diverse areas will help a youth worker to locate different groups of young people. Although some young people establish their 'territory' in a location that can be easily accessed, meeting regularly in a specific area or shelter, others may seek out more private locations, particularly if they are hiding or running away from families, carers or other authorities. A youth worker who leaves the area at 8:00 p.m. may miss the group of homeless young people who occupy the park at night or the young sex workers on the streets. Youth workers who take time to observe what is going on in an area will also meet parents, caretakers and others related to young people including friends and enemies, partners and employers. These contacts can inform the development of appropriate 'intervention strategies' and provide ideas for future interactions with young people (see also Box 3.3 for some different practice examples of outreach work).

Box 3.2: Examples of outreach activities

- Make new contacts with young people and their communities through door knocking, leaflet drops, poster campaigns and provide publicity about youth work opportunities
- Talk about youth work with young people who do not know about what is on offer, who choose not to access current activities or who may be prevented from participating to identify needs and interests
- Discuss youth work practice, options and developments with detached groups, groups in schools, users of particular services to promote understanding of the role of a youth worker
- Conduct research to identify barriers to participation, community concerns or changes that could be made to improve participation to plan future work
- Involve young people in planning and developing new activities and services and evaluating existing facilities
- Network with other professionals to identify opportunities for new developments, partnerships, overlaps and gaps in provision.

Reaching out to all young people

Paying attention to the identities of the young people who are being contacted, which groups of young people are reached or are excluded and which places are most suitable for making contact, can be part of anti-oppressive practice. Whilst some young people can be found in familiar settings or existing groups, others may be more isolated, detached and previously 'unreached' by youth work or other services. Some young people face barriers to participation created by established societal oppression whether overtly or unwittingly. Others may be in circumstances where their needs are not addressed due to neglect or ignorance. A youth worker needs to make a positive effort to reach such individuals. Rather than labelling young people as 'non-attenders', 'hard-to-reach' or 'not interested', youth workers should attempt to locate such individuals through adopting a range of different ways to make contact.

Some organisations target particular groups of young people, such as those who have been excluded from school or who are not in paid employment. Projects may target particular types of behaviour, particularly that which is, or is perceived to be, dangerous, illegal, 'anti-social' or 'risky'. Care needs to be taken to ensure that targets address genuine needs or interests and are not based on a deficit model, which perceives certain young people as 'disadvantaged' or nuisances.

Such focused practice can be useful to ensure that the needs of a particular group are addressed. However, youth workers need to be cautious about targets that assume youth work is easily predictable, defined or quantifiable. Youth work can be constrained by reliance on measurable and tangible outputs. Evaluation that only looks at the number of groups or individuals contacted can provide a false picture of the success or failure of youth work. Young people's learning and development through involvement in youth work will vary according to the individual and the group. More qualitative research methods may be required to recognise and value these changes. (See chapter 10.)

Box 3.3: Practice examples: Outreach work

Outreach at 42,
Parental support is really important in this community because the young people depend on their parents for transport to the sessions. Also most of them need parental permission to attend. My role as an outreach worker often takes me to their homes – so I see them in an environment that they are familiar with. Usually everyone is more relaxed if I meet them at home – rather than if they have to come into the centre before they know anyone. I also find that if I can create a bond with other members of the family, the young people tend to attend the youth sessions more regularly.

Outreach as detached work
Most of the young people I work with would not come to the youth centre so I generally contact young people outside in the parks or on the streets. Some of them have attended the youth centre before and have been excluded because of alcohol or drug abuse or violent behaviour. Some of them just don't like the youth club environment. I was given some funding to work with targeted groups of young people to reduce 'juvenile nuisance' in the area. After making initial contacts, we developed a good relationship which allowed the young people to say what their needs were and gave me some ideas about possible activities. After a while, I told them why I got funding for my work and we had a useful discussion about community living, rights and responsibilities. The young people became involved in developing the local park, which eventually went some way to bridge the gap between young people and other community members.

Outreach as multi-agency or co-operative work
We use the local health centre to make contact with young people. We find that a large number of young people come to the health centre for advice and services about drugs, sexual health and sexual activity, concerns about weight and mental health. We developed a support group on site that is very well used. I don't think that they would have come to a 'mainstream' youth work group and they certainly wouldn't have felt comfortable raising these issues in a youth centre; they come to this group because it is accessible and related to their needs.

Outreach as networking

I gather suggestions from other professionals about relevant organisations and specific contacts who might be useful. I always ring up first to see if I can get an invitation to observe or talk with a meeting. I've talked in school assemblies, joined discussions in probation groups, visited prisons and met with groups of care organisers. If I am going to give a presentation, I discuss how I will be introduced so that it is clear that I am from an external organisation. I generally join in any activities going on and exchange small talk with all of the people I meet, such as secretaries, building caretakers and other professionals.

Distributing publicity and information

The process of outreach work should be two-way so that when contact is made with individuals and groups, ideas about events or opportunities are discussed (see Box 3.4). Participation in relevant meetings and events provides opportunities to audit residents' opinions about relevant issues. Initial forays into communities with publicity and information about youth work may develop into 'off-site' projects targeted to reach particular groups, such as detached work and outdoor activities. Publicity distributed through newspaper, television or e-mails should include offers of opportunities to meet. Using a range of methods, such as texts, websites, e-mail lists, chatrooms, leaflets, posters and public events, can help to reach different groups.

Box 3.4: Practice example: Door-to-door outreach work

Noticing that a large number of young people were 'hanging around' outside a block of flats, a youth worker approached the group to talk about activities at the youth centre. Although the centre was only a few streets away, the young people said that their parents had instructed them not to venture beyond the immediate vicinity. The youth worker decided to go door-to-door around the flats to distribute information about the youth centre.

The majority of residents were fairly friendly and almost all had something to say about the young people, usually 'somebody needs to do something about those young people always getting into trouble'. She responded lightly with 'I've really enjoyed meeting the young people downstairs.' Or 'They seem quite lively and interesting'. Or 'It's hard, isn't it, for young people these days – because everything is so expensive'. Although she felt a bit uncomfortable about declining invitations, her refusals to come inside were accepted politely.

Box 3.4 - Cont'd

Reflecting on the exercise in supervision, the youth worker was reprimanded for not taking another worker with her to provide back-up should she have an accident or be physically attacked. While the youth worker explained that she didn't feel she had been in any danger and that working solo had enabled her to have more natural conversations than would have been possible with accompanying colleagues, her supervisor was adamant that a partner was essential and would not negatively affect her work. The youth worker agreed that any future outreach would be undertaken with greater attention to safety.

The supervisor and youth worker agreed that the outreach work had been useful. A number of new contacts had been made and informed about the youth work activities. Quite a few individuals had identified themselves as parents of the target age group. Providing telephone contact numbers, sample programmes and photos of the facilities seemed to go down well. Negative attitudes towards young people had been discussed and a couple of residents had expressed interest in volunteering at the centre.

In the short-term, attendance at the youth centre was unaffected. However, about a month later, the youth worker (with a partner) went around the flats to invite the residents to an event at the youth centre. About a dozen people who had been personally contacted through the visits attended. Over the following weeks, attendance increased dramatically as young people came and brought their friends.

Bearing in mind the potential for domestic relations to affect a young person's access to youth work, tact and diplomacy is a requirement in young people's homes. In general, a non-judgemental approach to who they are living with and how they are living is appropriate. For the most part, youth workers greet others living with the young people and discuss their work with whoever seems appropriate. Some youth workers find this difficult, particularly if young people are living in circumstances different to their own experiences (see Box 3.5 for

Box 3.5: Practice example: Making inappropriate judgements

During a supervision session, a youth worker described his reactions to a visit to a young person's home carried out with another worker. 'I was sitting in the living room when his mother offered to make me a cup of tea. I had to refuse, because there were dog hairs all over the furniture, piles of old clothes and papers all over the room and dirty plates on every surface. I hate to think what the kitchen was like.' The supervisor asked the worker whether he knew how many people lived in the house. When the worker identified that there were seven people, including three adults working full-time, two adolescents and a toddler as well as the dog, the supervisor asked the worker how maintaining a tidy environment was practicable. Given that the house only had two bedrooms, it was likely that the other downstairs room was being used as a bedroom – and the living room was additionally functioning as a laundry room, storage space and dining room. It was quite possible that the plates were from a recent meal and that the clothes had just been washed and were waiting only to be ironed. When comparing the situation with his own living arrangements, the worker was able to identify the stresses and strains impacting on this household. He agreed that his impressions could have been an over-reaction and that even if the room had been unhygienic, it was really none of his business.

an example of a youth worker making inappropriate judgements). Some young people may live in poverty or without due care and attention, which may be outside the expectations of a youth worker's experience. Whilst providing opportunities for young people to talk about their circumstances and choices is appropriate, youth workers rarely intervene to 'fix' young people's lives. Should a young person appear to be in genuine danger, most youth workers would raise this with the young person prior to alerting any other authority, such as the Police or Social Services. (See also the discussion about confidentiality in the Introduction to this book.)

Getting to know existing groups

For a youth worker new to an area, existing youth work activities can provide instant access to contacts. New workers will need to establish their own relationships with the young people. Whether quietly and slowly or with a splash will depend on the youth worker's own individual style and on the type of facilities or activities going on. In a youth centre with a laid-back approach to provision of various leisure activities, a new youth worker can often simply observe and mingle without the need for formal introductions. By joining in conversations or activities, a youth worker can be gradually integrated into the setting. In some youth centres where young people are encouraged to take 'ownership' of the management and facilitation of activities, they may also take part in the selection and induction of new workers.

Contacting young people already accessing facilities needs to be recognised as a limited exercise. Over-reliance on existing members for 'word-of-mouth' recruitment can lead to rather homogenous groups who are unwelcoming to individuals perceived as 'different'. Apparently superficial or even indiscernible distinctions can sometimes lead to bullying or clique-ish behaviour. Most groups benefit from regular new membership to avoid becoming static.

Meeting young people at school

An awareness of issues affecting youth work within an educational establishment, such as attendance and protocols, can assist a youth worker to identify appropriate methods for establishing contact. While most young people attend school regularly, others only attend intermittently or not at all due to responsibilities at home, fears of various kinds or exclusion orders imposed by the school. Some young people have valid reasons for finding school an inappropriate use of their time. A youth worker based in a school or making contact with young people through school should have an understanding of the educational options available within the school and the area. Whilst information about the achievement, exam results, position within different performance leagues may be easily accessible, protocols about how to meet with young people may require more specific networking. Access to young people and introductions can be effected through school assemblies, having an office near the common room or arranging a specific time for work with certain groups. A job description which designates specific priorities may limit a youth worker's access to young people who are not in the target grouping.

Following-up directed contacts

Youth workers may be directed to contact certain individual or groups of young people by their employing organisation, other agencies or partnership work. Youth workers need to be cautious when directed to work with particular contacts as the nature of the relationship may no longer be voluntary or meaningful to the young person. Clarity about the purpose of such contacts is essential so that youth work principles are not compromised.

Presenting self

The initial contacts that a youth worker makes with young people can set the tone for future work and relationships. During the first connections with young people, a youth worker finds out about them by listening to them talk about their interests and concerns. At the same time, a youth worker passes on information about the organisation and what is on offer for the young people and their communities. Introductions with key individuals, groups, organisations and services are part of the process. Good listening skills and clarity about the role of the youth work and the organisation are therefore essential to this first stage of getting to know the young people.

In reaching out and listening to young people, the youth worker communicates to the young people the importance of their views.

Having an interest in learning from young people and enjoying their company are essential to youth work practice. Those youth workers who enjoy being with young people and finding out what they have to say are rewarded with new learning and positive relationships with a wide range of individuals. Often young people have had poor experiences in their previous relationships with adults. A youth worker who meets young people on their own terms may be very different from what they have been led to expect from adults. Whatever time is necessary to establish the relationship between a youth worker and young people is generally worthwhile.

Contact with young people assists youth workers to plan, facilitate and evaluate youth work activities, services and projects. Identifying where young people live, what music they listen to, their religion or ethnic group, their peers, their school, what clothing or sports they like, and so forth is not simply a way of getting to know the young people. It is also a way of identifying which young people may be on the fringe of communities or feel excluded. By finding out about young people and being open to what they have to say, youth workers begin to identify some of the barriers faced by young people and their needs.

Having conversations

Conversations that take place in and around other enjoyable activities are the mainstay of youth work. Youth workers and young people get to know each other, identify interests and pass on information through causal conversation while more serious discussions provide opportunities to challenge each others' assumptions and raise awareness of issues. Although a youth worker provides space for conversations and brings in issues for discussion, the power is with the young person to 'dis-engage' and the youth worker accepts that relationships may take time to develop. Box 3.6 has some suggestious about ways to engage in conversations.

A calm and confident approach to conversations with young people is conducive to two-way communication and is generally easier than when a worker presents a false persona in a mistaken attempt to curry favour

---

Box 3.6: Practice examples: Starting conversations

- *Identify what is going on: observe the young people and listen to any on-going conversations. Take notice of what is going on and identify key ingredients such as the setting, the current topics, who is involved, any emotions being displayed, body language, new jargon or slang. You don't need to use their language; you just need to understand it!*

Box 3.6 - Cont'd

- *Listen to the young people's stories. Hear what they have to say.*
- *Think about what you are going to say: identify a topic that has been raised and you find interesting. Respond to their conversations rather than changing the direction.*
- *Join the conversation as an equal rather than asserting your right to speak, being confrontational or offering advice. Try not to interrupt anyone. A question may be perceived as intrusive. Acknowledging agreement with something that has been said can be an effective way of communicating that you are listening respectfully, are interested and have understood.*
- *Allow the young people space and time to respond. Listen.*
- *As the conversation progresses (if it does) stay within the topics that the young people are discussing. Don't raise questions about issues or facts that are outside of the immediate subjects or arena of the discussion.*
- *Don't collude with anything that you're not comfortable with, such as laughing at sexist jokes or condoning illegal behaviour. You don't have to express your views on every issue, but don't agree if you disagree. Be yourself and express your opinions without expecting everyone to be in agreement.*
- *After the conversation, reflect on what happened. 'Replay' the conversation to identify any issues, points at which the conversation could have happened differently, particularly your own interventions. Think about whether there were any issues raised to cause concern and your feelings about the topics and dynamics of the conversation.*
- *Discuss the issues and feelings in supervision and consider issues raised that could be returned to if the opportunity arises or handled differently next time around.*

---

or be accepted. When a youth worker feels positive about the young people and interested in what they have to say, initiating and responding can be an enjoyable part of the process of getting to know each other. Whereas worrying unduly about one's own 'performance' or finding the young people unresponsive, inattentive or aggressive can make this stage quite difficult.

A youth worker needs to recognise that young people grouping in outdoor spaces, whether open to the public or just available for access, usually consider themselves to be in their own territory. Many young people do not have alternative access to spaces where they can invite friends, socialise with others or express their opinions freely. An appropriate and effective way to communicate with young people does not convey collusion with illegal or risky behaviour and recognises the young people's rights to their own space. Unless good relationships are already established, conversation with a group of young people on a street corner should not imply that the youth worker has power over their behaviour. For example, *'Do you think you should be smoking that joint?'* or *'Aren't you a bit young to be out at this time?'* would rarely be effective intervention strategies in this setting. A youth worker who 'joins' such a group will soon find that the young people can and will walk away unless 'their space' is clearly recognised and respected. A better intervention would be responding to an issue raised by a young person or to something that one of the young people had said. Discussions about behaviour may need to wait for an opportunity related to the young people's discussion. For example, a young person saying that he had a bad cough or was feeling tired could provide an opening for a discussion about smoking or sleep; worries about not having any money may lead to conversations about jobs and careers. Finding the right moment can mean responding to topics arising, sometimes rather creatively, rather than having a set agenda.

Detached work usually starts with initial observations and low contact visits to identify the best approach with a group. Establishing group routines, such as when and where they meet, protocols within the group and any activities that might require risk assessment can help youth workers to make best use of their contacts. Interactions build up gradually through greetings and non-intrusive 'small talk'. Different 'intervention strategies', such as offering information or options for opportunities or events, would follow.

Identifying risk

Youth workers need to balance an optimistic approach to work with young people and communities with an awareness of potential pitfalls or dangers. This balance can be achieved through on-going assessments of risk and the development of associated protective measures. Any youth worker who goes out into unknown communities may be considered to be 'at risk'. Not much youth work would be carried out if concerns about workers' safety were allowed to take over and create an atmosphere of fear.

Lack of experience, negative experiences or the reputation of certain individuals or groups can contribute to insecurities taking over in certain situations. An assessment of the risks associated with going out into a community could begin with an understanding of the youth worker's own feelings, experience and knowledge. A starting point can provide direction for necessary preparations to alleviate or address worry, which will vary with individuals. If a youth worker is worried about personal safety, further precautions could be taken. Just as any individual would think twice about venturing into an isolated and unknown territory in the dark, so should youth workers consider reasonable precautions. Some sensible safety measures, such as the identification of support and emergency routines, may assist an anxious worker to overcome unreasonable fears.

An essential skill of youth work practice is to find a way to work with young people without being afraid. A youth worker who is scared of young people or frightened of a particular area is unlikely to be able to carry out useful youth work. Feelings of fear can be analysed to identify causes and come to an understanding of whether they are realistic or prejudicial. Negative stereotypes can be created by certain negative media images, distorted history and lack of experience. For example, a youth worker with a 'racial' identity that is different to a group's may be afraid because of stereotypical notions of their behaviour. Confidence can be developed through gradual exposure to the new group, discussion of fears with other experienced youth workers with knowledge of the group and reading to challenge attitudes.

Making arrangements for safe practice

The potential conflict between responsible protection and safety with necessary risky behaviour and activities is not always easily resolved. Employing organisations may require a 'risk assessment' to protect their workers and avoid high insurance costs and litigation if a youth worker is hurt or injured whilst working. Managers of youth workers are aware that while any setting carries an element of risk, the consequences of injury or harm are more far-reaching when an individual is at work. Overprotection can have its downsides. A requirement for the use of brightly coloured all-weather gear, for example, may well protect against wind, rain and traffic accidents, but may also give an inappropriate impression of being part of a uniformed security or police service.

Some health and safety procedures can reinforce negative views of certain groups of young people and limit opportunities for positive work. For example, youth services often have policies prohibiting work with young people without others present. The policy is seen to protect the young person from abuse from the youth worker. The youth worker is also protected from false accusations because a colleague is present as a potential witness. Making home visits or taking young people in their cars on their own is often discouraged or prohibited due to concerns about accident or attack. The policy protects the organisation, but may also limit the scope of work through preventing or inhibiting one-to-one conversations.

Youth workers with greater levels of confidence and experience can be encouraged to work alongside others with less. Recognising the difference between young people who are expressing strong opinions, anger or other negative emotions and individuals or circumstances that could be personally dangerous may only come through experience. Youth workers develop antennae to pick up indicators that someone may be about to switch from expressing themselves through words to violent behaviour. This ability means that youth workers can be more confident in their interactions with young people, a skill that will develop through praxis, co-working and supervision.

Organising safe detached work

As detached work aims to provide opportunities for positive interactions with young people and communities, safety precautions that serve to create an atmosphere of fear or perceive young people or members of their community as dangerous are generally ill advised. Youth work organisations may require detached youth workers to undertake additional precautions to ensure their well being as well as comply with risk assessment, health and safety procedures or the demands of insurance. (See Box 3.7 for an example of the precaution that one organisation takes to attempt to ensure safe detached work.) A balance between intrusive or excessive measures to ensure safety and sensible arrangements needs to be found so that youth workers can approach young people with confidence and a relaxed manner. Although some youth workers prefer a more

---

Box 3.7: Practice example: Precautions for detached work

Our manager requires us to carry emergency phone numbers like organisational contacts and legal advisors, a personal attack alarm and change or petty cash for public transport. We have a phone card for emergency telephone calls and a choice about whether we carry a mobile (cell) phone. We have to wear identifiable clothing with the organisation's logo and carry an identity card. We always work in pairs or small groups with an established meeting point with other team members. We have a pre-planned escape route and leave details about where we are going with a colleague who isn't out with us who we report to at the end of the shift. We all have to be trained in handling needles, first aid and self-defence. Once I got into a routine of doing all this, none of it seemed intrusive except for the 'corporate' raingear, which I think makes us look like officials.

I always leave any valuables, money, expensive clothing and my car at home. I'm not sure what messages certain labels give out and I don't want to worry about damage or loss. Not because I think the young people are thieves – it's just once less thing to think about.

As a team, we make sure to be aware of isolated places or risky hiding places. Basically it's street sense. We don't split up and we make sure that we can see a co-worker at all times. We always have someone delegated to be particularly observant, to watch what's going on around us. We're always more cautious if a situation or group is new to us and let the others know if anything is worrying us. We try to define the area of work prior to going out and stick to this and agree specific start and finish times and stick to them. We also keep our

> **Box 3.7 - Cont'd**
>
> *eyes open for accessible venues in the area for respite both for ourselves and for young people. Sometimes a local key member of the community will offer an emergency contact point or access to a toilet. We are also on the lookout for alternative accommodation in case a group wants to get involved in some activities like discussions or games.*
>
> *Having said all that, I do detached work because I really enjoy talking with young people in a relaxed setting! We have a real laugh and they seem to enjoy the fact that we don't come across with authority or try to control their conversations and behaviour. We get to know more about them through talking with them in the park than we could ever have in the centre. I know that I will always remember some of the conversations that we have had.*

flexible approach and perceive certain precautions as interfering with practice, they need to be aware that not adhering to an organisation's requirements can result in the withdrawal of support or dismissal should an accident or dangerous incident occur.

Assessing risk for the young person

Managers of youth workers and volunteers also need to be aware of the potential risks or consequences for young people in relation to engaging with youth work or youth workers. New experiences can bring physical, emotional and other stresses or danger for which some young people are not fully prepared. Taking reasonable precautions whilst enabling young people to experience new situations can be a difficult balance. Involving young people, their communities and youth work colleagues in risk assessment can also provide a more secure foundation for understanding planning needs. (See Box 3.8 for some examples of planning methods that can assist in addressing risks.)

Box 3.8: Examples of methods for addressing risks

- Involve young people in risk assessment and planning
- Induction, training and supervision for youth workers and volunteers
- Use experienced staff
- Monitor behaviour, attitudes and practice of staff and young people
- Have adequate insurance for staff and young people
- Plan carefully, particularly for new or different activities
- Be clear about any limitations in relation to capacity, skills, safety
- Be available to listen and talk about issues arising
- Involve young people in evaluation and review of activities

Although some young people are supported by families and friends when they attend youth work activities, this is not always the case. Some may attend against parental or carer's wishes. Young people may encounter individuals and groups who have different perspectives, experiences, belief or value systems from their families or communities. Being exposed to challenges and changes to their ideas, language, knowledge and experience can be difficult for some young people. The physical or emotional challenges of trying out new activities are usually exciting, but can be overwhelming. They may find out about risky or illegal behaviour that is new to them. Providing opportunities for young people to talk about these issues and feelings and make sense of them is an important aspect of youth work.

Not letting the contact be the end of the story

Youth work depends on establishing relationships, which take time to develop. Unfortunately, funding for youth work is often limited to short-term programmes, which may mean that making contact with young people is the beginning and end of the story. Pressures to demonstrate statistical success can lead to meaningless collection of superficial contacts. Rather than providing time to establish relationships and develop group work, some projects are terminated after the initial contact and distribution of information. Some youth workers are frustrated by being pulled out to work with another group that has been identified as 'a problem' when they have only just begun to establish links with the community. Others can carry out this limited role in creative ways that involve young people and other community members so that the whole community benefits. For example, peer education projects can involve young people in passing on the information so that the work has longer-term impact.

Essential skills for making contact

- Going out to where the young people are
- Locating the young people
- Reaching out to all young people
- Distributing publicity and information
- Getting to know existing groups
- Meeting young people at school
- Following up directed contacts
- Presenting self
- Having conversations
- Identifying risk

- Making arrangements for safe practice
- Organising safe detached work
- Assessing risks for the young person
- Not letting the contact be the end of the story

Further reading about reaching out

Burton (1993); Driskell (2002); Hart (1992); Shier (2001); Weil (2005).

CHAPTER 4: Voluntary relationships

Youth work is based on building relationships with young people that recognise individuals and respect the reality of their lives. Youth workers foster the independent nature of their relationships with young people through maintaining professional boundaries. This chapter explores the early stages of developing these relationships with young people through establishing dialogue and working together.

Establishing the voluntary nature of the relationship

Young people choose whether to become involved in youth work. This basic principle affects the nature of the relationship between youth workers and young people as well as the practice of youth work. (See Box 4.1 for a definition of youth work relationships). Youth workers work with young people who decide whether to participate in the activities, discussions and projects. Young people can come or go, accept or reject suggestions or advice, participate fully or refuse to join in. Young people retain a level of power and control and they are encouraged to exert control over decisions about whether and how much to participate. This approach makes youth work unlike most other situations in many young people's lives. Attendance at school is generally obligatory, often a legal requirement and sometimes a costly privilege. Most teachers or parents demand or expect at least a minimal level of compliance. Youth work offers young people options. The activities may be exciting and creative or safe and secure. Through their participation, young people become motivated to undertake more challenging activities.

Box 4.1: A definition of youth work relationships

'A key aspect of Youth Work is 'to build relationships with young people which enable them to explore and make sense of their experiences, and plan and take action'. From the UK National Occupational Standards for youth work.' (PAULO, 2002: vii)

The approach and skills that youth workers use to build relationships with young people can be useful in a range of situations, including those

To37929

which do not correspond with the voluntary nature of youth work (see, for example, Box 4.2). When young people do not participate or are perceived as difficult by other professionals, a youth worker's skills in building relationships may be recognised and valued. Other services which require or coerce young people to participate may call upon youth workers for assistance. Clarity about differences between the voluntary relationships in youth work and other types of work with young people is essential. The distinction needs to be clarified with managers or colleagues from other perspectives or professions. In order to maintain their professional identity and approach, youth workers need to insist that some level of choice be provided for the young people. (See also Chapter 2 about work in different settings).

Box 4.2: Practice example: Establishing a voluntary relationship in a prison

I work as a youth worker in a prison for young offenders. In the evenings when they have 'leisure time', we set up activities in the common room and they can come over and talk to us when they want. We don't invite the young people over. This is their 'free time.' When they do approach the table, I always make sure to acknowledge their approach with a nod or some facial expression. They know that I know they have joined the group, but it is never a big deal.

Lots of them don't ever come over. I've never even met some of them. Sometimes someone will join in a few games and not really say anything. Quite a few though have real issues that they need to discuss and the table with the activities provides an excuse for them to come and talk – as well as a distraction from the reality of what is going on around them.

Welcoming

When young people make contact with youth workers, a welcome that respects and accepts them as individuals is an important first step. Young people are welcomed to their first youth encounter with a youth worker and any subsequent meetings whether the visit is a regular occurrence, following an unexplained gap or after an enforced absence. The welcome communicates a belief that whatever has happened previously, there is an opportunity to move on from that position. A youth worker should not harbour, or at least, not communicate, ill feelings or negative attitudes towards a young person. If a young person was aggressive or disruptive in a prior meeting, that individual needs to be offered the opportunity for a fresh start in a new session. A youth worker would rarely demand explanations or apologies for prior experiences during a welcome as the new encounter needs to be able to start positively with reasonable expectations for success on both sides.

Welcoming is not always an action. Young people are often welcomed simply by being accepted rather than elaborate greetings or induction procedures. Recognising the barriers that can prevent young people from accessing activities, youth workers attempt to provide positive images and information from a wide range of perspectives to communicate that diverse young people participate, individuals from marginalised groups are welcome and a wide range of issues and questions can be discussed. Box 4.3 provides a practice example from a young person's perspective.

Box 4.3: Practice example: A young person's first impression

When I first came to the youth group, I didn't know what to expect. At first I couldn't even see any adults. It looked like the whole place was just kids. At first it made me nervous. I kept looking around for somebody to tell me off, keep quiet or stop putting my feet on the furniture and I wasn't sure what would happen if some of the scarier-looking kids started giving me a hard time. After a while I noticed a couple of youth workers playing pool with some kids and another one was sitting with some others playing some kind of game with a board and cards. I felt better when I saw one of them break up an almost fight without any shouting or big deal. I also saw some interesting posters – particularly ones about different types of families – including ones with just grandparents and small children. And in the toilets there was a list of emergency phone numbers that included numbers to ring if you were worried about suicide, rape, pregnancy and all sorts. There was some great music going on and next door, kids were playing basketball. It was all very exciting.

The level of warmth and method of communicating welcome will vary according to individual workers (see Box 4.4 for some examples of different styles of work). The gender, cultural background and individual style of a worker may well affect how they interact with young people. While one youth worker may view another as detached, aloof or aggressive with young people; others, including the young people, may recognise that worker even-handed, clear and genuine. Confidence and individual preferences will clearly influence the ways in which a youth worker builds relationships with young people.

Box 4.4: Different styles of work

Some youth workers and young people may:
• Find it easy to make themselves heard in a group while others prefer quiet chats in a corner.
• Share personal experiences and opinions while others find that talking about themselves gets in the way of finding out about others

Box 4.4 - *Cont'd*

Same youth workers and young people may: Smile, laugh, tell jokes and stories while others have a calm and receptive exterior
- Join in competitively with all of the activities while others stay in the background
- Get everyone's attention and rally them around to engage in an activity while others watch and observe what is going on.

Ideas about acceptable ways to interact with young people will vary greatly between individual workers and particular organisational cultures. Most youth workers use lighter comments with a sense of humour rather than lectures, thought-provoking questions rather than accusations, and honest expressions of opinion rather than directives. These youth workers would not feel the need to establish their views at the beginning of a relationship. Other youth workers have no difficulty in establishing rapport with young people despite expressing quite opposing views and engaging in robust arguments.

This range of styles can be accommodated because of the flexible nature of youth work. As relationships are voluntary rather than assigned, a young person can approach different youth workers – perhaps at different times – whose styles fit their specific circumstances or needs. Young people's choices can also be informed by the clear definitions of expectations from the organisation (see an example of welcoming in Box 4.5).

Box 4.5: Practice example: 'Matching the mood'

A young person had been attending a youth centre for some months without becoming involved in any of the activities. He tended to sit in a quiet corner rather than interact with others or use any of the games or equipment available. A youth worker made a point of welcoming him to the session and spending some time each evening sitting next to him. After a few attempts to make conversation, it seemed clear that the young person did not want to talk. This decision was recognised and the youth worker did not demand responses. However, the young person continued to attend the sessions and the youth worker continued to spend a part of the time in the young person's company. While the young person did not seem interested in conversing, he did not appear to object to sharing the sofa and seemed content to observe the youth worker's interactions with the others. Without pressuring the young person to talk or join in the activities, invitations were always extended to him and his decision not to participate was respected. One evening, the young person began to talk with the youth worker about some of the seriously unhappy feelings he was experiencing.

Following the young person's disclosures, the youth worker explored the approach that he had used with the young person with his supervisor. They agreed that the reason the young person was eventually able to talk with the youth worker was because he had come to trust that the youth worker would not push him further than he wanted to go. The youth worker was not sure whether more direct questioning at an earlier stage would have enabled the young person to 'open up' more quickly. The process seemed to have taken rather a long time. Subsequent chats with the young person confirmed, however, that he would not have attended the sessions if he had been 'forced' or expected to talk and that he had been unable to discuss his feelings with anyone else up until that point.

Responding to individuals

Youth workers see young people as individuals and try to avoid labelling, making judgements and identifying solutions to their problems (see, for example, Box 4.6). The role of a youth worker is to encourage a young person to take responsibility for their own actions, to identify their own options for change and development in relation to the choices they make in their lives. Youth work provides opportunities for young people to find their own ways forward. A 'deficit model' perceives young people as needy and often inferior receivers of services, which is not appropriate for youth work. Youth workers tend to have a more positive approach to individuals.

Box 4.6: Practice example: Responding to an individual

A young mother of a young baby came into an Information and Advice service facilitated by youth workers. She said that was having difficulties finding enough money for baby clothes, nappies, a cot and a stroller. The youth worker suggested that he refer her to Social Services who might be able to help. The young woman strenuously rejected the idea saying that she they had been to her house before and that they weren't able to help. The youth worker gave her some leaflets about baby clinics in the area, referred her to a local church that he knew had recycled baby clothes and furniture, said that he would try and find out some more information and asked her to come back in a couple of days. He felt pretty good about what he had been able to do for her.

After the meeting, the youth worker asked a colleague from another agency who worked in the same building whether she knew anything about the young woman. The colleague said that she had heard a lot about the local Travellers community. There was massive overcrowding and unemployment, very low attendance rates in the school and educational attainment, continuous problems with the Police being called out to settle domestic abuse situations and high rates of crime and recidivism. She also stated that 'most of them are here illegally anyway and shouldn't be entitled to any state benefits.'

Following this conversation, the youth worker reflected on his first session with the young woman and worried that he had given her a leaflet that she may not be able to read, sent her to a church that she might not believe in and

> **Box 4.6 - *Cont'd***
> she had more or less stated that social workers were involved with the family. What about the baby's safety, their housing and food?
>
> His supervisor suggested that he find a way to build a relationship with the young woman that was based on what she asked for rather than labelling her with the prejudices that Travellers tend to encounter. The supervisor advised him to find out where some cheaper baby clothes were available as this was what the young women had requested. Some research about Travellers' communities was also recommended.
>
> The next time the youth worker met with the young mother, he struggled to rid his mind of the picture of her circumstances painted by his colleague and welcomed her back. Although he had managed to learn a lot about Travellers that contradicted what his colleague had said, he still didn't know whether she was from that community. He asked her how she was doing and admired the baby. He waited to hear what she had to say rather than making enquiries about her circumstances.

Youth work practice is based on attempts to hear and understand what young people wish to communicate about their lives. This approach 'starts where the young person is at' and generally requires a great deal of flexibility. Youth workers listen to what young people are saying, discuss their ideas and work on issues related to their expressed needs and interests. (See Box 4.7 for a youth worker's explanation of the importance of listening.) Unlike some other professions, youth work is not governed by restrictive procedures or rules that are sometimes used to maintain authority or security.

Some agencies working with young people do have procedures for practice. Concerns about the safety of equipment, accidents on excursions and potential allegations of sexual or racial harassment can lead to the imposition of extensive rules and procedures. 'Clients' details are recorded. Interactions are monitored and recorded on a computer

> **Box 4.7: Practice example: The importance of listening**
>
> *I think that listening is definitely the most important thing that a youth worker can do. Listening and making sure that young people have a good time. Young people have so many things going on in their lives: adolescence and transitions to adult lives – emotional and hormonal swings and changes. They have to adjust to changes in family relationships, things going on in school and friends – all kinds of issues related to sexuality and health, including drugs, HIV/Aids, having babies. They think about leaving home, housing, employment, discrimination, inequality and exclusion. The thing about coming to the youth centre is that they can talk about these things and their views and ideas are taken seriously and sometimes even acted upon – but only when they want them to be.*

that compiles statistical data, which is then made available to a range of agencies. Young people are carefully instructed about regulations, rights and any constraints to confidentiality. Assurances are provided that any information disclosed will be treated in the same way as that of any other young person. Parental and care-provider permissions are sought with great frequency. Checklists ensure that policies cover every eventuality. Some organisations may believe that with these policies in place, young people will be protected from unequal treatment or gaps in information.

The effect of policies that are designed to protect the organisation against litigation and disciplinary action can be detrimental to the aims of youth work. Key aspects of youth work, such as flexibility, spontaneity or informality can be undermined by organisational anxiety. The emphasis on procedures, professional language and competence can also work to devalue the contribution of professional decisions or input from untrained volunteers alike. Dictating too many procedures and an overcautious approach could create barriers to exchanges of views and ideas on a level of equality on the wide range of topics that may concern young people (see Box 4.8 for an example of a youth group with no rules).

Box 4.8: Practice example: Working without rules

I started a football session with a mate of mine on Tuesday nights because we liked football and we knew that the kids around here had nothing to do except get into trouble. I managed to get permission to use some grounds attached to a religious centre nearby. We can't use their toilets and we don't have anywhere to get changed or shower, but they said that we can use their field. So anyway, about a dozen kids show up – not always the same ones, but pretty much. They just found out by word of mouth. Everybody around here knows us anyway. We don't have any club rules; we just have football regulations. Except we don't have teams – they change every week. And we usually don't bother keeping score. Actually, that's not true. We did have one rule. No hitting – or else you can't come back the following week. Then one week one kid hit another kid. We all stood around in the rain shouting about it. Then everyone said. 'See you next week.' So we got rid of that rule.

In some contexts or situations, a welcome may be quite short-lived. Once a young person's arrival is acknowledged, some organisations or youth workers have certain expectations about acceptable and unacceptable behaviour and attitudes, particularly when a youth work activity takes place inside or whilst on a supervised excursion. Rules should, whenever possible, relate to attempts to ensure young people's safety rather than simply to control or for no genuine purpose. Some facilities or organisations ban or eject young people who are clearly under the influence of mind-altering substances, attempt to bring such substances into premises where youth work is taking place, are physically violent or verbally abusive towards others, engage in risky behaviour or behave in ways that are unsafe or are dangerous to others or bully or intimidate others. Other organisations have very few rules, but manage to convey their expectations of considerate behaviour through example and discussion (see also Chapter 8, which discusses ways to make group agreements).

Maintaining dialogue

Youth workers engage in dialogue by listening and learning in order to hear what the young person is saying before responding. A dialogue can be initiated by either party; youth workers are responsible for ensuring that the lines of communication are open and conversation is welcomed. Maintaining a dialogue where power rests with the young person means that the youth worker minimises the focus on self. Checking understanding could help dialogue to become more equal and should encourage a full exploration of issues so that each party comes to recognise more about the other's perspective. Youth workers use what is sometimes called 'democratic dialogue' in the fields of community development or conflict resolution (e.g. Pruitt & Thomas, 2007). (See Box 4.9.)

Box 4.9: Why democratic dialogue?

'The more conceptual frameworks differ, the more the interpretations are likely to be at odds and the greater the challenge of achieving understanding. What is needed in these situations is not necessarily more communication but more understanding.' (Pruitt and Thomas, 2007:16)

While the starting focus of a conversation is on the young person's understanding rather than an analysis from the youth worker's perspective, judging when to interject and help to steer a discussion or offer an opinion is critical to youth work. In certain circumstances, a youth worker can provide an alternative perspective or analysis of a situation, which can be enlightening or useful for the young person. Box 4.10 provides some suggestions for ways to maintain democratic dialogue.

A young person should have the choice whether to ignore, challenge, avoid or circumvent not only what is happening to them outside, but also within the youth work setting. Youth workers provide support for individuals facing unjust treatment in many different ways according to the situation and the youth workers' own experiences, which will inevitably affect their perspectives, analysis of what is going on and ways to handle situations. Youth workers with a range of responses can

---

Box 4.10: Practice example: Suggestions for maintaining dialogue

- Focus on the young person
- Provide opportunities to ask questions or find out information rather than always providing the answer
- Approach young people positively rather than prejudging or labelling
- Take time to listen rather than worrying about your own situation, work and schedule
- Attempt to understand the meaning of what someone is saying rather than listening without hearing
- Allow young people to find their own examples and demonstrate their knowledge rather than showing off and scoring points
- Expect to learn from the young people rather than telling them 'like it is'...
- Check understanding of the situation rather than interpret possible meanings
- Acknowledge what the young person says rather than disagree
- Ask about opinions rather than providing them; ask for suggestions rather than giving them
- Check young people's own feelings or responses rather than demonstrating your own
- Allow young people to think 'out of the box'; don't resist new ideas or perspectives
- Design activities with high levels of participation and creativity; don't just control or divert attention and energy
- Invite feedback; don't resist criticism
- Encourage young people to express themselves; don't talk too much
- Allow young people time to explore their ideas; don't move into decisions or actions too soon
- Encourage young people to share their experiences and feelings; don't problem solve.

---

provide that choice for young people, who will drift towards a youth worker and young people's organisation that suits their needs.

Most youth workers listen to young people's experiences of injustice so that the young person can find ways to deal or cope with what happens. Some however, place more emphasis on the positive effects of pursuing diversionary interests and not dwelling on life's inequities. A youth worker may demonstrate an understanding of the context in order to assist a young person to outline the options. Another youth worker may not react. Not only because situations are familiar and therefore un-shocking, but because this youth worker feels that the focus should be on young people's experience of the issues. One youth worker may have a more emotional response, showing warmth and compassion. Whilst another will be more intellectual – encouraging the young person to consider options and consequences. Finding the appropriate level of support will enable a young person to identify what is going on in a situation and make choices in relation to any action, reaction or coping mechanism (see Box 4.11 for an example).

A youth worker's relationship with young people is not simply responsive. Youth work has a positive and proactive role in promoting social justice, recognising discrimination and addressing barriers to equality of opportunity. A youth worker raises and discusses issues such as racism, sexism, disabilism, heterosexism, class oppression, ageism and unfair treatment of individuals. The attitudes and practices of young people, colleagues and other agencies working with young people may provide barriers to participation that need to be addressed. Through positive images, supporting individuals experiencing discrimination and challenging oppressive attitudes and practices, a youth worker encourages young people and colleagues to have an active approach to addressing inequality (see also Chapter 7 on Anti-oppressive Practice).

Box 4.11: Practice example: Providing appropriate support

A young man told a youth worker about the 'bullying' he received from a teacher at school. The young person said that no matter how hard he tried, he could not understand the course work. He was constantly in trouble for not completing his assignments and the teacher was always 'going on' at him. The youth worker, who was experienced in working with excluded young people, wondered whether, the young man had undiagnosed learning difficulties. Although the youth worker thought that the young man might well have been unfairly treated, he did not reveal any anger about the situation. He provided the young man with the opportunity to express his feelings, describe his learning experiences and explore his options. The focus of the discussion was on what the young man could do to change the situation that he was in and what the consequences of different choices might be. Possible options included making a complaint, asking for help or ignoring his teacher. During this discussion, the teacher's apparent unfair treatment became less of a concern than the possibility of being able to find a way to complete his school work. The youth worker provided the young man with information about dyslexia. They talked about the possibility of being screened and discussed his feelings about this – as well as the advantages and disadvantages of this process. Decisions about his first steps, such as talking with his parents, asking the Head of Year for an appointment and talking with his teacher, were also discussed. Through this process, the youth worker provided support for the young person to make his own decisions so that he could take more control of his situation.

Respecting young people

Respect plays an important role in youth work and relates to the young people, the youth worker and their relationships. The process of building a relationship based on respect starts with 'respect for the person' rather than the person's status, beliefs, opinions or history. To do this, youth workers separate the young people from their reputation and previous actions to provide them with opportunities to express themselves. In general, youth workers do not expect instant respect from young people as this respect may need to be earned. Most youth workers recognise the value of having respect for themselves, their professional value base and boundaries rather than demanding this from others.

Youth work respects others' potential for change and development and recognises their achievements. Demonstrating a respect for others' basic human rights to dignity, privacy and equality of opportunity is the first step. Youth workers are often involved in encouraging young people to recognise the rights of individuals to free speech and assisting them to see a distinction between respect for the person and respect for what they have to say. A youth worker does this by supporting young people's rights to say something even when others strongly disagree. Through a range of responses and activities, youth workers foster young people's abilities to respect themselves, each other and other people in their lives, including the youth workers.

The level and degree of respect demonstrated and demanded between a youth worker and young people should be mutual and even-handed. Most youth workers do not expect or demand respect for their own achievements, knowledge or strengths; the emphasis is to pass these on to young people if they are interested or want them. Attempts to provide a positive role model, for example, can be based on a perception of a young person's current role models as immoral or operating on an inferior value-base, which is not a respectful approach. Demanding respect from young people as an older, wiser, more mature or successful individual can be counter-productive to establishing a youth work relationship, which is generally on a more equal level (see Box 4.12 for some examples of these varied approaches to practice).

Box 4.12: Practice examples: Different styles of work on respect issues

Challenging disrespect: *If I overhear a young person disrespecting another or if someone disrespects me, I point this out. I might ask them how they would feel if someone treated them like that or tell them that the particular behaviour is offensive or explain how it makes someone feel. I don't think you can ignore it when someone is rude or uses offensive language or puts someone else down. We have to pass on an understanding of basic human rights and the need to treat others' fairly and humanely. I show respect to them so they show respect to me.*

> **Box 4.12 - Cont'd**
>
> **Showing respect:** *I know that many of the young people's experiences are about not being respected – so I don't expect them to show me respect. I try to demonstrate respect to them. I hope that over time this will 'rub off.' I think that young people have so many authority figures telling them how to behave all the time and I'd rather try something different. It may take time, but I respect where they are coming from and take it from there. Eventually they respect themselves. Eventually, they come to respect me.*
>
> **Analysing respect:** *Sometimes young people don't realise how their own behaviour contributes to the situations. So we talk about rights and responsibilities – choices and consequences – and try to link these themes into how respect can be earned. We talk about what goes on in their interactions with teachers, parents and the police and talk about their reactions, unfair treatment and being ignored and how they can handle it.*

Respect for young people as individuals is generally linked to an understanding that young people are capable of making choices and taking some control over the decisions that they make. Some interventions or interactions may be more useful with specific groups or situations – and most youth workers will use a variety of 'standing by' approaches as well as 'getting involved'. Young people often ignore frequent challenges, which can communicate a negative stance. Appropriate encouragement and praise can help to counterbalance interventions that point out mistakes. Deciding when, how, why and where to intervene may require a number of factors to be analysed. An individual's confidence and responsiveness, the potential effect on the individual and others, and whether alternative actions may prove more effective, may all determine what might be said or whether to say anything at all.

Youth work practice is contextual, based on the realities of the particular young people with whom the youth worker comes in contact. While different youth workers may use their own individual strengths in quite varying ways to engage with young people, build credibility and/or provide alternative perspectives, the relationships start with the specific young people and their experience, preferences and realities.

Use of self

Youth workers tend to be cautious when utilising their own experience, opinions and personalities in their interactions with young people. Being honest and open with the young people with whom they work does not mean telling the young people everything about themselves. Clearly not everyone thinks in identical ways, has the same experiences, learns through similar methods, has comparable interests or shares perspectives.

On occasion, however, an example from one's own experience can be useful. Rather than prescribing a specific course of action, a thought-provoking example may help or encourage individuals to think differently about a person or issue.

The Johari window (Luft, 1982; see the figure in Box 4.13) can be used in self-reflection or supervision to identify the issues that may be appropriately disclosed in youth work. The 'open window' contains information and issues that could be appropriate for discussion with young people. The 'hidden window' contains the experiences that are not relevant to a youth work relationship – or for that matter anyone else – and therefore would not be disclosed. These windows might be quite different from the open and closed windows used at home or out with friends, where self-disclosure generally increases with close relationships. Young people can be very open about providing feedback and help to reduce the 'blind window'. The young people's perspective on how youth workers present themselves may be quite educative. Use of the 'unknown window' may also be enhanced through youth work. Shared enjoyable activities with young people could serve to reach as yet untapped creativity normally unknown and in the subconscious.

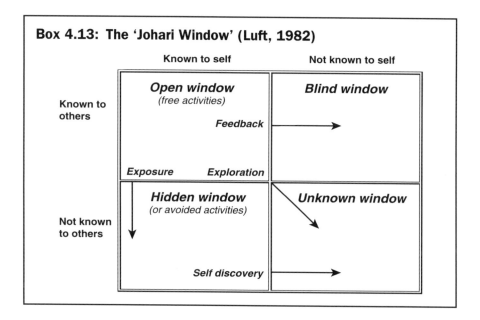

Box 4.13: The 'Johari Window' (Luft, 1982)

Locating self

'Location of self' involves identifying one's role and experience in order to have a clear awareness of self and identity and to be 'comfortable with who we are'. An awareness of political and personal power, experience of privilege or oppression can help youth workers to recognise how they are perceived by others. Individual personal histories can provide experiences that may be significant. Relevant experiences could range from a secure or a chaotic upbringing, religious and political ideologies or unstructured hedonism, the safety of a family or domestic violence, serial or long-term relationships or poverty, war, gangs and riots. Identifying a personal standpoint in relation to such social constructs as class and 'race' or prejudices, such as sexism, disabilism and heterosexism, can enhance a youth worker's understanding of similarity or difference with the young people who join in the youth work activities. Supervisors, colleagues, family members, reading and reflection can be used to 'locate self'. Considering identity, strengths and weaknesses and developing self-knowledge is a part of professional development. Taking time to reflect on identity and practice can help youth workers to analyse their assumptions and the context of their beliefs (see Box 4.14 for some examples of ways to 'locate self').

Box 4.14: Some suggestions for 'locating self'

Youth workers can 'locate self' by identifying and evaluating:

- Their experiences, identities, abilities, skills knowledge and values and how this shapes or affects their perspective and reactions to young people, issues and colleagues

- Their strengths

- Their weaknesses or gaps

- Their identity in relation to age, gender, race, class, ability, religion, politics

- How they might be perceived by others

- The differences between their own experiences and perceptions and those of the young people

- Their role as a youth worker

- How their role relates to the young people, the organisation, the community, the society

- Self-disclosure and how much information about themselves is necessary to pass on or reveal

- The core values of youth work and their anti-oppressive perspectives, including feminism, a black perspective, a social model of disability

- How the core values of youth work and own personal values or perspectives relate to each other

- How they would define appropriate relationships with individuals and groups of young people

> **Box 4.14 - *Cont'd***
>
> • How they perceive professional behaviour with other workers
>
> • Their own power – whether personal (due to their experience), locational (due to their identity) or positional (due to their job status)
>
> • How they can be clear about the above without remaining stagnant.

A youth worker's previous experiences can affect reactions to situations, understanding of issues and relationships so that location of self in relation to experience can be useful for professional development. Self knowledge and clarity about any similarities or differences between their own and others' identities can assist a youth worker to understand how this can affect relationships. This self-knowledge comes about through considering one's own identity and how this relates to others.

Maintaining professional boundaries

Professional boundaries in youth work relationship include concerns about power and autonomy. Youth workers must maintain a strict boundary between actions taken in youth work practice and any actions intended to gratify their own sexual desires. A sexual relationship, even if the young person becomes the age of a consenting adult, will interfere with the youth worker's relationship not only with the individual, but other members of the group. Developing a close relationship with a former member of a youth group or a close relative of a current or former member is also ill advised. Youth workers can be friendly and listen; in some instances they may be supportive or caring, but the relationship should not overstep into a friendship. Young people should be allowed to make their own mistakes and to take control of their lives. A worker provides guidance and 'detached' support rather than becoming embroiled in a situation as another 'player'. In order to maintain these boundaries, youth workers need to reflect on their practice in the light of youth work principles and make use of supervision to discuss any situations where dependency, sexual desires, or friendship are impacting on the youth work relationships.

The boundaries for appropriate youth work practice are established by youth work principles and defined by youth workers through reflection on practice with experienced supervisors. Inappropriate relationships with young people abuse the trust that they, other youth workers and society as a whole should be able to expect. If a young person seeks an inappropriate relationship with a youth worker, the youth worker must tell the young person that such a relationship is not possible. In addition, the youth worker will need to consider ways to distance themselves from the situation without making the young person feel rejected or worse about themselves. In these situations clarity of role as a youth worker is important to explain why it would be unethical to continue such an association. (See Box 4.15 for some suggestions about professional boundaries.)

Box 4.15: Some ways to define professional boundaries

The boundaries of youth work practice require a youth worker to:
- Be aware of the position of power and responsibility that they have in young people's lives and not abuse this
- Steer clear of exploitative or preferential treatment for individual young people
- Avoid close, dependent or emotional relationships with young people
- Not engage in work-related activities for personal gain
- Understand the difference between an inappropriate gift and a token acknowledgement
- Not accept gifts that would lead to preferential treatment or compromise integrity
- Take care that behaviour (inside and outside of work) does not undermine the confidence of the young people in the profession
- Be aware that individuals may wish to discuss personal and private matters that they are unable to discuss with others
- Recognise the difference between a professional approach that is based on developing a positive independent relationship and emotional involvement
- Take care not to develop close personal, particularly sexual, relationships with the young people they are working with
- Alert a supervisor about any concerns over relationships which may breach professional boundaries.

Letting go

Enabling a young person to move on from youth work into other arenas is an essential skill and helps to define an appropriate youth work relationship. If a relationship has not been co-dependent or overly emotional, letting go will usually be a natural and easy progression. Some youth work organisations have more formal leaving strategies, such as identifying skills for the next stage via exit interviews. The process of disengaging with young people could also include an exit strategy. Some youth workers find Tuckman's (1965) definition of stages of groups a useful tool for recognising the need to celabrate or mourn at the end of a relationship to enhance the ability of the individuals to move on. (See also Chapter 5: Bringing young people together.)

A youth worker respects and promotes the right of an individual and group to make decisions and choices about their lives based on their own understanding of their own needs. This does not mean that youth workers have a passive role or that they watch others endanger others or themselves without comment or intervention. Youth workers are involved in raising young people's awareness of the range of decisions and choices open to them and offering opportunities for discussion and debate on the implications of particular choices.

Essential skills for developing appropriate relationships with young people

- Establishing the voluntary nature of the relationship
- Responding to individuals
- Respecting young people
- Use of self
- Locating self
- Maintaining professional boundaries
- Welcoming
- Maintaining dialogue
- Letting go

Further reading about youth work relationships

Banks (2006); NCVYS (2007); Rogers and Farson (1988); Smith (1994); Thompson (2006).

PART B Working Together

Working Together has four chapters examining group work practice with young people. Chapter 5, *Bringing Young People Together*, looks at forming groups that address basic needs and stated interests and enable young people to learn from each other. Chapter 6, *Having Fun*, examines examples of enjoyable group activities and the importance of developing positive experiences in young people's lives. Chapter 7, *Issue-based Practice*, focuses on a planned approach to working with young people in addressing some of the issues that they face through individual circumstances, their development needs and societal discrimination. Chapter 8, *Working it Out*, explores working with groups to address any differences and relationships within those groups.

CHAPTER 5: Bringing young people together

Using various methods to bring young people together, youth workers facilitate the development of groups where young people can enjoy themselves, share experiences and learn from each other. Some of the stages required to develop groups based on genuine need are discussed in this chapter, such as identifying resource requirements, considering barriers to participation and prioritising conflicting demands.

Youth work provides enjoyable opportunities for young people to come together in groups to socialise and develop their interests. Shared activities enable young people with similar circumstances, identities or experiences to develop positive relationships, learn from each other and have a voice in issues that affect them. Collectively, they identify and articulate their own experiences in discussions with others who have a genuine understanding of their perspectives and can provide the support and/or direction to develop realistic plans for change. A youth worker brings individual young people together through organising contacts, creating warm environments for meetings and working with groups to acquire resources. Young people gain confidence through collective decisions and gain an appreciation of the consequences of various actions to inform future social action.

Young people participate in youth work activities for various obvious and more hidden reasons. Developing one-off activities and complete programmes of sessions as well as fixed term projects and ongoing groups requires youth workers and young people to work with each other so that motivations and interests are addressed. Some young people join groups for sports, arts or learning activities. Others may use resources, such as a play facility, computer suite or leisure facility. Some require services, such as support, advice or practical assistance. Understanding what may motivate young people to join a group or make changes in their lives can provide direction for the development of viable youth work activities (see the table in Box 5.1).

Recognising young people's needs

Youth workers often prioritise work with young people whose needs have not been met through other social structures, such as families or

Box 5.1: Reasons why young people may participate in youth work

For enjoyment	• To relax, have fun, play, be with others, share enthusiasms or interests, be happy, express themselves • To meet other people, get to know them, make friends, talk about selves, find out about others, gossip, fall in love • For adventure, excitement, new experiences
For specific activities	• To carry out outdoor pursuits, rock-climb, play sports or chess • To socialise, pray, discuss, listen to music, become involved in arts, dance or drama, keep fit, learn something, try something new
To fill gaps and/or address needs	• For praise, recognition, love, security, self-esteem • To feel needed, belong, be listened to, respected, treated fairly, keep busy, get involved, be responsible, achieve, gain status • To influence, change or assert control over social, economic and political issues that affect them • To gain confidence, boss others about, express themselves, feel powerful • To talk about issues arising in their lives, e.g. worries, concerns, fears, about the many emotional, physical, mental, domestic, sexual, behavioural and social changes and transitions going on in their lives • To adjust to changes in their dependence on others for boundaries, value-base, opportunities, responsibilities, finance
For a cause	• To work together, campaign, effect change, improve the environment, build community links or spirit, combat drugs/crime, have a say about current affairs and politics, access and participate in the provision or improvement of services, opportunities and resources
For services, advice or support	• For education or training, answers to questions, to gain specific skills, knowledge or awareness • For condoms, childcare, counselling, mediation • For advice and information about health, debts, drugs, alcohol, housing, employment, educational opportunities, family problems, domestic violence, peer pressure, bullying
For escape or refuge	• To get out of the house, combat isolation or boredom, feel safe or relaxed, survive • For shelter, warmth, food, security, safety, protection • Because of desperation, there's no where else to go, fear, upset, conflict
Coercion	• Because of a court order or rehabilitation programme, a professional referral, it's part of the school curriculum, the teacher sent them • Because of peer pressure, their parents/carers sent or brought them, punishment.

education services. Maslow's (1943) hierarchy of human motivation (see the figure in Box 5.2), often depicted as a triangle rather than the rather dynamic situation he defines, recognises that most people are only partially satisfied in relation to their needs. This dissatisfaction can provide a motivation for change through attempts to address unmet needs or to compensate for them.

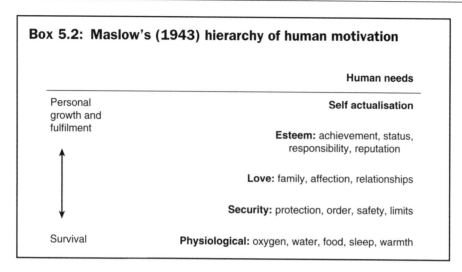

Box 5.2: Maslow's (1943) hierarchy of human motivation

Human needs

Personal growth and fulfilment — Self actualisation

Esteem: achievement, status, responsibility, reputation

Love: family, affection, relationships

Security: protection, order, safety, limits

Survival — **Physiological:** oxygen, water, food, sleep, warmth

According to Maslow (1943), the survival needs at the bottom of the hierarchy generally take priority over the other more intellectual desires for achievement. Different perspectives due to interest, age or circumstance can affect an individual's priorities. For example, someone interested in power may value their reputation over their need for love. Individuals whose needs are not met in one area may find satisfaction through addressing another. For example, musical expression may compensate somewhat for a lack of love and security. (For an alternative look at human needs, see Max-Neef, 1991, discussed in Chapter 9 Developing participation).

An awareness of the degree to which young people's needs are being met can inform practice, but does not drive it. Recognising that basic physiological needs are important and that they may not have been addressed elsewhere, youth workers provide a warm welcome and a comfortable environment. Refreshments may be provided with the activities that young people say that they want. As a general rule, youth workers respond to young people's expressed needs rather than diagnose deficiencies. For example, a young person expressing an interest in music would be responded to in a positive way, possibly by being signposted to relevant opportunities. A youth worker should not make a judgement about the young person's musical potential or abilities to pursue this interest. If the young person appears to lack the self-esteem necessary to pursue such options, activities that could widen opportunities for social relationships and feelings of self-worth would also be discussed.

Youth workers need to be aware of young people's development needs during their transition to adulthood as these issues often inform the development of relevant activities and groups. (See the table in Box 5.3, which list some examples.) Pringle (1980) suggests that the significant

Box 5.3: Issues related to young people's development

Areas of development	Possible issues arising
Identity location of self	• Self-esteem, self-image, groundedness (being secure and in touch with reality), self-knowledge and confidence • Political, cultural, ethnic, sexual and gender identity • Racism, xenophobia, sexism, heterosexism, disabilism, class, ageism, class • Morality, beliefs, religion, spirituality
Health Physical, mental and emotional well-being	• Changes in appearance, abilities, puberty, growth • Pregnancy, sexual health • Boredom, self control, anger, disappointment, shame, stigmatism, behaviour • Exercise, sports, healthy eating, caring for self • Accessing health services and advisers • Addictions, substance abuse (own and others) • Eating disorders, self harm, anxiety, depression • Ableism, disabilism, impairments • Illness, bereavement
Relationships • With family members • With friends, peers, lovers, partners • With the community and the public • With colleagues at work and school • With professionals and figures of authority	• Communication, negotiation and social presentation, confidence and assertiveness • Conflict, arguments, disagreements • Giving and receiving love, affection, care, attention • Bullying or being bullied, hate crime, cyber bullying • Divorce, family break up, running away, parenting • Expressing political views and opinions • Crime, domestic violence, forced marriages, sexual abuse, rape, violence, gangs, guns (as perpetrators or victims)
Looking after domestic arrangements	• Housing, finding a home or refuge, homelessness • Moving house, eviction, conflicts with neighbours • Being in and leaving home, care, prison, the armed forces • Seeking refugee status, asylum seeking • 'Financial literacy': handling finance, credit, planning, poverty, debt, repossession • Cooking, household management, repairs and maintenance, gardening • War, torture, environmental disasters
Education and work information about options, access and pathways	• Motivation and aspirations, creativity, satisfaction • Time-management, focus and planning • Participation, progress and achievement in learning, education and employment • School exclusion, under-achievement and failure • Literacy, numeracy and computer proficiency • Dyslexia, learning difficulties • Finding and keeping a job

developmental needs are love and security, new experiences, praise and recognition and responsibility. Youth workers address the need for love by bringing young people together for shared activities where they can develop friendships and other loving relationships. The need for security is addressed by providing a reliable, welcoming and safe presence in young people's lives. Youth work also provides both safe and adventurous environments for activities that enable young people to extend their assertiveness and survival skills. The need for new experiences can be addressed by broadening young people's understanding of possible life choices, going on excursions and trying new skills. Involving young people in planning and organising activities and sharing in decision-making enables young people to experience handling of responsibilities. Young peoples' identities, health and relationships are frequent topics for youth work discussions and activities alongside issues related to their environment and their careers. (See also Chapter 7, which focusses on issue-based and anti-oppressive practice.)

Identifying genuine and compatible interests is not always a straightforward procedure. Some young people may not identify or articulate their needs clearly. Whilst in some situations, several young people may have compatible reasons for coming together or joining a group, others may have conflicting interests. Evaluating levels of enthusiasm for activities is often based on expressed interests as these are the most obvious reasons for a young person choosing to participate. Other motivations may also play a part and can affect participation. Some young people have or express more rigid preferences and will only attend youth work for a specific activity. Such specific and overt reasons may be easily identified yet subject to change. For example, a young person's aspirations to be an actor may provide an impetus for joining a drama project, but not sustain sufficient interest if only a small role is offered. Another young person may attend the same sessions with a more hidden, unarticulated need for refuge from an oppressive or abusive domestic situation. This motive may provide rich sustenance for hard work. Young people who have a general desire to become part of a group and have a good time may be inspired by a group to perform. On the other hand, this group may prefer less demanding activities. Reflection on these possible influences on group development is essential to good group work practice.

Having a planned approach for bringing young people together

Bringing young people together may take place over a single session or over many months. Having established a level of communication with an existing group, large assembly or various isolated individuals, a youth worker may be able to identify some genuine needs and interests for a group. Possible options can be discussed with potential members so that they are involved in planning and developing viable activities and sustainable services. Depending on the evidence and level of interest, initial meetings of members may take place to discuss the aims before a more extensive resource allocation is made.

Youth work activities need to be of interest to the target group. If young people need employment, improved park facilities may not attract them. The planned approach to outlined in Box 5.4 should enable a youth worker to put together a case for resources to be allocated to relevant activities based on genuine interests and needs. While young

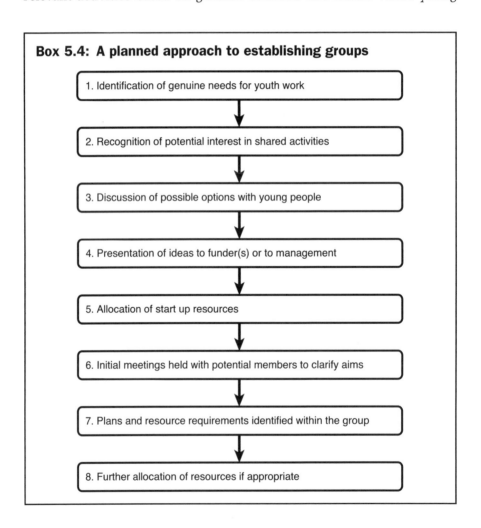

Box 5.4: A planned approach to establishing groups

1. Identification of genuine needs for youth work

2. Recognition of potential interest in shared activities

3. Discussion of possible options with young people

4. Presentation of ideas to funder(s) or to management

5. Allocation of start up resources

6. Initial meetings held with potential members to clarify aims

7. Plans and resource requirements identified within the group

8. Further allocation of resources if appropriate

people's ideas may change about their involvement in decisions, applying for and allocating resources can assist them to consider their choices more carefully.

The common interests of young people, community, organisation and wider society may come together to develop well supported and sustainable youth work. However, such congruence is not always the reality. Some groups are established due to organisational or societal priorities rather than young people's needs or youth work principles. Youth workers often find that the essential steps to establish genuine needs and interests have been bypassed. A romantic or idealistic perception of young people's needs or a social policy based on a political agenda may direct and finance particular initiatives. Attempting to address targets that do not relate to the young people's concerns can result in inappropriate allocation of resources and lead to difficulties in recruiting members or maintaining participation. A boring programme, an underused facility or unrealistic targets can result from attempts to start a group with insufficient consultation and involvement (see the figure in Box 5.5).

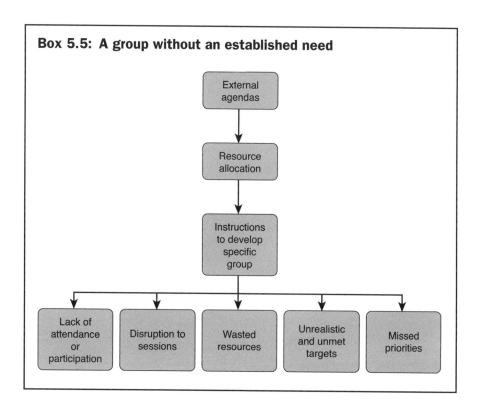

Box 5.5: A group without an established need

Identifying a need for a group can be established through outreach, networking and getting to know a community. (See Box 5.6 for a practice example and chapter 10 on using research.) Young people and other members of the community often suggest ideas. 'We don't get a chance to do anything with the boys around'. Young women may find it difficult to compete with boys for equipment or space so that a girls' group could ensure young women's access. 'Could we meet later on? Then it wouldn't clash with football'. A schedule that fits in with current activities respects the young people's life choices and in this case, could encourage their continued participation in sporting activities. If the youth worker can match these identified needs with existing resources or a funding opportunity, a successful group could result.

Box 5.6: Practice example: Identifying need through observation

A community worker enjoyed wandering around the local outdoor second-hand market during her lunch breaks and noticed that there was a large number of young women with small children wandering around. It was apparent that neither the young women nor the children enjoyed the experience. The worker was aware that employment in the area was low, that there was a high level of debt and that loan sharks were active in the area. She also knew that there was a high percentage of young single mothers under the age of eighteen. The worker was aware that there was a brand new community facility with rooms available for community use. She publicised a parent and toddler group through leaflets distributed in the market. Response and participation levels were high.

Youth work can also develop as a result of an awareness of gaps in existing resources, which may be unavailable, inaccessible, unresponsive or inappropriate (see the practice example in Box 5.7). An awareness of any community issues and sources of support for young people can help to identify whether a new activity or group is required. More extensive research, (such as that detailed in Chapter 10) can help to prioritise needs.

Box 5.7: Practice example: Addressing gaps for LGBT young people

Lesbian, gay, bi-sexual and transgender (LGBT) young people living in a rural area felt isolated because they had nowhere to socialise or find out information about LGBT issues. Only by going into the regional city centre could they find venues where they felt they could be 'out'. The distance to travel and the adult facilities on offer were generally not appropriate for the younger ones. Their main source of relevant information was through websites, some of which were unsuitable. The 'open access' generic groups and activities for young people in the area were limited and the young people reported that they did not feel safe to be themselves in these environments. The youth workers discussed the options with the young people concerned and it seemed that networked computers with appropriate firewalls and recommended sites could be a way for the young people to make friends and gain peer support away from the adult gay scene. When plans were being made for allocation of resources in the next financial year, they made sure to include LGBT young people in discussions. Meanwhile, the youth workers also began some issue-based work on heterosexism within the local generic groups. Publicity and information was put on display and discussed.

A change in a community, such as a sudden crisis, can provoke a range of needs for youth work. Some examples could be a natural disaster, war or explosion, or the closure of a resource. Youth work can bring young people and their communities together to address short-term or longer-term changes. Discussions about trauma, addressing the consequences or providing diversion from them can be provided through youth work activities and programmes. Youth action groups can be formed to address an issue; youth volunteers can offer services to a community; facilities for young people can be offered by youth workers (see, for example, Box 5.8).

Box 5.8: Practice examples: Developing work on drug mis-use

Version A: Addressing the issues
A flurry of young people's drug-related deaths galvanised young people's interests, community and political support as well as interest within a local youth centre. The youth workers involved young people in addressing the issues. Opportunities were developed to socialise without fear and to use needle exchange and advice services. The activities were well used, welcomed by the community and well supported by the organisation. The community issue focused attention on positive practice.

Version B: Conflicting approaches
In another community, conflicts of needs and interests led to disagreement about how the drugs 'crisis' should be addressed. Community leaders demanded tighter policing and curfews. When the young people asked for a needle exchange, the community was outraged. Without political support, the youth centre could not find sufficient resources for informal educational activities. The youth workers decided that developing closer links with community organisations and disseminating information about the reality of young people's lives may provide a more positive basis for future practice.

Using different methods to bring young people together

Whilst some young people will join a group or come to a meeting through reading a notice or being handed a flyer, most will require a closer relationship with others involved prior to attendance. The figure in Box 5.9 illustrates some different ways to bring young people together.

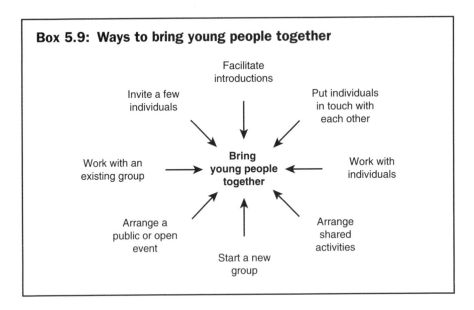

Box 5.9: Ways to bring young people together

Facilitate introductions

Invite a few individuals

Put individuals in touch with each other

Work with an existing group

Bring young people together

Work with individuals

Arrange a public or open event

Start a new group

Arrange shared activities

Working with individuals

Bringing young people together may start with work with individuals to build up their confidence and readiness to join a group while at the same time getting to know them and their needs or interests. A young person may benefit from getting to know a youth worker first in order to be ready for the next step or to identify what the next step might be. While groups of young people can provide excellent support and learning, some young people may require additional groundwork prior to or during their participation in groups. For example, an individual may need to discuss or move on from experiences such as poor relationships with other young people. A young person experiencing certain life transitions or trauma unrelated to participation in groups may require further support. A young person may need or want to develop particular social skills, such as non-violent interactions, confidence or assertiveness and language skills prior to joining with others (see Box 5.10).

Putting individuals in touch with each other

A youth worker who remembers individual young people's interests, such as a certain type of music, martial art, or other hobby, can make

> **Box 5.10: Practice example: New experiences developing confidence**
>
> A youth worker became aware that a young person had been bullied in school and was reluctant to join a local youth group because of fear that the experiences would be repeated. After several individual chats about 'non-serious' topics, such as favourite football teams and television programmes, the young man expressed some interest in a documentary programme about gravity. The worker remembered that an observatory in the area had advertised 'Summer Sleep-overs' for young people where they would have the opportunity to look through the telescope and find out about stars.
>
> With the youth worker's support, the young man made some enquiries and discussed his findings. He found out that the session would consist of quite a small group, which would be unlikely to make him feel lost and under-supervised. He would be on the older edge of the age range, which reduced his fears of being intimidated by older boys. The sessions were quite structured, which would lessen opportunities for bullying. He decided that he would go.
>
> When the young person returned from a positive experience, he felt ready to join the local youth group. The youth worker was aware of the need to keep an eye on him. However, the confidence that the young man had gained meant that he participated fully in the activities.

arrangements for those young people to meet and share their interests in one-to-one meetings or independent groups. Shared experiences or circumstances may also highlight an opportunity for encouraging contacts. Depending on the age, maturity and confidence of the individuals concerned, a youth worker may need only to identify the shared interest or need, check out willingness to meet, distribute contact details and allow meetings to develop as the individuals wish. In situations where the individuals may be inexperienced or vulnerable, a youth worker could offer guidance to safety, such as recommendations for safe and neutral meeting places, getting to know each other before meeting alone or at home or informing parents or carers about arrangements.

Putting individuals indirectly in contact with each other may be a useful method of bringing young people together when developing a sustainable group is impractical. A passion for an unusual topic or a minority interest may not lead naturally to a group activity. Individuals who live in a rural area may find it difficult to travel to a shared facility. Alternative organisational priorities or resource restrictions may mean that a youth worker is unable to facilitate these smaller groups. A self-sufficient group or independent communication between such individuals, perhaps by telephone or internet, may be more feasible and still provide opportunities for social interactions.

Facilitating introductions

Individuals may benefit from a managed meeting with an invitation to a specific time and place as a way to start building relationships.

The worker may need to facilitate introductions, move the conversation on and co-ordinate follow-up. This approach would be useful when individuals are under-confident or need supervision because of their age or history. Sometimes the basis of the shared circumstances is a topic that the individuals find difficult to talk about (see, for example, Box 5.11 on sharing experiences of bereavement).

Box 5.11: Practice example: Sharing bereavement

A youth worker was aware that two young people living within a particular area had both experienced parental bereavement and felt that they would benefit from getting to know each other. Without over-emphasising their shared circumstances, the worker told each individual some information about the other prior to the introduction and asked each about their interest in a get-together. The worker encouraged them to view the meeting as an opportunity to meet someone else their own age rather than primarily to discuss their bereavement. At their first meeting, the worker was more nervous than the young people and reflected afterwards that she had probably over-done her involvement in facilitating the introductions and conversation. The meeting felt rather stiff and formal. However, when the worker left the two alone to answer a phone call, she returned to find the two young people chatting cheerfully. They expressed interest in meeting again and the worker helped them to make the arrangements.

Concerns about issues related to circumstances or development, such as identity, health or relationships, may help to bring young people together but do not need to be the overt aims for a group or meeting. Involving young people in joint enjoyable activities may prove just as beneficial as exercises more explicitly related to their common concerns. For example, bringing together a group of young people who are in care ('looked-after' by others rather than their family) to play games may relieve some loneliness and lead to improvements in their relationships with others. A single parents group may benefit from socialising as much as educational activities about child-rearing. A starting point for work with young people who are in danger of gang reprisals may be a common interest in football rather than discussions about their fears.

Recognising barriers to participation

Many young people work and play alongside each other happily despite differences or difficulties outside the youth work arena. Others find that access is fraught with practical and emotional difficulties. Youth workers attempt to enable access and participation for all young people who need or want to participate. Consideration of potential barriers or hindrances to participation can identify areas for positive action. Society or individual attitudes, practices or policies may be at the root of some of the barriers to participation faced by some young people. Although youth work may not always be able to control, overcome or diminish exclusion, changes to practice may be able to address some of the effects.

An individual or smaller group may be prevented from participating or be unwilling to participate or contribute because of the identity or behaviour of the larger group. Involving the young people in identifying barriers to participation and ways in which they can be addressed can be a positive step. Taking part in positive action to address barriers can raise the level of young people's involvement and their confidence as well as effect genuine change. Communication with the young people about the best way to address the barriers may help to find ways to enable participation.

Discussing options with the young people

Checking with the young people about their needs and ideas is an essential part of developing a proposal or plans for further work. For example, youth work needs to take place in a setting that can support and promote participation, the forming of relationships and learning from the activities. The right environment for a group to function and grow includes a number of decisions about the venue, such as ownership, scheduling and needs in relation to facilities (see the figure in Box 5.12).

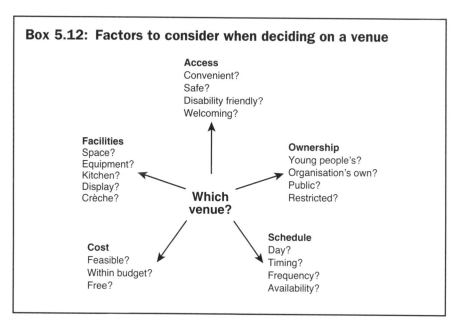

Box 5.12: Factors to consider when deciding on a venue

Access
Convenient?
Safe?
Disability friendly?
Welcoming?

Facilities
Space?
Equipment?
Kitchen?
Display?
Crèche?

Ownership
Young people's?
Organisation's own?
Public?
Restricted?

Which venue?

Cost
Feasible?
Within budget?
Free?

Schedule
Day?
Timing?
Frequency?
Availability?

The young people will have their views about the purpose of the group; who should be included and their requirements. Youth workers may need to encourage the group to consider issues for potential members as well as those currently involved and to identify who is excluded by their decisions and whether the membership is representative of young people in the area. The discussion can be used to raise awareness of barriers and anti-oppressive practice as well as issues in the area.

Factors affecting a choice of venue can be wide-ranging and contradictory (see the examples in Box 5.13). Some young people feel more confident or comfortable within their own space or peer group. Certain groups of young people may not wish to venture beyond limits defined by a school's catchment area, housing estate or other geographical features. Young people from a working-class housing estate may be reluctant to use the facilities of a youth centre situated on the other side of a main road in a more affluent area of town, and vice versa. Violence or the threat of violence within a 'gang culture' may define certain 'territories'. These boundaries may affect where the young people they might be willing to go to participate in youth work activities. Many young people need strong motivation to explore beyond an existing group of friends and will only participate in an activity if others from the group come with them. Coming to an agreement or a decision about arrangement is part of the process of establishing the group and can lead into longer-term work to assist young people to overcome any fears about going into new or different territories. (For more on working out disagreements, see Chapter 8).

Box 5.13: Practice example: Contradictory suggestions from young people

- *Fridays are great for me.*
- *I won't be able to come on Fridays because of Friday prayers.*
- *I have to pick up my sisters from school so we have to meet before 1.00 p.m.*
- *I work until 2.00 so I can't be here until 3.00.*
- *My parents would never let me come to this venue; it's the wrong religion.*
- *This is an ideal venue. My parents would be very happy to let me come.*
- *I can't go to that venue; it's next door to the Police station.*
- *The bus comes nowhere near this venue. Don't you have a pickup service?*
- *I don't want anyone to know I'm coming. Can you guarantee that no one will know?*
- *Someone needs to look after the baby or I won't be able to play badminton!*
- *This venue has no proper washing facilities in the toilets in keeping with sharia law. We need clean water available in the toilets.*
- *This is the only venue we can afford.*

Once a need has been established, a youth worker meets with the young people to identify how they will address their interests. Decisions about resource requirements need to be made to establish when and how the group will meet. Certain types of activities such as cooking, gardening or building, may require specific facilities or equipment. The scheduling of the meetings may also dictate availability and options. The life-span (whether short-term, fixed term, ongoing) may be fixed or unknown. The history and reputation of the group may also affect decisions. Clearly funding and resources, although not always static, are a factor.

Identifying and addressing appropriate childcare arrangements and related issues can be essential for a group to thrive. Some projects aim to promote positive parent/child interactions so that offering a crèche throughout a session may not be appropriate. Other activities may not be possible for a parent whose child is present. Although a safe and well staffed crèche may be an ideal way to enable parental involvement, resource requirements may be extensive. Alternative arrangements could include partnerships with childcare providers who may offer local or on-site services, expenses for parents to pay their own child-minders or a babysitting rota amongst the young people themselves.

The extent to which the young people can use a particular venue and stamp their own identify on to it are important considerations when bringing young people together. The degree to which displays, decoration and changes to the furniture and equipment are possible may affect a choice of venue. Other users may not appreciate the displays that youth workers see as vital, such as providing positive images of diversity, educational material about sexual health or guidance about harm reduction. While many youth workers value the opportunities that one-to-one work provides for identifying and addressing young people concerns, bringing young people together is an essential skill for youth work practice. Groups can inspire young people to explore new options. Through interactions with their peers, young people can develop the skills and confidence that will enable them to make their own choice about their lives, education and future careers.

Essential skills for bringing young people together

- Recognising young people's needs
- Having a planned approach to bringing young people together
- Addressing young people's interests
- Recognising shared circumstances
- Recognising the need for a group
- Using different methods to bring young people together

- Working with individuals
- Putting individuals in touch with each other
- Facilitating introductions
- Recognising barriers to participation
- Discussing options with the young people

Further reading about bringing young people together

Hunter, *et al.* (1995); Informal Education website; Mullender and Ward (1991); Pringle (1986).

CHAPTER 6: Having fun

This chapter looks at some positive and enjoyable activities that youth workers can offer. Examples of creative and sporting activities are examined to illustrate the range of enjoyable experiences, learning and action that characterise youth work. Some of the issues related to involving other professionals are also considered.

Whilst youth work should be more than just a service providing activity that young people enjoy, youth work should be fun! Involvement in positive and enjoyable experiences serves to address the human and development needs discussed in other chapters (Maslow, 1943; Pringle, 1980) and the voluntary nature of youth work, which, according to Plato, provides a better platform for learning (see Box 6.1). Young people want to come to youth work for the possibility of new and challenging experiences as well as familiar and friendly pursuits.

Box 6.1: Voluntary learning, Plato (around 375 BC)

'A free man ought not to learn anything under duress. Compulsory physical exercise does no harm to the body, but compulsory learning never sticks in the mind.' (Plato as construed by Lee, 2003: 269)

The general positive feelings that come from a nurturing and supportive environment can result in enjoyable youth work. Providing a warm welcome to all young people usually requires that a youth worker enjoys the company of young people and embraces participative and anti-oppressive values. Developing positive relationships is encouraged through a high level of social interaction and discussion. Some activities may focus on physical or individual achievements. A range of options are needed to address varied interests and needs for stimulation and reassurance.

Youth work typically includes this range of activities, which generally provide opportunities to socialise, dialogue and take action. The range of content and styles of youth work mirrors the diversity of young people's circumstances, motivations, sensitivities, preferences and interests. Flexible and responsive programmes of activities can be developed in partnerships between young people and youth workers. A youth worker attempts to adapt activities to address feedback from participants or the expressed interests of potential participants. Current interests and needs are a starting point from which to develop confidence in undertaking new experiences. Suggestions from young people may be augmented by youth workers' suggestions or options to avoid boredom or complacency. New challenges and learning opportunities are required for youth work to remain enjoyable. Perhaps the art of youth work practice is to find an appropriate mix of working within young people's 'comfort zones' and challenging their preconceptions about options that they may not have considered before. Involving other professionals or agencies can augment the range and depth of activities on offer.

Work with young people whose basic needs require attention can lead to a loss of focus on the enjoyable aspects of youth work. For example, youth workers may encounter individuals who would benefit from better homes, food and clothing. Rather than judging circumstances and rushing to provide a solution, youth work attempts to provide an environment where young people feel appreciated and can enjoy themselves as well as take up opportunities to learn new skills. Any educational or other social and community services that may be offered as a part of youth work should be informal rather than replicate services offered elsewhere.

Some youth workers view the activities as being merely a means to an end and describe their function as a 'vehicle for delivering youth work'. Providing opportunities to keep fit, for example, is seen as a method of 'delivering' messages about healthy eating or lifestyles. Other youth workers focus on the activities provided and describe their role as, for example, a sports, arts or outdoor educator. Whilst either approach is compatible with youth work, youth workers need to be clear that the activities on offer need to retain their voluntary and participative qualities. Young people should not be manipulated into undertaking activities that do not reflect their interests or become passive passengers using a service.

Developing arts activities

Taking part in performance arts, such as music, dance and drama, as well as making things such as crafts and cookery are often popular choices for enjoyable, creative and educational youth work activities (see the figure in Box 6.2 illustrating examples of art activities). The benefits of offering arts activities can range from developing a satisfying hobby to liberating self-expression. Individuals who have not had success in educational settings that rely on verbal literacy or numeracy may show more proficiency with other methods of communication and creation. Many young people do not have other opportunities to develop or explore their artistic talents. Schools, families or communities may not prioritise these areas, perhaps preferring that young people address subjects perceived as more 'useful', such as maths and science, technology or business. Clearly youth work has an important role to play in nurturing young people's participation in arts activities.

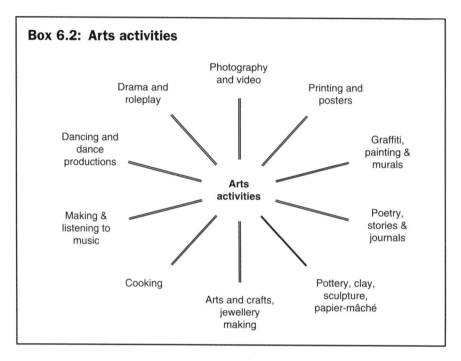

Box 6.2: Arts activities

Artistic endeavours may lead to more formal or public expressions such as exhibits, performances and competitions. Opportunities to dabble and play with materials and experiment with equipment are also valuable as a means of trying out ideas and getting used to the media. Part of the youth worker's skill is to determine when a group may benefit from the challenge of a more in-depth project. The foundation may emerge from previous work together or from a chance opportunity. Box 6.3 outlines an example of how a photography project developed when an informal educator was able to match the interests of young people with a successful bid for resources.

An individual, exhibit or performance can provide examples for young people's artistic development. Excursions to galleries, theatres or concert halls can provide inspiration and the direct attention and communication with artists that can be possible through workshops is also stimulating (see Box 6.4). Identifying a suitable individual to work with the young people is not always an easy process. Involving the young people in selection can help to find to someone who is good at their art as well as being accessible and communicative.

Box 6.3: Practice example: A photography project

I was an informal educator based in a community centre, which made a successful bid to a local art gallery to create an exhibition on the theme of 'Diversity in this Town' within a six-month timescale. Discussions about the bid led to the emergence of a core and diverse group who requested suggestions from all of the groups and classes using the centre. The consensus from the sixty respondents was to produce a photographic display, a presentation book with texts, a video film of the processes involved and paintings and drawings around the theme of living in the town.

Participants were given a disposable camera and asked to photograph things about their lives. As each photograph contained an amazing story, a visual and emotional collage gradually emerged. Everyone was asked to write a short piece of text in their first language or in English to support the photographs. The design of the presentation book, the photographic hangings, the video editing, the soundtrack and the design of the exhibition stand were completed in workshops. The group handed over their precious work to a committed and interested gallery team on the deadline. Invitations were sent to families, friends, tutors, youth workers, other artists and agencies with whom participants linked in their lives. The launch day was a remarkable chance to feel the results of networking, sharing life experiences and trusting in others, as well as a chance to recognise the work of other groups in the exhibition and be recognised by visitors in turn for the commitment and creative energy the project released.

The project provided participants with a means to enhance individual skills. For example, some used their creative eye with a stills or video camera; some found the confidence to share and talk about their lives in pictures. Some enjoyed being able to express themselves confidently in their first languages because they were clearly valued by others; others functioned in English with support from English-speaking volunteers. Sharing individual artistic skills, taking risks by talking with a newspaper reporter about the project and contributing to a group statement about the project involved a steep learning curve for everyone. The group experience presented challenges about ownership, communication, commitment, skill-sharing, learning to trust others in different roles, taking risks with trying new skills, negotiation and reaching a consensus, being together in new settings, being seen as a group and meeting other groups – not to mention the joy of celebrating together!

By the end of the project, participants could handle a camera with confidence, ask critical questions about what they watch on film and enjoy the public recognition of their important message to the town, which was to be kind to each other and live in peace. The project brought the individual skills and group experience alive while promoting participants' growth in being able to relate to others and the deepening of relationships.

Using drama and roleplay

From a discussion where a youth woker says 'imagine you had to say that to him now....' to a fully fledged film or stage play, drama is a powerful tool for youth work that examines issues. Being able to take on a 'role' rather than directly talking about experience can be a liberating

---

Box 6.4: Practice example: Music as transformation

A group of young people that I was working with was involved in planning and organising a music festival with professional musicians playing alongside young people in a composed set of pieces. Some of the young people had never even picked up a musical instrument before. But they learned quickly! They spent months practising their parts, ringing up and emailing other groups, talking about their different pieces. It all culminated in a public performance at a concert hall attended by the local government officials, parents and friends. It had such an effect on them. They got such a kick out of being on stage and it was videoed and put on the web as well. I really think that they will be much less likely to be involved in the risky and destructive behaviour that they used to get up to. It was a truly transforming experience. The project involved young people who had no access to music lessons, no experience of performance, very little contact with people outside the suburban village where they lived. Most of the professional musicians had come from an entirely different kind of background of economic privilege and high educational qualifications. This festival made such a difference to both groups' understanding of the world.

---

opportunity for a young person to explore and release emotions. Drama exercises in everyday practice (such as those outlined in Box 6.5) can enable young people to develop their social and presentational skills and to practice their responses to difficult scenarios. Dramatic play may also develop their assertiveness and confidence as well as helping them to see the consequences of certain actions.

Full dramatic productions can emerge from roleplay exercises and can be organised in the same way as any other project (see Chapter 11). A youth worker would need to assess a group's readiness for a long-term

---

Box 6.5: Practice examples: Drama and roleplay exercises

'In the manner of a word'
We use a game to help develop awareness of body language. One person selects a card at random and has to carry out actions as requested by the rest of the group 'in the manner of the word' written on the card. The requests could be as simple as 'walk around the room in the manner of the word'. The other participants have to guess the word on the card. Examples are 'cheerfully', 'angrily', 'slowly', 'loudly', 'sadly', 'wisely' or 'rhythmically'. You have to leave enough time to discuss how to portray the more positive words, such as 'confidently', 'proudly' and 'assertively'. These are the most difficult to portray yet the most useful to them! We have enough cards for each player – or sometimes, one team prepares the cards for the other team. You have to be careful with literacy issues though. It can be embarrassing for someone who can't read the word or doesn't know its meaning.

Box 6.5 - *Cont'd*

'Backstory' or 'What happened next?'
We have a collection of unusual photos, postcards and posters that we use to stimulate story-telling. Everyone has to say something or act out something that could happen just before or just after the picture. The images prompt thinking about situations that may be unfamiliar to them – some of them are well known but show different perspectives and identities have something different about them. The game helps with self-presentation and conversational skills especially with young people who are not used to being in the spotlight for positive reasons.

'Acting out'
We have a group that loves to develop and perform scripts based on their own lives. They form groups that take turns to act out scenes from their experiences. Then they talk about how each felt during the scene and discuss how they could have dealt with issues differently. I would only use this exercise with a group that I knew well. They need to feel that they could trust me to 'rescue' them if it got too heavy. They have looked at such a wide range of issues, from sibling rivalry to pressure to join gangs. The best thing about the approach is that they can have a laugh about some of the ways people behave as well as try out different responses to situations.

---

commitment before undertaking such a production. Considerable amounts of time and other resources are usually required, not only to organise the event, but to build up young people's confidence in performance. A partnership with an experienced individual or organisation aware of what goes into producing and directing plays or films could provide the young people with some useful guidance. Youth workers need to be clear about whether the production will be handed over to another professional's approach or will be cooperatively managed.

Planning games and sports

Youth work offers opportunities for engaging in games and sports to provide activities that many young people enjoy and that may also lead to healthy mental and physical development. Much youth work consists almost entirely of physical and sporting activities (see the figure in Box 6.6 illustrating some examples). Some youth workers have additional training and qualifications in specific areas, such as coaching and outdoor pursuit certificates, to enhance what can be offered. However, many youth workers undertake such activities with groups of young people despite a lack of sports training. Although 'extreme sports' and more risk intensive activities may require proper preparation, a youth worker's lack of proficiency may provide a young person a rare opportunity to excel, for example, with a game of pool or running races.

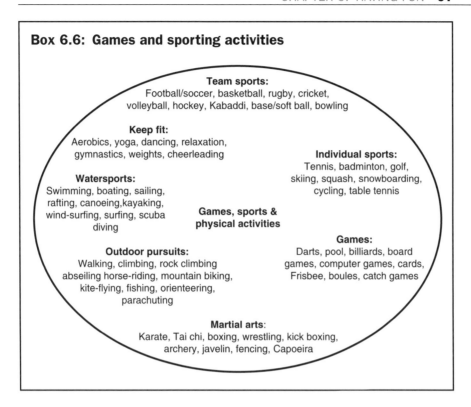

Box 6.6: Games and sporting activities

Team sports:
Football/soccer, basketball, rugby, cricket,
volleyball, hockey, Kabaddi, base/soft ball, bowling

Keep fit:
Aerobics, yoga, dancing, relaxation,
gymnastics, weights, cheerleading

Individual sports:
Tennis, badminton, golf,
skiing, squash, snowboarding,
cycling, table tennis

Watersports:
Swimming, boating, sailing,
rafting, canoeing,kayaking,
wind-surfing, surfing, scuba
diving

**Games, sports &
physical activities**

Games:
Darts, pool, billiards, board
games, computer games, cards,
Frisbee, boules, catch games

Outdoor pursuits:
Walking, climbing, rock climbing
abseiling horse-riding, mountain biking,
kite-flying, fishing, orienteering,
parachuting

Martial arts:
Karate, Tai chi, boxing, wrestling, kick boxing,
archery, javelin, fencing, Capoeira

Some activities require a considerable amount of resources whilst others, such as 'clap and rhyme' or 'stickball' (see the Street Games/ Street Talk website) are played in the streets without any preparation. As long as health and safety issues are addressed, a wide range of sports can be organised without the 'proper gear'. Of course, certain activities are enhanced by having relevant equipment and facilities and others require the involvement of trained professionals to avoid danger. A youth worker who overcomes a fear of abseiling, for example, may be a better model for a similarly challenged young person than an 'expert enthusiast'.

Teamwork and achievement in an individual sport can both be valuable experiences for young people. Coping with pressure and disappointment as well as success are further beneficial outcomes. Most youth work may not be particularly appropriate for the development of 'serious' competitive athletes because of the emphasis on participation by all members of the group whatever their abilities. For those individuals who are able to achieve excellence in sports, youth work can provide a first step and the inspiration and direction required for further training. For all young people, participation in games and sport should lead to learning about taking responsibility, making choices and working with others as well as having an agreeable time.

Involving young people in planning for games and sporting activities can increase accessibility and full participation. The wide range of young people's skills, abilities and preferences need to be taken into account to ensure that as many individuals as possible can participate. Addressing issues of exclusion requires consideration of potential participants' needs rather than simply those of an existing group. For example, thinking about how a young person using a wheelchair would play a game can help suitable alterations to be made when required. Accessibility is usually improved by planning some co-operative as well as competitive games and team activities as well as individual ones.

Young people will be drawn to different sports, games and facilitators, often on a personal level. Keeping an eye on whether young people are enjoying the activities is essential to youth work practice. A youth worker's enthusiasm should not cloud judgement about the young people's level of interest. For example, a youth worker keen on basketball may participate in pickup basketball games in the park that develop into local tournaments. Some groups develop into highly competitive teams, but this should depend on the individuals' interests. A different group of young people may prefer to carry on in their own less structured way.

Some young people are clearly motivated to be involved in physical activity and some perform well whilst others may require encouragement and support to develop their motivation, confidence and skills. A variety of other factors can affect interest in sports, including self-image and prejudice. Young people who feel that they are the wrong size, gender or shape may be encouraged to take up physical activities through the provision of different options and role models. Issues that can arise include bullying and exclusion when a competition goes wrong or feelings of inadequacy that arise from losing. Part of the role of a youth worker is to ensure that less able or confident members are not left out or abused, to provide alternative and perhaps less typical images of individuals enjoying a wide range of sports and to support a positive approach to competition and 'having a go.' (See the practice example in Box 6.7 that illustrates this role.)

Youth workers emphasise the aspects of the activities that relate to youth work principles, such as participation and anti-oppressive practice to enhance young people's enjoyment and self-esteem. Work with groups often requires a youth worker to promote awareness and appreciation of everyone's contribution. Physical activities and games can provide more structured opportunities for groups to interact and develop confidence. Through team sports, young people learn to co-operate and work together in planning their tactics, organising competitions and trips to other facilities. Similar benefits can emerge from the individual sporting activities undertaken as a group. Community involvement through parents and other members of the community

---

Box 6.7: Practice example: A young women's football project

I worked with a young women's group carried out some research and found that many young women were not engaged with sport, particularly those viewed as 'boys' sports. They decided to hold a residential to provide opportunities for young women to try out different sports. The women-only environment seemed to make them less embarrassed. Even though many had not kicked a ball before, the most popular sport proved to be football.

A women's football project was formed and regular sessions started at the beginning, for example how to kick and pass. Help came from professional sports coaches from the two local professional teams. Sometimes increased competitiveness and aggression lead to sexist comments amongst each other such as 'you kick like a girl!' During the project, the young women started to challenge these and other stereotypes about 'girls' sports' and 'boys' sports'.

The group found out about an international women's football competition and decided that they wanted to go. They fundraised for nine months with cake sales, car boot sales, karaoke and band nights, held a sponsored triathlon with cycling, swimming and a five kilometre run and made funding applications with the help of youth workers. Getting a passport, flying across the Atlantic, seeing new places and feeling homesick were all new experiences for some of the members. The young women had never been outside their own city before. At the event, the team didn't win any matches but were presented with a trophy for sportswomanship.

One year later, two of the women have joined a local women's football team and two others now go to the gym regularly. Many of the young women cut down on smoking and drinking and began to do other types of regular exercise. They are producing an information leaflet about healthy eating and exercise for other young women. The group runs fortnightly football sessions and has played in some tournaments. They are also planning some sports taster sessions next year in wrestling and cheerleading! Additional benefits have been life skills and organising skills, such as getting to practice and to the airport on time, as well as a massive increase in self confidence and a greater understanding of their own bodies and healthy living.

---

acting as coaches, cheerleaders or uniform and transport providers can further enhance a project. Box 6.8 provides an example of how a martial arts co-operative developed to promote a youth work approach to sporting activities.

Usually the choice of a sporting activity depends more on the young people's enthusiasm than on a youth worker's interest. However, many young people have been excluded from participation in sports through access issues or a lack of self-confidence. Stereotypes based on race or gender, fitness or ability may prevent many from participating or enjoying certain activities. A youth worker who has a genuine enthusiasm for the sport may help young people to break free from these images and participate with enjoyment.

> **Box 6.8: A practice example: Martial arts for everyone**
>
> Several individuals interested in different approaches to martial arts used the same community facility to train and provide exhibitions relating to their field. Chance conversations about mutual interests gradually led to the development of ideas about how the centre could be used more effectively as a resource for young people, martial artists and martial arts educators. A vision for the centre emerged as a place where young people could explore different sports and activities within a holistic approach to assisting young people to develop into more productive members of society. The ideas developed because the martial artists recognised a potential role for martial arts that not only developed physical and mental skills and stamina, but enhanced leadership qualities and life choices.
>
> A conference or meeting was called and parents, teachers, coaches and artists were invited to discuss core values for the centre. The themes that emerged included the need to:
> - Provide a space for young people to grow and mature
> - Focus on learning and development as well as success in competitions
> - Work with all young people, regardless of mistakes, lack of experience or ability, or identity
> - Link the sporting challenges of strength of purpose and confidence, focus and dedication, time management and cooperation to all aspects of life and life choices.
>
> The strategies were:
> - To provide leadership training through mentoring youth in leadership roles
> - To develop women in coaching roles
> - To move away from a coach-centred model towards an athlete-centred approach aimed at helping all participants improve their performance over time.

Playing games

As Singer (1994) says, play is valuable for a number of development areas (see Box 6.9). Playing games also performs a number of functions in youth work: they can be fun, provide an excuse for interactions and can be used to raise a number of issues. The competitive nature of sports and many games suits some young people and youth workers more than others. Some young people thrive and learn more from a disciplined approach, whilst others find this constricting or even frightening. In a similar way, some young people find much needed safety and security with a youth worker who provides a clear structure for learning particular skills and developing strength, whilst others need more freedom. Different youth workers and different activities can provide a range of options, from those who constantly alter the rules, those who have no rules and those who insist on playing by them. Valuing these differences within a team and a programme can help young people to explore and find activities that they enjoy.

Box 6.9: A definition of the value of play

'I propose that children's play, with its repetitive and exploratory characteristics, represents not only fun but a critically important feature of their development of cognitive and emotional skills. Considering the various forms play takes, it is easy to identify the possible value of sensorimotor games for enhancing physical skills and even of games with rules for modeling early forms of orderly thought or even morality.' (Singer in Goldstein, 1994:6)

A wide range of games can be used to encourage an alternative approach to play without the pressure of points, rules or winning and losing that inhibits some people's enjoyment. In some cooperative games, such as parachute games (for examples see Le Fevre, 2007), creative thinking, participation and enjoyment are clearly valued. The competitive elements of a particular game can also be circumvented by constantly switching team members or refusing to count the score. A fiercely competitive young person playing a more anarchic game might be initially frustrated and then begin to enjoy more free play (see Box 6.10).

Board games and computer games as well as pool are staple provision in much centre-based youth work. Many young people find them enjoyable and the activities are generally viewed as harmless entertainment (although most organisations will monitor internet and computer games for appropriateness). Games that can be played by several players simultaneously have similar benefits as the sporting activities in relation to providing opportunities for communication

---

Box 6.10: Practice example: Games with no rules

We used to have games of 'running bases' where the young people ran between two points like cricket players – but without any batting – while two catchers continuously threw an object back and forth. The runners could be 'tagged out' by the catcher holding the object by tagging (touching) the runners before they reached the base. Initially the young people thought that the point was for the runners to keep score of how many runs they made and how many outs. We kept randomly adding points to some runner's scores ('there's two more points for you for running in a zig-zag line') and taking them off others ('that's minus two points for wearing a red shirt') and we never made anyone stop. So the game would last as long as they could keep running and we kept throwing. There was usually at least one who wanted to know who was winning and what score everyone had and we would just tell make up numbers in response. The great thing about it was that if you got the right atmosphere, everyone was involved at their level and tried really hard – because there was a notion of competitiveness – but winners and losers didn't exist because we showed no interest in the rules.

---

and co-operation. Any arguments and disagreements, which are also part of the 'package', can be learning experiences as well. Allowing young people to find their own ways to share equipment and resources is part of youth work. The degree and type of intervention from youth workers in relation to young people's interactions and decisions about taking turns and clearing up does vary. Most youth workers will step in so that bullies are not allowed to dominate all of the time. However, some will step in simply to be a presence and play alongside the young people for a period; others may hold a discussion about groundrules (see also Chapter 8 on Working it out).

Developing partnerships

Establishing or developing partnerships between young people, other members of staff and other organisations to carry out an agreed piece of work can enhance the resources available for activities. Collaborations can lead to shared expertise and ideas, a wider range of perspectives on issues and different approaches to problems. The organisation of more demanding projects beyond the remit or capability of a youth worker, such as an extensive artistic production or a challenging sporting expedition can often benefit from the involvement of other professionals or individuals with specialist training and certification. However, partnerships with some professionals and 'experts' with little or no experience or desire to involve young people in decision-making or address anti-oppressive practice may constrict practice. Their notions of professionalism or standards for productions may also get in the way of the group's enjoyment of the activity.

In general, strong or effective partnerships are based on a common understanding of aims and objectives and good communication between the partners regarding their roles, values and approaches. A partnership may develop organically through a network of individuals who offer mutual support or be established with a contract made between agency managers. Some partnerships involve reluctant parties forced to work together due to pressures from others or financial constraints. All too often, lack of time and poor management can lead to partnerships which take up more time and work ineffectively. The figure in Box 6.11 illustrates a planned approach to establishing a partnership that could be more effective.

Clear lines of communication, accountability, planning, mutual trust and allocation of tasks and responsibilities need to be maintained throughout the lifetime of a partnership. Some of these elements can be difficult to support. Conflicts may arise at various stages over perspectives, culture and values, as well as practice. For example, young people may

---

Box 6.11: A planned approach to establishing a partnership

1. Establishing a recognised and agreed need

Potential partners identify and agree each partner's potential contribution as well as the aims and benefits of the partnership and acknowledge any barriers, difficulties or concerns about working together.

↓

2. Establishing clarity of roles and responsibilities

Partners discuss and understand the partners' roles within their own organisations as well as establish who does what within the partnership.

↓

3. Developing a co-ordinated approach

The partnership establishes compatibility of values and practices and builds on their different strengths by recognising and accepting the different skills, knowledge, approaches and perspectives that each contribute.

↓

4. Ensuring agreed purpose, aims and objectives

Partners establish mutual agreements and understanding of what is being attempted.

---

find it difficult to work with individuals who do not show them respect. An artist, actor or athlete who has been involved in disciplined training for years to establish their technique may have little patience with young people who appear to lack motivation or skill. However, when these partnerships work well, young people and their partners can genuinely enjoy each other's contributions.

Essential skills for organising enjoyable activities

- Understanding the need for youth work to be enjoyable
- Enjoying young people's company
- Developing different activities

- Developing arts activities
- Using drama and roleplay
- Planning games and sporting activities
- Playing games
- Establishing partnerships

Further reading about organising enjoyable activities

NCVYS (2007); Street Games, Street Talk website; The FreeChild Project website; US Scouting Service Project website.

CHAPTER 7: Issue-based practice

While young people develop their abilities to make positive choices in their lives and understand their options, they face the realities of inequalities in relation to privilege and societal oppression. This chapter looks at a planned approach to issue-based and anti-oppressive practice in the immediate, short, medium and longer terms.

On-going anti-oppressive practice as well as issue-based youth work attempts to address the effects of inequalities by focussing on specific issues or targeting particular groups in order to have a more transformative function than simply offering support to young people during their transition from childhood to adulthood. Anti-oppressive practice demands that attention is paid to attitudes and practices within youth work organisations as well as communities and society as a whole. Youth work can address some of the effects of the inequalities arising from opportunities being provided to certain privileged minorities often on an unearned basis that are denied to other individuals and groups. Relevant issues, for example, include racism, sexism, heterosexism, class, ageism and ableism, which can prevent equal access to activities and services and prevent basic needs, such as for safety, security and love, from being addressed. (See also Box 5.3 in the previous chapter that outlines relevant issues.)

Oppressive and discriminatory attitudes and practices that affect young people are often embedded in and promoted through legal, political and educational systems. Societal and institutional oppression involves power being exercised in discriminatory ways, which can affect an individual's opportunities, experiences and self-esteem. Recognising oppressive practice and distinguishing situations where individuals may be able to exert more control can assist young people to understand and make choices about their responses. Identifying when and how their actions may be able to make a difference to how they are perceived or treated can assist them to make life choices that are both positive and practical. (Box 7.1 has some examples of oppressive attitudes and practices that can affect young people, ranging from passivity to violent expression and including internalised oppression, which is a product of them.)

> ### Box 7.1: **Types of oppressive practice**
>
> **Passivity:** Indifference, acceptance of unfair treatment, not addressing the needs of particular individuals or groups through programme provision or staffing, not examining oppressive attitudes and behaviour.
>
> **Lack of action:** recognising yet ignoring oppressive attitudes, behaviour or practices, avoiding confrontation on the issues.
>
> **Active:** unwelcome remarks, name calling, insulting pictures, drawings or signs, symbols and publications, not delivering a service or goods, not hiring or promoting someone, not recognising someone's contribution.
>
> **Violence:** Hate crimes, bullying and cyber-bullying, verbal abuse or threats, domestic violence, forced marriage, slavery, colonialism.
>
> **Internalised:** adopting oppressive attitudes and practices and directing these towards oneself and others who share the characteristics or situation.

Working at different levels

Anti-oppressive practice includes work a different levels, that is with individuals, groups, organisations, societal structures as well as the youth worker's own professional self-development (see the table in Box 7.2 for some examples). Affecting change at some levels can be as simple as presenting an alternative perspective or way of working. Welcoming and involving an individual from a group that has been traditionally excluded from participation can challenge preconceived ideas and provide a model for practice for young people, colleagues

Box 7.2: **Anti-oppressive practice at different levels**

	Examples of practice
Individuals In the community, members of groups, colleagues, other professions	Reach out to new members; target marginalised, detached or excluded individuals; raise awareness of issues and provide alternative perspectives; promote positive images and role models; recognise contributions and alternative experience; discuss options and support participation in new experiences.
Groups Of young people, community groups, working groups	Initiate, support and develop groups; reach out to under-represented groups; enable participation of marginalised individuals in groups; facilitate communication, stimulate thinking about issues and develop issue-based activities; respond to oppressive language, attitudes and practices; pass on information, establish anti-oppressive groundrules, promote interactions (excursions, sporting events, festivities) with other groups to widen experience.

Organisations Employing agencies, networks, forums	Initiate and value responses and challenges to oppressive and discriminatory attitudes and practices; develop targeted provision and allocate resources to these; ask questions, disagree and make proposals; develop inclusive anti-discriminatory policies and procedures, widen participation in decision-making, promote representative staffing, promote and provide awareness raising information sessions for staff, share experience and joint work with other organisations representing different identities; encourage participation and feedback from a wide range of perspectives.
Social structures Educational, political and criminal justice institutions, the media, housing providers, commercial bodies and employers or religious bodies	Campaign, inform, challenge, promote and provide alternative images and perspectives; support young people's participation, particularly from marginalised groups.
Own professional development	Discuss, read, use supervision, undertake training, attend conferences, network, seek out information and critical feedback from a range of sources and perspectives.

and the organisation. On the other hand, more in-depth or long-term strategies at different levels may be required to create real changes to an organisational culture that will improve employment practices.

Working with individuals

Anti-oppressive practice attempts to counteract negative messages about skills and abilities that young people may have absorbed from the media, the family and other social structures. The alternative perspectives presented by a youth worker can transcend this restricted social conditioning. Passing on information about other perspectives, such as femimism, a black perspective or social model of disability to colleagues or members of the community can also begin to counteract societal and institutional negativity. Some youth workers may focus more on young people's practical needs arising from particular issues such as poverty or exclusion while other focus more on raising awareness of individuals who perpetuate oppressive attitudes.

One-to-one conversations with young people experiencing the effects of oppression can provide them with strengths to value themselves and their lives. When young people are listened to, they begin to articulate their genuine interests, goals and life plans. Young people are individuals with varying experiences and may benefit from different methods of raising their confidence and self-esteem. Some simply require that their aspirations are taken seriously and need information about potential options.

Some may be better able to deal with 'slings and arrows' after exploring methods of handling themselves, including self-control and focussing on a goal. Others may benefit from seeing the differences between minor difficulties or short-term setbacks and more serious or longer-term problems. Two-way conversations and some flexibility can help youth workers to find an approach that works well with a specific individual.

Youth workers also work with individuals who have absorbed or internalised oppressive attitudes that they then impose on others. Youth workers are often well placed to form positive relationships with individuals who have been misled or have fallen into negative patterns of behaviour. Individual conversations can be a powerful way to find out what is behind a young person's discriminatory views and address some of the causes. Ignorance is a frequent cause of oppressive behaviour and many young people are not aware of the origins or meaning of the language or opinions that they express. Relevant information may change some young people's ideas or deter them from continued use.

A different approach may be required for work with individuals who are not ready or willing to change their entrenched views. Some individuals recognise and enjoy the power of their negative views or actions and may not be prepared to give them up. Many youth work organisations ban young people who become involved in fascism, gangs or other kinds of violence. Some youth workers will simply 'draw the line' at certain behaviour – either refusing to work with young people acting in certain ways or not allowing them to express their views. These approaches may protect other vulnerable members and could effectively control those individuals motivated by a desire to participate. Such acquiescence could be a positive exercise in self-control rather than evidence indicating a new position on oppressive behaviour.

Positive practice requires a range of approaches to address individuals' needs. Getting to know people from a wide range of backgrounds and experiences, enjoying the company of people who were previously unknown or feared, and learning about different histories and cultures can be effective tools for perspective transformation. Individual conversations with open and honest discussions about where certain negative ideas come from may also serve to open a young person's eyes. A young person may not recognise issues related to oppression until the opportunity to identify their own experiences of bullying or abuse, lack of opportunity or prejudice has an impact.

Anti-oppressive practice means working with young people in various situations so that they can identify their own, often difficult choices about managing changes in their lives. However, youth workers need to recognise the reality and extent of the changes that some individuals would need to make to change their lives for this exercise to have any meaning. Having aspirations for alternative pathways and the wherewithal to take them may require individuals to completely change their circumstances. Some may need to move to a different area, find new friends, get a job, study for qualifications, escape addiction and/or face retaliation from a gang to make a fresh start.

Developing one's own understanding of oppression

Continuous professional development through supervision, critical feedback and research can assist youth workers to continue to develop their awareness and practice related to oppression. Youth workers who are not directly affected by issues may have to work hard to identify the implications and fully understand what young people who are directly affected are saying. To use MacPherson's (1999) description of 'unwitting' racism, 'unfamiliarity with the behaviour or cultural traditions' of individuals and groups by a youth worker whose 'lack of understanding, ignorance or mistaken beliefs' can lead to 'well intentioned but patronising words or actions.' (Macpherson, 1999: 6.170). Considerations of identity in relation to the various oppressions as well as anti-oppressive practice need to be part of 'locating self' (see Chapter 4). Professional practice requires recognition of how identity affects thinking and perspectives, as well as how others perceive them. Unless proactive efforts are made to recognise an issue, learn more about it, and address it through policies and practice, youth workers can become part of the problem rather than the solution. (See Box 7.3 for a quote from Eldridge Cleaver's 1968 speech as a Black Panther.)

Box 7.3: A definition of responsibility

'What we're saying today is that you're either part of the solution, or you're part of the problem.' (Cleaver, 1969: 32)

Identifying the effects of oppression

Having an understanding of the context and effects of different oppressions can provide frameworks for practice. An awareness of institutional, societal and cultural oppression can inform youth work activities and the information that youth workers pass on. Young people may be liberated through an analysis of power in society, using for example, Thompson's (1993) model of personal, cultural and structural oppressions to see that their negative experiences are not specific to them. Some may benefit from the knowledge that their reactions to situations, such as abuse, domestic violence, bereavement, may be common or expected. Recognising the effects of direct and indirect discrimination on marginalised groups may help to illuminate issues that may not have been clearly linked previously. Young people who experience stress, difficulties in pursuing educational and career opportunities and low self-esteem may appreciate opportunities to discuss them.

Recognition of a lack of positive images and knowledge of different groups can provide a particular arena for practice. Individuals from both dominant and oppressed groups are often deprived of the rich and varied knowledge of cultures that are different from the mainstream. Young people and youth workers may not know much about marginalised groups whose history and cultures are not taught in schools, represented in the media or valued by political and social leaders. Some youth workers undertake research with young people to find out about diverse groups and to address gaps in educational systems or individuals' learning from those systems. Mentoring may also provide relevant informal education and role models.

Separate lives and experiences can also create divisions between different groups that youth work may be able to address. Fear, enhanced through lack of contacts and negative images, can divide communities, inhibit 'cross-cultural' communication and prevent mutual understanding. Inappropriate actions or ignorance of customs can also cause unintended offence. 'Cultural competence' or confidence in cross-cultural interactions or a 'valuing diversity' approach that accepts and respects differences are potential frameworks for practice in these areas.

Youth workers who focus on oppression and the effects of personal, cultural or societal prejudices may not gain a true or real picture of the actual experiences of specific individuals or groups. In youth work practice, identifying the potential effects of discrimination on individuals and groups means developing openness to others' experiences and an awareness of societal and cultural influences rather than seeking out disadvantage or inferiority. Information about a particular group's 'lack of achievement' in education is recognised as a consequence of various factors rather than any direct result of inadequacy. Generalising about the experiences of 'oppressed' or 'oppressing' groups due to concerns about unfair treatment could in itself be prejudicial. Recognising the existence of oppression, the strength of oppressive practices and then the specific contexts in which oppression takes place is not the same as having generalised and low expectations of certain groups, which can lead to further discriminatory practices.

Addressing societal oppression

Individual youth workers have different experiences of social and political inequality and sometimes have conflicting ideas about ways to address these realities. Some youth workers become involved in campaigns for legal rights or arguments about changes to the law or organisational policies. Many youth workers find themselves challenging other organisations to improve their services for young people, particularly in relation to individuals who do not seem to be receiving adequate attention. Others believe that attempts to adjust an oppressive system are exhausting or even counter-productive. Some believe that although they may not be able to make systemic changes, working for individual success or improvement is worthwhile. Many youth workers have political or philosophical beliefs that underpin their work. For example, a belief that only conflict or revolution will enable everyone to benefit from world and social resources might sustain one youth worker while another may have a religious vocation.

The natural impulse of caring adults is to protect children or young people in difficulties. The realities of oppressive and unequal circumstances mean that even well intentioned steps do not always have the desired results. An innate sense of responsibility and legal requirements for ensuring for young people's safety often mean that professionals attempt to take positive action when young people reveal issues related to basic human needs, such as safety, hunger, homelessness or burdensome care responsibilities. For example, it is not uncommon for abused and neglected young people to find themselves further abused in foster 'care'. Youth workers sometimes need to recognise the boundaries of their practice and the limitations of their role. Working with young people to consider their options is the role of a youth worker; unless there are very good reasons for an alternative approach, the young person should make the decision about which route to take. (See Chapter 9 for more discussions about different roles.)

Having a planned approach to issue-based practice

Issue-based practice requires youth workers to develop appropriate responses to issues that arise through action and reflection. Applying Lewin's (1946) spiral process provides a structure for a planned approach (See Box 7.4.) Practice starts with a general idea about the need to address a particular issue. The issue is examined carefully and researched to devise an overall plan. The next step is deciding on appropriate action or actions, for example, putting certain policies and/or practices into place. Immediate, short, medium or long-term action is undertaken. Monitoring and evaluation of the action could identify further issues requiring a response. So the spiral of steps: planning, action and evaluation, continues. Involving participants and individuals directly facing the issues assists the practice to maintain relevance.

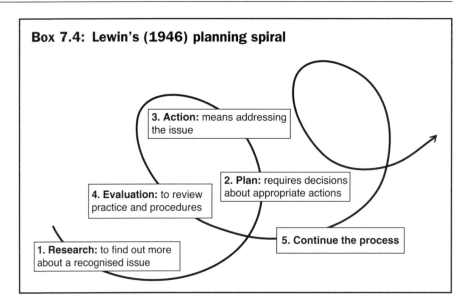

Box 7.4: Lewin's (1946) planning spiral

Recognising that an issue exists

Youth workers develop their awareness of a particular individual or group's interests by listening to young people and observing their behaviour. Statements may display ignorance; questions may indicate fears or curiosity; language and actions may demonstrate gaps in understanding. A chance remark may provide an opening for discussion of important concerns. Individual youth workers also bring their awareness and interest in a range of topics to their practice and use conversational topics, materials on display and activities to stimulate further focus. Recognising different types of oppression can enhance open discussion. The table in Box 7.5 outlines some examples, which can assist identification of prevalent issues, causes and effects, those which are under the control of the individual and those which are maintained through societal or institutional attitudes and practices. Consideration can also be given to how the issues can be addressed or combated by individuals, groups or organisations.

Deciding on an appropriate plan

Appropriate responses to evidence of oppressive attitudes or practices will vary according to the situation and to suit different youth workers. In order to be able to address issues appropriately and carry out suitable responses to the attitudes, practices or policies that relate to an issue, youth workers decide whether an appropriate response should be implemented immediately and/or whether a plan for short, medium or

Box 7.5: Examples of oppression

Perceived area of difference	Examples of oppression
Identity	Class or caste systems, sexism, racism, disabilism, heterosexism, ageism; discrimination against Deaf people, people with dyslexia, or dyspraxia or who are mentally or physically impaired or in ill health, transgendered people, transsexuals, transvestites
Ethnicity	Xenophobia and nationalism, such as discrimination or prejudice against religious groups, speakers of other languages or people from other countries
Life-style or choice	Discrimination or prejudice against single-parent families, young parents, large families, streetworkers, commune-dwellers
Circumstances	Discrimination and prejudice towards asylum-seekers, refugees, economic migrants, homeless people, residents in a particular area or in temporary or inferior accommodation, also people experiencing: • poverty, low wages or low economic status, inferior housing • being in care, in prison or remand centre • high levels of health, drug and alcohol problems or substance users and abusers • mental health problems, such as low self-esteem, high rates of suicide, self-harm and anorexia or bulimia • illness, who are chronically ill, with mobility problems • low academic achievements, dyslexia, different learning styles or attention spans

long-term action is appropriate. Some issues are better addressed immediately in reaction to a current situation with a quick remark, digging out a relevant piece of information or exercise or initiating a discussion. Other issues may benefit from a longer-term project, such as informal education, collective action or an excursion. Youth workers need various ideas and strategies to take the initiative for a proactive approach to promote anti-oppressive awareness and understanding.

Responding immediately

A youth worker may identify that an issue requires immediate action. Responses could include snappy one-liners to contradict what someone has said, a speech that outlines a different view-point or perspective or a joke or question to provoke alternative thinking. A quick response, such as a one-line reply to something that has been said, can provide information to address gaps or misunderstandings. A piece of information can be delivered in a humorous or thought-provoking manner rather than as a contradictory or negative put-down. Such responses can be planned and thought out beforehand in a readymade and flexible tool kit.

Some may be employed with a full range of individuals including young people, members of the community, other youth workers, managers, other professionals and friends. Developing new responses to different situations and positions is an essential skill for youth work practice. An experienced youth worker or team of youth workers can establish their protocols for diagnosing issues and the appropriacy of different responses based on an increasingly sophisticated set of 'templates' (Boreham, 1988), trial and error, research, discussion and evaluation. Box 7.6 contains some practice examples of immediate responses that could be made to appressive remarks that could provoke thought or challenge attitudes.

Box 7.6: Practice example: Immediate responses

- **Informative:** *I've heard that mothers under 16 years of age – and their babies – tend to have worse health than when the mother is over 16.*
- **Thought provoking:** *So what would you say if you knew I was gay, she was lesbian and he was born a girl?*
- **Signposting:** *You could have a look at this leaflet .... talk with so and so .... ring the 'X' organisation.*
- **Humorous:** *So you think that if someone doesn't wear the kind of gear you approve of, they shouldn't be allowed to come to this youth group? Should we make that a new rule?*
- **Enthusiastic:** *That's an interesting point of view. I'm not sure I've heard that said before. Tell me more .....*
- **Probing:** *Why do you think that is the case?*
- **Projecting:** *Do you think that everyone should have to stay in the country they were born in?*

A short-term plan may be appropriate for particular instances or settings. In the short term, a youth worker can address young people's lack of information, provide a certain level of support and signpost them to appropriate resources. An activity or project can be carried out that raises awareness or provides useful information. Some issues can be addressed through an effective short-term plan. A young person may only require a piece of information from the youth worker or an opportunity to think through some options. In some settings or projects, a youth worker may only have a short and fixed period with an individual or group. Devising an activity or small project to raise awareness may be all that a youth worker can do. A typical reactive short-term plan to address an issue is to first listen and show interest, encourage analysis of options and then 'leave the door open' for further discussion. (See Box 7.7 has a practice example of a short-term response to oppressive practice that could have real impact on a young women's experience.)

Box 7.7: Practice example: A short-term response

A young Muslim woman said that she was being harassed at school for wearing a niqab (a face covering veil), she was too distressed to go to school. The teachers seemed unsupportive and asked her to remove the garment – especially during science and PE classes. The youth worker allowed the young woman to tell her story and express her views while attempting to offer a listening rather than a judgemental ear. The youth worker encouraged the young woman to consider and evaluate various issues arising from her account, such as motivation, practical steps and their consequences. By the end of the conversation, the young woman was still planning to attend school despite her distress and said that she had a number of options to address her concerns.

   The following week the youth worker asked the young woman how she was and gave her the opportunity to talk some more. The young woman indicated that she felt less distressed about attending school. The worker gave her some relevant news articles about students' experiences in challenging school polices and also about different types of religious dress. She also made sure that the young woman knew she could return to talk with her about these or any other topics.

Designing specific issue-based projects

Youth workers can play a proactive role in raising issues and do not always wait for young people to bring issues to their attention. A youth worker may provoke a discussion or plan an activity that is designed to raise a particular issue, particularly if it is known to be a local concern. If young people in the area are victims and perpetrators of crime, failing their school work or having difficulty finding employment, youth worker cannot ignore these issues. Whilst youth work activities may provide a safe haven from external dangers, young people's defences and alternatives also need strengthening.

   A youth work project may be set up to address particular issues in young people's lives, for example an anti-bullying campaign, a clean up the environment scheme or a project looking at self-image. Involving young people in discussions of issues that affect them provides opportunities for young people to share problems from a perspective of equality. Within a group of young people, shared experiences can be identified and discussed in order to develop understanding as well as options for ways forward. The 'solutions' can be based in a young person's reality and thought through from their perspective. Youth workers may have never experienced the issues faced by the young people with whom they work. What they can do in a particular situation is act with the authority and skills gained through experience.

   A multi-agency response can be an effective way to address certain issues, particularly when other agencies or services have relevant resources. Youth work projects may be funded to work on an issue due to media interest or government policies, such as 'under-age' pregnancy or 'teenage nuisance'. Rather than hampering the project by specific targets linked to resource allocation, a multi-agency approach can allow each organisation or professional to contribute their particular area of expertise. Rather, than is sometimes the case, straight-jacketing youth workers to carry out services, such as surveillance or training that might be better addressed by others. A multi-agency organisation that supports youth work to contribute their strengths can be a worthwhile partnership (see Box 7.8).

Box 7.8: Practice example: A multi-agency approach

A youth worker was employed within a youth work organisation to work with young people on the issue of domestic violence. Research had identified that organisations in the area were dealing with a high number of cases of domestic violence and that they felt ill-equipped to work on the issue or discuss options with young people. After making contact with different groups of young people in schools, on the streets and in youth centres and networking with other agencies, the youth worker decided that a multi-pronged approach to the issue and its effects was required. Awareness-raising sessions were planned within the local schools and youth centres. A drop-in session for young women was developed at a local health centre. Girls and women only sessions were held in the youth club. A programme for work with young men was developed with other youth workers. Partnerships with other agencies were established to share information and highlight good practice.

Challenging attitudes

The challenge for youth workers is to bring an anti-oppressive perspective to their practice without resorting to one-way communication that undermines their relationships with participating young people or colleagues. Youth workers are involved in mutual learning, not teaching or training and share information rather than tell others what to think. Finding effective methods of not colluding with discriminatory attitudes or practices often requires an alternative perspective to be presented. Whilst some workers 'take off their hats' when associating with friends and family, most find that ignoring racist jokes or tolerating homophobia becomes impossible whether they are on or off the job. An anti-oppressive approach generally becomes part of all interactions whether with young people, members of the community, other youth workers, managers or funders, other professionals, friends and/or family members.

Retaining a positive, participative and anti-oppressive approach to practice must be part of the process of addressing issues. Having a range of possible responses, some of which may be more appropriate in specific situations than others, can be helpful. One situation may warrant an immediate and quick response, while another may require further reflection, a longer-term response and a more effective situation in which to carry it out. A youth worker with a proactive anti-oppressive approach may find that challenging oppressive attitudes can become a full-time occupation. Varied responses, such as the examples in Box 7.9, may also be more effective than a 'broken record', which can lose meaning.

Box 7.9: Practice examples: Responses to heterosexism

Attitude
Lesbian and gay people could just keep it to themselves. They don't have to tell everyone what they do.

Possible responses
- *So you think that a young person would volunteer to get a hard time from their friends?*
- *Straight people talk about their boyfriends or girlfriends, kiss in the street, dance, get married, go on holiday together. Why should lesbian and gay people have to hide?*
- *Most lesbian and gay people do keep their relationships and sexuality to themselves – and this kind of self denial leads to high levels of suicide, drug use, dropping out of school, homelessness ...*
- *Most people know about their sexuality when they are five years old. Do you really think a five-year-old shouldn't be able to talk about this?*

Challenging language

A typical situation facing youth workers is the use of offensive or oppressive language. Young people, colleagues as well as society as a whole use words and phrases that convey prejudicial attitudes through offensive labelling that demeans and belittles. Rather than challenging everyone every time certain language is used, youth workers need to find a range of responses to suit the particular terminology, its use and the speaker. The offensive nature and the power of particular words to offend changes over time and can be quite subjective depending on the setting or the identity, personal circumstances and lifestyles of the individuals involved.

A youth worker who recognises that a group of young people frequently uses a word that is offensive is likely to find that a challenge on each occasion that a young person used the term would be ineffective and possibly counter-productive. The youth worker would need to identify whether the young people are aware of the word's meaning and effect as well as their underlying attitudes towards the group that is apparently being labelled. What might be clearly a pejorative term to some people may be everyday language within other groups. A group that is aware of the meaning and using the term to abuse or create an effect would require a different approach than a group that uses the word as a form of speech in a thoughtless manner or without intention to target a specific group. Appropriate responses could include pointing out its oppressive nature, raising the profile of the group being labelled, asking the group for appropriate alternative words and challenging the underlying attitudes.

Youth workers need to find ways to address oppressive practices that challenge thinking, raise awareness of the effects of oppression and support positive action. An intervention that points out or contradicts an oppressive remark or action requires considerable calm and confidence. Simply pointing out that something is offensive can create additional problems, such as defensiveness. Explaining why something is offensive may be difficult to articulate and may not come easily if the situation causes feelings of upset, anger or fear. Expecting others to recognise that their own actions have been oppressive can be rather ambitious. Putting someone on the spot to admit responsibility or guilt may not have a positive result. An analysis of the dynamics or causes of what happened can lead to a more appropriate response.

Challenging actions

Youth workers sometimes 'challenge' young people to understand the implications of their actions or to change their ways in order to reach their goals. Noticing risky or anti-social behaviour, a youth worker may challenge the action rather than seeming to agree or collude by ignoring it. Challenging usually introduces a different perspective to a situation, but may also be a reminder of a previous conversation. Generally challenges are made to maintain safety, raise important issues and promote changes to behaviour. To maintain a positive approach, an explanation of why a challenge is being made is good practice (See Box 7.10 for some varied examples from youth workers about challenging young people's oppressive behaviour.)

Raising awareness of options

Lack of awareness or confidence and internalised oppressive attitudes can limit young people's prospects. Youth workers raise awareness of options through challenging prejudices and providing new experiences. Knowledge of potential opportunities and the practical steps that may need to be taken to learn new skills, gain employment or acess better housing can stimulate both interest and action. Youth workers encourage young people to consider jobs or roles that they may not have envisioned for themselves. They assist young people to identify different ways to tell their friends, parents or teachers about mistakes they have made. Visits to new settings provide first-hand experiences of different ways of life,

---

Box 7.10: Practice examples: Advice about challenging behaviour

- *If you get to know the young people first, you will know when to intervene and what they will hear.*
- *Recognise that it is not always possible to change a young person's behaviour; it's a real achievement to get someone to stop and think for a minute. That has the potential for a long-lasting impact.*
- *You don't need to challenge every instance; choosing to walk away is an option on both sides.*
- *Don't collude; you can express your choice not to be involved.*
- *Don't preach; you need to be heard.*
- *Get to know the young people; don't judge them.*
- *Don't over-react to behaviour; most young people are inclined to take risks.*
- *Separate the behaviour from the young person; you can react to the behaviour as a stupid/risky/rude rather than label the young person as such.*
- *Choose your time and place for raising an issue. You can't challenge everything they do.*

---

cultures and communities. Youth workers need a range of ways to widen horizons to suit different needs and interests. (See Box 7.11 for some varied practice examples from different youth workers.)

An essential skills for youth work practice is being able to work with young people to support their efforts to address the issues that arise in their lives. Youth work can widen young people's opportunities for developing skills and access to

---

Box 7.11: Practice examples: Ways to widen horizons

- Ask why certain jobs are associated with a specific gender, class or age group
- Ensure that sufficient examples of positive images and 'non-traditional' role models appear in materials, displays, information
- Network with other organisations to provide access to alternative resources and experiences, particularly those that would challenge stereotypes
- Discuss the sources of attitudes and stereotypes, such as the influences of the media, education, friends, parents, community on individual choices
- Express the point of view that the experiences or aspirations of parents, carers and communities do not necessarily need to limit their own choices
- Find ways to introduce issues related to equality of opportunity in conversations about television programmes, local issues, national politics
- Establish targeted work with particular groups to build confidence and promote discussion that might be stifled in mixed groups
- Visit prisons and universities - art galleries and homeless shelters - to experience firsthand what these are really like
- Arrange mentors with shared experiences to provide alternative pathways
- Focus on building specific skills to develop confidence through work experience, teambuilding and training

---

employment and education as well as other services and activities in practical and tangible ways. Making a difference requires attention to the personal, cultural and structual oppressive frameworks (Thompson, 1993).

Essential skills for anti-oppressive practice

- Being clear about anti-oppressive practice
- Working at different levels
- Working with individuals
- Developing one's own understanding of oppression
- Having a planned approach to issue-based practice
- Recognising that an issue exists
- Deciding on an appropriate plan
- Responding immediately
- Designing specific issue-based projects
- Challenging attitudes
- Challenging constructively
- Raising awareness of options

Further reading about issue-based practice

Freire (1972); Hill (2007); Oliver (1996); Mullaly (2002); Thompson (1993); Unks (1995)

'From Gandhi we can learn about non-violence, self-determination and political organisation; from Kwame Nkrumah we can learn about the independence movements, national youth movements and Pan-Africanism; from the Rani of Jhansi we can learn about leadership and resistance; from Martin Luther King we can learn about civil rights; from Mary Seacole we can learn about dedication and compassion; from Marcus Garvey we can learn about the principles of organising in the Diaspora; from Augusto Boal we can learn about the techniques and methodologies of art and theatre in tackling oppression.' (Joseph et al., 2002: 26)

CHAPTER 8: Working it out

Working out disagreements, making decisions and addressing barriers to participation are part of building cohesion and strength for groups and individuals. This chapter looks at different ways to enhance communication and shared decision-making that can create positive group work experiences that enable young people to enjoy, learn from and effect changes in their lives.

Recognising group processes

An understanding of group processes can assist a youth worker to plan and carry out work with groups. The simple group process illustrated in Box 8.1 shows a cycle of debate and discussion that characterises most functioning groups. For some groups or for some group experiences, the cycle can be smooth. The group comes together around an issue or question, perhaps to agree on a way of working, define some options for a decision or carry out some work. They can become more cohesive as they share new experiences together and 'bond' through explorations of new territory, even when disagreements are part of their journey. Returning to 'basics' for these groups, which could entail discussions about roles and future plans, enables them to review what took place and take on further new challenges.

Other groups or experiences may face or provoke greater fragmentation and disagreements between members. Members may respond to new ideas at different rates so that any new territory brings a greater challenge to the group identity. New experiences may expose uncertainty and conflicts. These groups may need to go 'back to basics' with greater frequency – perhaps every few minutes or every few sessions – to discuss 'ground rules' or their interactions. This part of the cycle, which may also provide a reminder about group aims and purpose, can provide an opportunity to make sense of the differences, incorporate any learning or simply find some basis of agreement. The group can then settle into working together in identifying what the differences are or what the next steps should be. Working together may give them greater confidence or allow them to progress so that they can explore different perspectives in the next round of the cycle.

Box 8.1: Group process

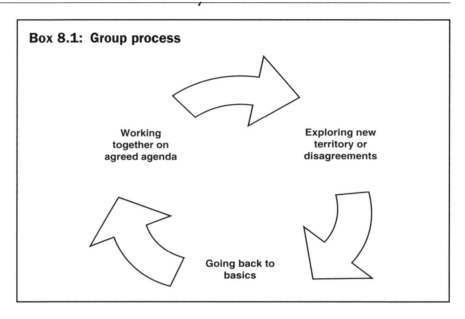

Working
together on
agreed agenda

Exploring new
territory or
disagreements

Going back to
basics

Poole (1983) describes a group process as intertwined threads developing at the same time but at various rates. When the group is involved in the analysis of problems and solutions, gathering information and choosing solutions, a 'task thread' is being followed. A focus on the content of the group activities, the issues and arguments discussed, is when the group follows a 'topical thread'. Concerns about the interpersonal relationships between the group members means the group is concentrating on a 'relational thread'. 'Breakpoints' occur when a group switches focus from one thread to another through normal changes of topic in the conversation, adjournment or postponement, delays caused by going back over previously settled matters, or disruptions caused by conflicts or failures in communication. When the group develops in a co-ordinated way on all three threads at once, problems are identified and addressed. When the threads are not co-ordinated and the focus shifts repeatedly, an analysis of the process may assist the group to progress.

Being able to identify changes and patterns in groups enables a youth worker to anticipate development and support positive change. Tuckman (1965) describes stages of group development that can enable cooperative and team work (see Box 8.2). His theory was that if groups did not explore the stages fully, co-operative working and progression would be limited. The definitions can provide a useful framework for a group to consider in order to identify and review their own development.

Deciding whether to intervene

A group of young people that works together well knows what to expect from a situation and each other. A youth worker encourages sharing of

---

Box 8.2: Tuckman's (1965) stages in groups

Stage One: Forming
The group is a set of individuals rather than a group. The stage is characterised by talk about the purpose of the group, the definition and the title of the group, its composition, leadership pattern and life-span. At this stage, each individual tends to want to establish their own personal identity within the group – to make an individual impression.

Stage Two: Storming
Most groups go through a conflict stage when the original agreements about ways of working are challenged and re-established. At this stage, personal agendas are revealed and a certain amount of interpersonal hostility is generated. If successfully handled, this period of storming leads to a new and more realistic setting of objectives, procedures and norms. This stage is particularly important for testing the norms of trust in the group.

Stage Three: Norming
The group establishes norms and practices about when and how it should work, how it should take decisions, what type of behaviour, what level of work, what degree of openness, trust and confidence is appropriate. At this stage, there will be a lot of tentative experimentation by individuals to test the temperature of the group and to measure the level of commitment.

Stage Four: Performing
When the previous stages have been successfully completed, the group is at full maturity and is able to be fully and sensibly productive. In Tuckman's view, although some kind of performance can be achieved at all stages of development, other growth processes and individual agendas will get in the way if the other stages have not been completed.

Tuckman went on to make a fifth stage called *Mourning* or *Adjourning* – depending on whether the individuals in the group move on to new experiences or stagnate wishing that the group was still in existence. Often a *Celebration* of what has been achieved can assist a positive ending for a group.

This summary is adapted from Handy (1995).

---

ideas and participation amongst these groups. When changes occur, such as questions are raised, challenges are made and new information is brought in, the group is less sure about what to think or expect and has to explore new territory. This period can be a time of great creativity, confusion and conflict with new ideas, discussion and activities. At this time, a youth worker makes choices about whether and how much to step in. Some groups will benefit from a youth worker's intervention, whether to contribute ideas, assist negotiation or support individuals. Most youth workers have a light touch. Interventions tend to be limited to reminding a group about any previous agreements, such as those concerning bullying or oppressive behaviour. Returning to original agreements about safety matters or how the group should operate may take place through this type of intervention or the group may naturally go back to basics to integrate their new ideas into the way that the group works.

A youth worker can simply observe group changes and development, which often continues at the same level as new members come and go, or provide a 'nudge' into the next stage or part of the cycle so that a group does not become 'stuck'. Most youth workers see a need to intervene when a group is unable to work together, negative behaviour is in danger of becoming a pattern or more vulnerable members are persistently excluded. Group interventions can include providing suggestions for the next stage, initiating opportunities for a change or facilitating an exercise to move a group on. Excursions and residentials, for example, often used as a tool bring young people together to experience planning and participation (see also Chapter 9), can also be offered as an opportunity to explore new experiences and territory together or to have a meeting to discuss basic group functions and plans. Some examples of group functions and how they might be tackled are provided throughout the chapter, for example establishing agreements, making decisions, working with conflict, challenging attitudes and practices and reviewing group development and progress.

Establishing agreements

Whether the agreements are unspoken or displayed on the wall, most youth workers communicate boundaries for acceptable behaviour through their responses to young people. Some youth workers rely on self-presentation and the creation of a positive environment for practice. Others facilitate discussions about issues arising to establish 'ground rules' or group agreements. The process of agreeing on 'do's and don'ts' can be a useful tool for stimulating thought and debate amongst a group of young people about how the group should work. The discussions can be used to start a group or referred to regularly as part of the ongoing process of group development. The agreements can play a key role in the induction of new members, fostering group relationships, planning the content of future sessions and establishing and reviewing the aims and objectives of the group (see Box 8.3 for an example of some ground rules).

Youth workers often negotiate agreements with and between young people about the ways in which a group works and plan activities together. This consultation and cooperation provides young people with a positive stake in the activities and involves them in maintaining youth work aims and values. As youth work practice is informal and participatory, agreements are usually oral rather than written, flexible rather than rigid and negotiated rather than imposed. Issues and practice are discussed and

> **Box 8.3: A practice example: Group 'ground rules'**
>
> • **DO** listen to each other
> • **DO** allow others time to express themselves
> • **DO** receive comments without criticism
> • **DO** maintain confidentiality outside of the group
> • **DO** think about what you are saying and doing
> • **DO** let others know if you disagree
> • **DO** include others in the discussions.
>
> • **DON'T** think that someone else will do all the work
> • **DON'T** expect everyone to agree with you
> • **DON'T** be upset if all of your suggestions are not taken up
> • **DON'T** become distracted from the purpose of the meeting
> • **DON'T** interrupt or criticise
> • **DON'T** be aggressive
> • **DON'T** ignore other members of the group
> • **DON'T** allow others to do any of the above without saying something.

any actions are agreed upon by consensus. The process means that members understand and participate in group decisions and their implications.

Agreements can be useful at different points in the life of a group. Some youth workers always start a new group or project with a discussion of ground rules so that members are included in the identification of how the group will function. The discussions can be used to establish boundaries of acceptable behaviour, such as defining appropriate relationships or interactions between members. A project-oriented group could identify issues related to timing of sessions, coffee breaks, keeping to agreed agendas, what to do if missing a session. Some youth workers and groups keep the ground rules on display and refer disruptive members to them. More indirect reminders of the discussions and agreements that took place can work well with some individuals. Reviewing the guidelines both individually and collectively, especially when new members join, can keep the agreements current and is a good basis for monitoring how the group is getting on. A review at the end of a group project can help to identify learning outcomes or group development.

Discussions of issues affecting participation are important exercises for developing a group. The support of the group in condemning certain behaviour and supporting rights to participate fully can be a powerful method of developing young people's confidence. Sharing experiences or opinions about issues such as bullying, abuse, assertiveness can strengthen the bonds between young people. Sometimes the issues have more relevance outside of the group. Young people may face racist abuse at work or their home life could be affected by alcoholism. Having the opportunity to discuss appropriate behaviour can be liberating (see Box 8.4 for an example of a group agreement).

Box 8.4: Practice example of a group agreement

1. *We all take turns washing up.*
2. *We don't have to answer questions about our lives outside this group.*
3. *We do have to respect each other as people.*
4. *We don't have to agree with someone else's opinions.*
5. *Everyone should welcome new members.*
6. *We don't use abusive language or bullying behaviour.*

The process of establishing the guidelines may be more important than the specific outcomes or rules themselves. Working with a group of young people to establish ground rules is a way of enabling participation and raising issues. Discussions about issues affecting participation and ways to address them can enable individuals to express their hopes and fears and establish a group identity. A ground rule may clarify human rights issues such as rights to privacy, to participate, to be free to express themselves or to be free from oppressive behaviour. Drawing up the guidelines is a useful way to discuss feelings about a group or programme and to develop a sense of common purpose. The process actively encourages participants to take responsibility for the direction of the group, the level of challenge taking place and the support that may be necessary (see Box 8.5 for some methods for establishing agreements).

Box 8.5: Practice examples: Ways to establish group agreements

- *Provide a good example for members of the group in relation to listening, negotiating, sticking to agreements and fulfilling responsibilities.*
- *Facilitate discussions about ground rules.*
- *Discuss issues such as confidentiality, appropriate behaviour and relationships, rights and responsibilities.*
- *Ask the group to share their hopes and fears.*
- *Encourage young people to talk about their experiences of non-participation.*
- *Have everyone answer the question: 'How could I ruin a session for someone in this group?'*
- *Ask the group to identify barriers to participation and consider ways in which the group could address them.*
- *Organise role-plays of situations in the group that members have found difficult to handle and discuss about ways to address these.*

> - *Promote bonding in the group through team activities, group or line dancing and co-operative games. Healthy relationships within the group enhance regard for others' feelings and rights.*
> - *Review the aims and objectives with the group and talk about what hinders progress in relation to them.*
> - *Break into smaller groups to make proposals that are then discussed in the larger group.*
> - *Provide sheets of paper on a 'suggestions wall'.*
> - *Ask individuals to draw up lists of 'I would like this group to …..'; I would not like this group to …' and then share them.*
> - *Have the group consider their rights and their responsibilities as members.*

When negotiating agreements with a group, it is important to distinguish any imposed rules made by the venue or organisation from those established by the group. Drawing up agreements about ways of working may be a useful time to highlight any regulations that already exist due to legal or organisational constraints. Some organisations deny participation rights to someone under the influence of illegal or prohibitive substances or carrying weapons. Fixed rules such as these are often imposed to protect staff and other members. In most organisations, these rules are stated as non-negotiable. Youth work organisations need to look carefully at any rules, particularly in relation to their target groups, to make sure that any restrictions are genuinely required or essential. Unnecessary statements that insult, irritate or suggest negative behaviour are clearly counter-productive and may interfere with good youth work practice (see for example Box 8.6). A useful way to determine which rules are superfluous could be to consider what, if anything, might happen if a rule was breached or non-existent.

Box 8.6: Practice example: Boundaries to detached youth work?

I find that rigid restrictions saying that I shouldn't work with someone who is under the influence of drugs or alcohol can get in the way of good practice as a detached youth worker. While I agree that there is no point in carrying out a discussion with a young person who is out of control or unable to carry out a conversation, there are situations where I don't feel I can walk away. I feel that I have to consider the options available before I signpost a young person who needs safe refuge. If a young person is experiencing difficulties with dosage or dealers, I would want them to come to us rather than be deterred. If our target group includes alcohol or drug users, we have to be able to make contact with them. The right time and place to reach certain young people to discuss these issues, such as harm reduction or appropriate housing and health services sometimes means being in the midst of a group that includes young people 'under the influence'.

Recognising different ways to make decisions

The ways in which decisions are made are part of the process of developing group and individual autonomy. Procedures, policies and practice may be discussed and decided upon by a whole group, part of a group or by one person (see the table in Box 8.7 for some examples of different types of decisions). A group may not recognise that their actions are decisions or that individuals have been excluded from the process. Sharing an analysis of the group's methods for making decisions can provide opportunities for members to suggest improvements to both the process and the outcome.

Box 8.7: Types of group decisions

Non-decisions
  Decisions are avoided, ignored and/or left to someone else.
External decisions
  Decisions are made by someone or a body outside of the group.
A leader's monopoly
  One person makes the decision.
Minority decisions
  A smaller group makes decisions from within a larger group.
Majority decisions
  A decision is made on the basis of which option has the most support despite other views being expressed.
Democratic decisions
  All members have an equal right to participate.
Unanimous decisions
  Everyone agrees on the decision made.
Consensus
  Individual differences are thoroughly explored and negotiated to arrive at an agreement.

A decision-making process can be complex and contain elements of more than one type of decision. A youth worker needs to observe who is participating in discussions and whether minority interests are considered or understood by the group. In some groups, a decision which appears to be made by consensus may actually have been engineered by a powerful bully. Dissenting voices, which could help decisions to be fully informed may not be heard or encouraged. An analysis of membership participation and compliance can assist a youth worker to identify what is really going on in a group (see for example, Box 8.8).

Box 8.8: Practice examples: Deciding about an outing

- **No decision – or a decision to leave it to someone else?**

A group discussed different options at length but was unable to agree which option was the best. Eventually the youth worker realised that the group could not handle the conflict or responsibility involved in making the decision and made the selection for them. Over the following weeks, the youth worker helped the group to develop their communication and negotiation skills through smaller decisions about the outing, which increased their confidence.

- **A minority decision or a unanimous decision?**

An experienced group of members said that a particular venue was a good idea and the others 'went along with the flow'. Everyone seemed to agree that this was the best option although only the more confident individuals contributed to the discussion. The youth worker recognised that the decision was far from unanimous and that a small group had felt pushed into compliance. The worker planned to make sure that sufficient opportunities were provided for the less confident members to participate in future discussions and decisions.

- **Is this a majority or a minority?**

The members discussed the benefits and drawbacks of several options and then voted. Option 'C' had the most votes so the group was about to book this option. One member of the group complained that the majority, or 55% of the group, disagreed with this choice. Option 'A' had 25% of the vote; option 'B' had 30%; option 'C' had only 45%. The group realised that the majority decision had not been followed and realised that the implications of voting needed to be explored more fully.

- **A minority option that becomes a majority decision?**

A group decided to vote on different options. After the vote, one venue had a clear majority (over 70%) but a significant minority of the group supported one of other options. When the minority pointed out that they would be unable to go on the outing if the majority option was selected, the others agreed to forgo their first choice. The group realised that a majority decision ignored the minority interests. In the end, they reached a consensus to choose the 'minority' option.

- **Consensus or chance?**

A group spent a long time exploring different options and felt that a number of possibilities were viable and of interest. Some options were preferred by certain members of the group, but there was no clear majority. The group decided to select the option by rolling a dice – assigning an option to each of the possible numbers. The decision to use chance was a consensus of opinion. Although the option was selected by 'chance', the method was agreed upon unanimously.

Moving decisions on

The process in which a group of young people makes and takes responsibility for decisions can be facilitated or supported by a youth worker. The degree to which a youth worker becomes involved will vary depending on the particular young people and the type of project. Whilst a group of young people left to their own devices could make and learn from the same mistakes as any other group, in a youth work setting, a youth worker observes the process of decision-making and will sometimes facilitate, intervene or mediate to move the group on. The aims are to enhance the learning experiences for the group and to make sure that youth work principles are addressed. For example, a youth worker may intervene to assist a group to make decisions with an inclusive approach rather than developing elitist factions or adopting bullying tactics.

A group needs to experience some form of agreement on process or goals in order to make any progress in planning. The example of a group attempting to plan publicity for an event without having established agreement on how they are going to work or where they are going (see Box 8.9) illustrates how these questions will continue to get in the way of making any further decisions. Rather than progressing through decision-making stages (as indicated in the left-hand column), the group continuously returns to the 'basics' without any real advance to agreement or exploration of new territory. A youth worker may allow these circular discussions to continue, or suggest that the group go back to stage one to establish some goals so that the group can progress.

Box 8.9: Practice examples of not making a decision

Possible Stages	Examples of incomplete decisions
1. Establishing goals: Ok, should we look at the plans for publicity now?	• Do we need publicity? I thought we were going to have a fun day just for us. • There's no point in planning any publicity until we know what the budget is. • I think we should make a start on what we want to do for publicity – then we'll know how much we need for the budget.
2. Clarifying objectives: So, who do we want to attract to this event?	• Do the numbers matter? It's no good if just a bunch of parents come – isn't this just for kids? • We need more members. Anyone who comes can get word around to somebody who may want to come.
3. Identifying and discussing options: So what are some of the ways you would like to attract people to the event?	• If we use leaflets, it's bad for the environment. • Should we see if we can get something on the buses? • It's a waste of time putting up posters; no one reads them. • I think we should use text messages and blogs. • Let's just have a go at designing some kind of logo that we can use in different ways.
4. Deciding on a way forward: So, what's next?	• Let's vote on it! • Voting's stupid. We don't have to have just one way to do publicity. • All we ever do in these meetings is just argue.

Working with conflict

Assisting young people to find ways to deal with conflict and disagreement are key and important areas for youth work practice. For example, issues of power and control can be difficult areas for young people to comprehend or handle. A youth worker may work with young people to assist them to understand the sources of conflict, to articulate their point of view and to find ways to cope with the reality of inequity. Youth workers can provide young people with opportunities to gain a better understanding of their own ideas and perspectives as well as others' positions. At the same time, a youth worker needs to ensure that their own practice is clear, fair and equitable.

Recognising the difference between conflicts and disagreements can assist young people and youth workers to find ways of working together in groups. When the source of a conflict is a clash of principles, a continuous battle for limited resources or contested power where neither party will back down, resolution is generally impossible and needs to be recognised as such. Unless either or both parties are willing to give up or give away their side of the argument, which is unlikely in a conflict over values and principles, a conflict cannot be 'won'. Progress is generally only possible through avoidance or some form of accommodation, such as an agreement to disagree. In such situations, cooperative working will require an alternative focus away from continued battles over issues that are not possible to resolve.

Disagreements, on the other hand, may be worked out to arrive at some form of more genuine cooperative progression. Negotiation, sharing information and improved relations can all help to move participants towards agreement or shared understanding. Whilst a conflict involves opposing principles, disagreements can arise about issues, a situation or a relationship based on a misunderstanding, negative patterns or experiences. These patterns may dissipate with more positive interactions, better communication or different circumstances. Often the various parties find that their positions are not such polar opposites and managed to find common ground.

Identifying own 'comfort zone'

Youth workers are individuals who react differently to arguments and disagreements. One youth worker with a high level of tolerance may perceive a particular incident as 'usual horseplay' whilst another might sense a potential for a violent outbreak. Some prefer to negotiate a resolution to any arguments that arise whilst others have a more laissez-faire (leave it alone) approach. Experience and temperament clearly play a part in the type of response a youth worker decides to take although understanding the sources of conflict (see the table in Box 8.10) can assist the development of a more calm and considered approach.

Box 8.10: Sources of conflict or disagreement

Area of difference	Possible causes	Possible ways to address
Perspectives: groups that refuse to co-operate with each other, individuals that constantly fight	• Conflicts between value systems, religions, ways of life, ideologies, beliefs • A lack of understanding or knowledge of the other's perspective • A history of interpersonal conflicts and disagreements, such as membership of opposing gangs	• Create an inclusive environment that welcomes all values and perspectives • Allow parties to disagree; point out that resolution on certain issues is not possible or necessarily desirable • Identify areas of commonality and don't focus on differences • Explore differences without judgements about right or wrong • Concentrate on interests rather than positions • Discuss the origins and effects of prejudice and stereotypes • Encourage working together on an agreed and common goal.
Interpersonal relationships: individuals who don't like each other and refuse to work co-operatively, fighting	• Previous arguments • Differences in styles, preferences, interests • Competitiveness • Misunderstanding • Disagreements about decisions	• Encourage members to accept that friendships are not essential for cooperative work • Listen to both sides; encourage them to listen to each other; encourage both to focus on what is being said rather than who is saying it • Identify whether the positions are misunderstood, conflicting or just different • Use ground rules or group agreements to govern the group • Provide alternative activities, such as games, that can build and develop communication between members • Find other avenues for co-operative working, such as physical or artistic activities • Encourage the group to identify and address the issues • Discuss the effects of being misunderstood or stereotyped.
Intrapersonal dilemmas: an individual's repetitive negative behaviour, such as withdrawing or domineering	• Individual in security or inability to communicate • A history of abuse or abusive relationships • Lack of opportunities to exert power elsewhere • Personal crises or uncertainly	• Use exercises that build up individual confidence rather than expect group cohesion • Provide opportunities for individuals with similar concerns to meet and find common ground • Identify whether the behaviour is a 'cry for help' by providing opportunities for one-to-one conversations.
Structural barriers or inhibitors: such as competition over actual or perceived unfair treatment, unequal distribution of resources or ownership	• Unfair treatment • Unequal distribution of resources or ownership • Lack of transparency about decisions and decision-making • Misinformation, different interpretations of information • Organisational culture or procedures	• Clarify procedures and information and find ways to share information and enhance communication • Alter the roles within the power structures or assign roles to new individuals • Provide suggestions for changes to the ways that decisions are made • Widen the group's knowledge of opportunities and access to alternative resources • Provide a change of environment or experience to enable changes to roles and patterns.

Many youth workers are worried about losing control of a situation that turns violent. The possibility that young people in their care or themselves experience injuries can be a real concern. The depth of understanding of the dynamics of conflict and the ability to recognise the potential for danger will often depend on the youth worker's experience and analysis of that experience. Youth workers need to develop an understanding of what will inflame an argument, incite violent reactions and deepen conflict. A useful method of identifying the warning signs and the ingredients is reflection on events in supervision and discussions in team meetings (see for example, Box 8.11).

Box 8.11: Practice example: Responding to a fight

Two members of a group each wanted a turn on the pool table and started a fistfight. After the session, the team of youth workers reviewed the session to identify the events and decided to identify some shorter and longer term options that they could have used. They came up with the following list:

1. Step into the middle of the scuffle and tell everyone to disperse.
2. Ignore the fight as the individuals needed to vent and express their anger.
3. Insist that each party calm down and apologise to each other for their bad behaviour.
4. Exclude one, both or everyone from the session either temporarily or permanently.
5. Remind all concerned about the centre's groundrules about sharing and no violence.
6. Hold a group investigation into what had led up to the violent behaviour – either immediately or later on.
7. Take the two individuals out of the situation, either together or separately, to discuss a way forward.
8. Initiate some 'anger management' training to discuss triggers, consequences and outlets for anger, either in the immediate, short, medium or long-term.
9. Involve the whole group in a discussion about allocating time on the pool table, the ground rules or which of the above options to take.

The workers' actual response had encompassed aspects of many of these options. Even though the session still had nearly half an hour to run and clearing up usually only took about ten minutes, one of the workers stepped in and shouted at everyone to 'Clear up, it's time to go home – show's over – we can't have any violence here!'. The worker then put a hand on each protagonist's shoulder and said: 'Come on – apologise to one another or I'll knock your heads together – and we'll have to ban you.' This produced some mumblings from both parties. The two did not seem to be hurt and both seemed to be consoled with a free packet of crisps. The groups mostly dispersed and took extra time to clear up so that the session actually finished at the usual time.

> **Box 8.11 - Cont'd**
>
> In the evaluation session, the other youth workers said that they would not have put their hands on the young people or used the same language. They all agreed that exclusions were not appropriate and that a greater presence around the pool table would be useful to review whether the young people wanted to initiate a different system for taking turns.

Analysing the 'ingredients' of an argument

A confident youth worker recognises the benefits of discussing disagreements and conflicts. Although conflict is often portrayed as divisive or dangerous for a group, a good discussion about an argument or a conflict can assist recognition of important issues and help to bring a group together. The outcomes of such discussion in relation to a group or individual may depend on the factors that contributed to the differences being expressed. The incident in Box 8.11, for instance, could have erupted into irreconcilable differences between the young people and the staff. Evaluation and team supervision can lead to issues being handled more confidently. Identifying the 'ingredients' of an argument or a conflict can help to determine its nature and potential for benefit or harm (see Box 8.12 as an example).

> **Box 8.12: Practice example: Advice about analysing an incident**
>
> *If you see an argument between some young people:*
> 1. **Don't say too much.** *Listen to what is going on. Move towards the people arguing and present yourself calmly. Communicate with body language, tone of voice and a few words that you are interested in and respectful of the person(s) as people.*
> 2. **Find out what's going on** *through observation. Don't ask too many questions and don't say anything unless you really know what's going on. It would be useful to notice:*
>   * *Who is involved*
>   * *How they see the situation*
>   * *What seems to be in their way*
> 3. **Don't get involved or caught up in the conflict.** *If you must say something, share your own thoughts or observations, for example, saying quite calmly: 'I can see that you are feeling quite angry at the moment'.*
> 4. **Identify and consider a range of possible options**, *for example:*
>   * *Acting, speaking, responding or doing nothing*
>   * *Approaching the situation positively. You could tell them what you would like to happen, for example, 'I would like us all to still be here tomorrow having a conversation about our favourite football team'.*

- *Getting them involved in a solution: For example: 'What would you do if you were in my shoes?'*
- *Changing the focus slightly: 'Right, so if we focus for a minute on the ideas here rather than the people, what do you think the other person(s) is saying to you?'*

5. **Don't expect the argument to be resolved right away.** *A lot of arguments have all kinds of elements that may not be immediately obvious. The argument may be temporary or have deeply conflicting roots. Your objective is to enable the participants to express themselves without physical violence. This might be difficult in the short term.*

Reviewing group progress and development

Individual members' learning and group development occurs when a group learns from their experience; recognising these changes can help a group to feel positively about the group. Kolb and Fry's (1975) experiential learning cycle (see the figure in Box 8.13) could provide a useful method of analysis of learning experiences whether by a youth worker or the group. Following a new experience, observations and reflections on what has taken place help to make sense of what has taken place. The shared experiences and reflections can help a group to come together. Articulating what has been learned can help to form new concepts for application to new experiences or experiments. In youth work, this could occur through planning, monitoring and review. The role of this process in working out differences, changes and learning can be invaluable in work with groups, whether or not the cycle is referred to overtly.

Box 8.13: Kolb and Fry's (1975) learning cycle

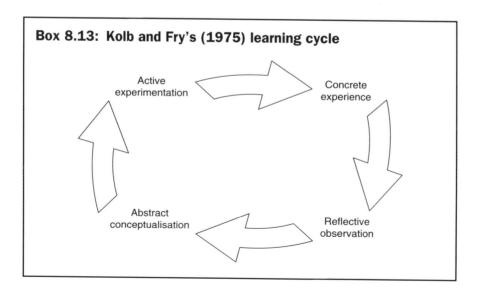

Essential skills for working it out

- Recognising group processes
- Identifying changes in groups
- Deciding whether to intervene
- Establishing agreements
- Recognising different ways to make decisions
- Moving decisions on
- Working with conflict
- Identifying own 'comfort zone'
- Analysing the ingredients of an argument
- Reviewing group progress and development.

Further reading about working it out

Belenky *et al.* (1986); Informal Education website; MacBeth and Fine (1995); Seeds for Change website.

PART C Making an impact

Making an impact on young people's lives and enabling them to make positive changes to their own and others lives as well as their communities can be enhanced through a planned approach to enabling participation and managing youth work practice. Chapter 9, *Developing Participation* focuses on strategies to involve young people in the evaluation and management of youth work organisations, relevant services and communities. Chapter 10, *Identifying Need* outlines a structure for research to support appropriate youth work practice. Chapter 11, *Managing a Project* explores the relationship between youth work values and management practice. Chapter 12, *Using Supervision* looks at supervision for professional development from the vantage points of a supervisor and a supervisee.

CHAPTER 9: Developing participation

Young people often have limited control over many of the decisions that affect their lives. This chapter looks at ways of facilitating young people's participation that provide opportunities for them to develop skills and confidence in making their own decisions and to participate in decision-making processes.

Focussing on the aims of youth work and participation

Youth work promotes young people's participation in decisions about issues affecting them, from relationships with their families and friends to environmental pollution and world peace. Participation by young people means ensuring that they have a voice and the opportunity to have a positive impact on the ways decisions are made. Young people's participation can improve existing services or make demands for new services to address their needs. Through youth work, young people have opportunities to express themselves socially, artistically and politically in ways that can make a difference. Young people who are brought together to learn from each other can find ways to improve their lives. (Box 9.1 outlines some examples of youth work practice at different levels. The aims of young people's participation).

Box 9.1: The aims of participation and examples of related practice

Aims of participation	Work with young people	Work with communities	Work with services and organisations	Self-development
Young people have more control over the decisions they make about their lives	Providing opportunities to develop confidence and responsibility	Raising awareness of community issues with young people and enabling them to influence these issues	Enabling young people to feedback and contribute to the decision-making process and decisions that are made	Learning from young people and involving them in relevant research

Continued

Cont'd

e's ~re and ~e	Developing and promoting opportunities for young people to become involved in evaluation and development of services	Raising awareness of young people's needs for accessible services	Developing structures and opportunities for young people to affect service development and management	Networking to develop multi-agency links and services; Developing an understanding of the barriers and shortcomings of services
Society develops positive attitudes towards young people	Developing their awareness of others' perspectives and any impact they may have on how they are perceived and treated	Raising awareness of young people's positive actions through	Challenging negative and oppressive attitudes and practices and enabling young people to do so	Researching to understand power, oppression, social structures
Young people are able to participate in decision-making processes	Involving young people in cross-generational work; Enabling young people to develop the skills and knowledge required for participation	Providing opportunities for young people to be heard	Developing structures for participation and enabling young people to participate in existing decision-making structures	Researching to identify relevant issues, resources and opportunities for participation

According to Max-Neef's (1991) analysis (simplified here in Box 9.2), participation is a fundamental human need. If young people's needs for participation are not satisfied, the effects can interfere with other aspects of their lives. For example, if they are disempowered or alienated, the sense of belonging and self-esteem that comes with identity can be adversely affected. On the other hand, if young people participate and have the opportunity to behave responsibly, they can be empowered in other aspects of their lives. The skills and confidence developed through cooperative action or being able to dissent could have positive effects on their abilities to understand others within their social groups, families, schools, communities and employment. Box 9.3 provides an example of how participation in planning projects and activities can enhance young people's confidence and address a range of other human needs.

Addressing the barriers between young people and those in positions of power can involve youth workers in a variety of roles (see Box 9.4). Acting as an intermediary or advocate, youth workers can create links between young people and decision-makers. Youth workers need to be cautious about getting in the way of direct communication between young

Box 9.2: Max-Neef's (1991) fundamental human needs

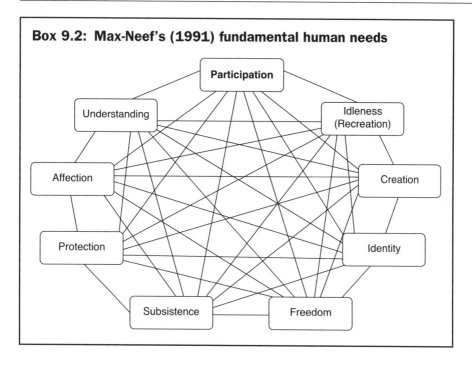

Box 9.3: Practice example: Developing skills through planning a camping trip

The young people learned the following skills whilst planning and organising their camping trip:

- **Research:** identifying preferences in relation to destination, activities and food; finding out about accessible and available campsites and transport; learning about insurance, parental permission and risk assessment requirements
- **Negotiation:** with local shopkeepers for donations of supplies, with campsite and transport for a good deal, with parents for permission, with each other to make decisions
- **Fundraising:** organising sponsored activities, seeking out donations
- **Budgeting:** planning and recording expenditure and resource requirements
- **Cooking and healthy eating:** identifying ways to address individual diets and health requirements, preparing meals, clearing up
- **Planning:** the registration process, the journey, the activities, the menus, the paperwork
- **Team work:** sharing tasks, joint decision-making, keeping each other informed, addressing responsibilities
- **Critical reflection:** evaluation of the project, of their learning, of whether they want to be involved again!

A youth worker's report

people and decision-makers and they speaking on young people's behalf rather than enabling them to speak for themselves. Passing on second-hand information, although clearly a second-best option, may be the only opportunity for young people's views to be heard. If called upon to be such a go-between, youth workers need to present young people's views as accurately and fully as possible.

Successful campaigns for organisational or structural change may depend on advisory or networking roles to gain support from others and keep them informed. Attempts to challenge organisational or societal ways of thinking or acting can provoke negative reactions. A youth worker who pushes or overextends the boundaries of a remit or job description to increase young people's involvement needs to involve others within the organisation. Otherwise, should employers disapprove, this activist role can leave a youth worker unsupported. Some situations

Box 9.4: Practice examples: Roles to develop participation	
Role	**Examples**
Advisor	I enable young people to participate by making sure that organisations know about different ways that young people could contribute to their decision-making. I have a number of proposals to address barriers to participation: structural changes, challenges to attitudes and examples of good practice.
Advocate	I enable young people to participate by making a point of acknowledging young people's contributions, ensuring that young people's views are taken into account and supporting young people in expressing their views. I always pass on young people's ideas to people who make the decisions and support or present proposals for structural changes that mean they have a greater say. For example, our organisation recently developed some procedural changes that delegated budgetary decisions 'downwards'. Enabling face-to-face youth workers to have greater control over their budgets means that young people have more direct access to decision-making.
Networker	I enable young people to participate by building links between organisations and groups of young people or organisations. I seek out organisations who wish to take account of young people's opinions and match them with youth-led organisations who wish to have their voices heard. I make sure that young people know about meetings, conferences and training events.
Researcher	I enable young people to participate by consulting with young people about their aspirations and interests, involving them in research to identify resources and funding, and making sure that they bring a global perspective to their planning, such as taking into account environmental issues and linking with young people from other countries.
Activist	I enable young people to participate by developing informal networks and forums that enable young people to influence and share in decision-making processes. I support young people to challenge those in power. For example, their campaigns to influence decisions. I structure my own practice so that young people have a direct say in decisions such as staff selection, organisational priorities and resource allocation.

benefit from a strategy that builds good relations with those in power. Providing viable suggestions for change that can be clearly understood may address or pre-empt resistance or backlash.

Recognising levels of participation

The level of power and control that young people experience ranges between passive recipient to active decision-maker. Various yardsticks to identify different levels of participation can be used (such as Arnstein, 1969; Hart, 1992) to identify young people's roles. (See Box 9.5 for a figure illustrating Hart's 'ladder'.) Whilst acceptable levels of participation do not require young people to be managers in control all the time, young people need to know where they stand. Clear identification of roles and communication can protect against false expectations.

Box 9.5: Hart's (1992) 'ladder of participation'

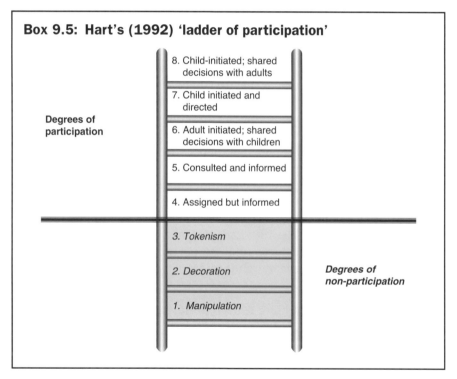

Degrees of participation

8. Child-initiated; shared decisions with adults

7. Child initiated and directed

6. Adult initiated; shared decisions with children

5. Consulted and informed

4. Assigned but informed

3. Tokenism

2. Decoration

1. Manipulation

Degrees of non-participation

The degree of participation that young people are able to exercise may depend on the particular activity or organisation or on what Shier (2001) defines as 'openings, opportunities and obligations' (see Box 9.6). Important factors are the commitment of the young people, the youth workers and the organisation. Support for the development of participation may come from the organisational culture and individual staff members as well as from positive policies and procedures. Clearly those same factors can also impinge on participation. Providing the

---

Box 9.6: Shier (2001) on 'pathways to participation'

'At each level, an **opening** occurs as soon as a worker is ready to operate at that level; that is, when they make a personal commitment, or statement of intent to work in a certain way. It is only an opening, because at this stage, the opportunity to make it happen may not be available.

The second stage, an **opportunity** occurs went the needs are met that will enable the work or organisation to operate at this level in practice. These needs may include resources (including staff time), skills and knowledge (maybe through training), development of new procedures or new approaches to established tasks.

Finally, an **obligation** is established when it becomes the agreed policy of the organisation or setting that staff should operate at this level. It becomes an obligation on the staff that they must do so. Working in a particular way, enabling a specific level of children's participation, thus becomes built in to the system.' (Shier, 2001:110)

---

right level of support at appropriate times without being overly directive is critical although not always easy to gauge.

Communication between youth workers and young people about the issues concerned in having a voice or making a difference needs to be regular and informative. The young people's understanding of the degree of influence or difference that their participation can make is often bluntly accurate. Experience of exclusion and being patronised, through age-ism as well as other oppressive attitudes or practices mean that young people's cynicism about participation cannot be ignored. A 'map of participation' (such as in Box 9.7) or other means of communication can assist young people to identify and communicate information about their experience and the level of their participation, whether that is being excluded or having leadership role.

Box 9.7: Practice example: A map of participation

We use 'maps of participation' to let young people tell us and other members of the community where they feel that they can make a difference and where they feel excluded. We use a large map of the area that shows the community centre, school, shops and their homes. Sometimes it's just a rough drawing – other times a printed one. For a group, we make one as big as the table. The young people decorate the map with symbols to highlight the places which are significant to them. Colours can show positive or negative feelings about certain areas. Sometimes we use stickers – a picture of a lion to be placed where they feel they can be leaders or a sheep where they feel like followers – although usually they decide on their own symbolism. Logos or grafitti 'tags' are put on areas are 'theirs'. The map gives them a powerful way to compile information about experiences–and a basis to work from to address the issues raised.

Promoting positive attitudes towards young people

Young people recognise that adults and their social structures tend to treat young people differently from mature adults. They experience the fact that adults generally have more political, social and economic power, which can be exerted over them to their benefit or detriment. Mutual mistrust between younger people and adults is often a result of reciprocal ageism, or generalised negative assumptions about different age groups. Ageism might be insignificant or oppressive, somewhat related to a truth or completely false. For example, assumptions are often made about the ignorance of a particular age group in relation to what is going on around them despite evidence to the contrary. If these assumptions lead to unfair or unequal treatment, abuse, exclusion or ridicule, then the ageism is discriminatory or oppressive.

The involvement of young people in local organisations or community activities can effect change in relation to ageist attitudes and practice. In certain communities, young people may be seen as problems and youth work as the solution or at least a form of problem intervention. Meanwhile, the young people may feel misunderstood and unclear about how to address their negative image. Developing the participation of young people in partnership with communities can enhance the recognition of young people as individuals and build positive relationships.

A youth worker can work with communities and agencies to support the participation of young people as individuals with certain perspectives. At the same time, work with young people to build on their strengths and seek out their ideas, encourage their questions, respond to their energy and enthusiasm and support their creativity can build up their confidence. All parties can emerge from a project (such as the practice example in Box 9.8) with very different and more positive images of the young people's capabilities.

Box 9.8: Practice example: Promoting positive attitudes

A new community facility was being planned in an inner-city area. Initially, the planning committee was managed by local political leaders and representatives from certain services mostly related to primary healthcare. A group of young people came by the building site one day when one of the members of the planning committee happened to be visiting. Following an animated conversation about the plans, the young people were invited to come along to a meeting to present their views. The young people were able to present a few ideas and ask a few questions related to the plans. The enthusiasm, ideas and creativity displayed by the young people impressed the committee, who were able to see the benefits of involving the young people in planning the facility.

> **Box 9.8 - *Cont'd***
>
> Whilst it did not seem appropriate to invite a random group to participate fully in the planning meetings, the committee decided to ask the local youth services to find a way to involve young people. The youth service recommended that a sub-group of the planning committee be set up as a forum for young people to discuss their ideas for presentation at future planning meetings. This meant that the young people's views could be contributed – without having to sit through all of the 'boring parts'. The planning committee acknowledged the value of the young people's contribution to the planning process.

Developing young people's control over their lives through participation

Different types of youth work provide different opportunities for young people to develop their capacity for taking responsibility and working with others (see the table in Box 9.9). In a 'young people's project', young people are in control. 'Youth work activities and projects' have different degrees of control depending on the level of their involvement. Whereas a 'youth service' may involve young people in participative youth work activities and projects or simply offer options from which young people select.

Through participation in youth work activities and projects, such as discussions and negotiations to make group decisions, young people develop clarity about the world and find ways to articulate and assert themselves. The previous chapters provide examples in which

Box 9.9: Roles and participation in different organisations

Organisation	Young people's role	Relevant youth work practice
Young people's projects	A group of young people decide on possible project options, select from them and carry out the work required.	A youth worker is in a supportive role, providing information, advice and access to resources as well as encouraging the development of the project so that it is inclusive and accessible to others.
Youth work activities and projects	Representative young people are involved at various levels of organisation to inform planning and management.	A youth worker consults with young people and encourages their participation. Decisions are made in partnership to provide options based on young people's expressed needs and interests.
Youth services	Young people select from options designed by others and feedback their views.	A youth worker provides a programme of activities and information, listens to the young people through monitoring and evaluation and makes reasonable adjustments to the programme.

Non-participation	Young people's role	Other kinds of work with young people
'Care', entertainment, diversion	Young people are involved in activities that they do not understand.	The worker has control, designs a project and allocates the young people to certain activities.
Training	Young people are told what to do.	The worker instructs the young people without identifying their previous knowledge or interest.
Coercion (court order, compulsory education)	Young people have no say in the activities.	The worker requires compliance for the project, which may also have enforced attendance and record-keeping.

young people are involved and develop a range of social and team-working skills. Being listened to and seeing the results of their contributions can be very positive learning experiences. For many young people, these opportunities to demonstrate capability provide useful and sometimes unique transitional experiences into adulthood and affect their confidence in other aspects of their lives.

Youth workers encourage young people to pass ideas and information between themselves to develop and manage projects. Role conflict can arise when the drive for participation comes from external funding criteria or organisational aims rather than the young people concerned. Attention needs to be paid to the aim of youth work, that is, to address their needs and interests and to the reasons for enabling their participation: to enable them to have more control over the decisions they make about their lives (see Box 9.1 on the aims of participation). Merton, *et al.* (2004) for example, define some functions of work with young people, which can conflict with youth work aims and values (see the table in Box 9.10). 'Participatory' projects can be more about

Box 9.10: Merton, *et al.* (2004) Functions of work with young people

Function	Application to work with young people
Integrative youth work	Is concerned with the socialisation of young people and introducing them into 'social norms, expectations, roles and institutions as preparation for the adult world. Seen in this way, social institutions remain broadly the same and it is the task of the young people and those working with them, to fit into what is expected of them.' (2004: 29)
Reflexive youth work	Recognises that local, incremental and individual instances of social change are necessary as 'social structures and systems may serve to exclude and disadvantage certain groups and individuals, and that one of the purposes of youth work is to ensure that the perspectives of young people are better accommodated within these institutions.' (2004: 30)
Redistributive youth work	Is concerned with social justice and social capital (e.g. Putnam, 1995) and 'counters disadvantage, by raising the sights of young people and directing resources to those least likely to receive them'. (Merton, *et al.* 2004: 30)

socialisation and control than young people's interests. Such projects may enable young people who enjoy taking on responsibilities to flourish while the others feel excluded because managing a project 'is just like school'.

Improving services for young people through participation

Decisions taken within a range of relevant structures, services and systems have widely varying expectations with regard to young people's participation; yet young people are affected by their decisions in most aspects of their lives. Assisting young people to identify where the power lies, how procedures work and how to participate in their decisions can be part of a youth worker's role. In particular, youth workers support young people dealing with the effects of inequalities (see also Chapter 7) within structures. Youth workers who are able to identify how power operates within society and its institutions, employing organisations, families and social groups can assist young people to find their way through these various arenas and enable them to participate more fully in decisions. Youth workers also need to be aware of their own power to identify whether their practice addresses or promotes oppression or liberation.

The ideas and perspectives of young people could usefully inform the design, development and implementation of services that they might use. When young people participate in management and evaluation activity resources might be more sensibly allocated. Services might become more accessible and relevant. In addition, the young people could develop more of a sense of ownership and responsibility for the services. Box 9.11 provides an example of the type of contribution that young people can make to a planning group. The young people could foresee a range of issues that may not have occurred to an adult planning group. In addition, they were able to make suggestions that were more feasible and interesting to the particular target group. Taking their ideas into account can give the young people a sense of pride that can precipitate their further involvement in maintaining a facility. If the young people had not been involved, the development may have been unused, dangerous and expensive. Their participation not only improved provision, but had the potential for benefits throughout the community. Through involvement in a socially responsible activity, the young people provide a positive image to their peers, families and community which could have far-reaching effects.

This model of young people's participation can be seen as 'market research' and lead youth workers and others to lose sight of the purpose of participation. Whilst improvement in services may be a worthwhile by-product, youth workers need to focus on enabling young people to have more control over the decisions that they make. Enabling participation is meant to be liberating for the young people, not providing more restrictions.

Box 9.11: Practice example: Young people's participation improves a park

Young people involved in the design of a local park were able to point out that a skateboard facility under discussion would:
- Be unlikely to interest the targeted age group unless certain design features were included
- Only accommodate a limited number of young people at a time
- Only accommodate one proficiency level at a time
- Require access to expensive safety equipment, which was beyond their means
- Need supervision to prevent younger children or alternative activities getting in the way.

Involving young people in organisations

An understanding of organisational structures, roles, relationships, power and decision-making processes can assist a youth worker to identify relevant practice to increase participation. The example in Box 9.12 demonstrates how a project can fall through with a lack of clarity about relationships and who has the power to make decisions.

Box 9.12: Practice example: Young people are duped

A Board of Directors for a youth organisation decided to set up a management group for a project made up solely of young people that would have responsibility for redecorating the youth centre, including the design and budget allocation. The Project Group put a lot of effort into considering different ways in which to involve other young people in the project. The final design included a mural with contributions from different groups using the centre. The centre was redecorated with a high level of participation by young people. A grand reopening was planned by the Project Group and the organisation's Board of Directors was invited. Several key members of the Board, who were also funders of the organisation, were offended by the content of the mural. At the next Board meeting, it was agreed that the mural would be painted over.

A youth worker could have made a difference to the practice example outlined in Box 9.12 above. Pointing out ways to enhance young people's participation at all levels of the project could have lead to more positive outcomes. For example, an experienced youth worker could have ensured that the Board of Directors fully discussed the implications and consequences of the brief prior to establishing the group. The Board's discussion might also have been enhanced by the participation of young people as representatives or members on the Board of Directors, which could also have improved communication and relationships between the two groups. Continuous representation from the Project Group on the Board of Directors would have helped to keep them informed about the development of the project. A youth worker or young person may have sought clarification from the Board of Directors about whether the Project Group's designs would need approval. Although this would limit the young people's power, a revised brief would more accurately reflect the views of the Board. The Project Group would also have been clearer about the consequences of their decisions.

A youth worker may also have been able to suggest a different approach to the way in which the Board handled the disagreement. For example, the Board of Directors could have informed the Project Group about their concerns and asked them to come up with alternative proposals. A youth worker taking on an advocacy or networking role may have suggested that the Board of Directors keep in touch with the young people to be in tune with their interests, styles and attitudes. Relationships could have been based on two-way communication. Then the young people's views may have been valued and the Board may have been able to communicate their own values to the young people.

The example highlights a number of issues about enabling participation. For participation to be positive, young people need to be treated with respect. In this example, the young people may have known that the mural was offensive yet have gone ahead in order antagonise the Board or to highlight the bogus power on offer. Alternatively, they may not have known that the mural was offensive and have been denied the opportunity to put the situation right. Youth workers need to question who has the right, the power and the access to knowledge and who makes the decisions over who will have access. This analysis of groups, organisations and society will assist the identification of meaningful participation.

Whilst conflicts about power can be inevitable, a number of structural changes could enhance young people's participation. Identifying different structures and different ways in which young people can participate on committees can provide options for organisations looking to increase young people's participation. A youth worker may be able to advise young people about effective contributions in committees and provide an understanding of the implications as well as the limitations of various roles. Participation in committee discussions from the initial allocation of funds to a project may enhance all of the members' understanding of possibilities and limitations. Or young people's ongoing participation on an Advisory Committee could contribute a relevant perspective to policy development.

A youth worker can also set up structures to enable young people's participation. Relevant structures could be based on informal youth groups or more formally constituted groups and committees. The aim will usually determine the levels of formality and young people's influence – although sometimes the history of the group is also significant. The remit and procedures of a group established by young people are likely to be quite different from an adult group that young people join. For example, young people on a youth council would set the agenda themselves; whereas the contributions of young people invited to attend the board meetings of a housing trust may well be limited to certain agenda items (see the table in Box 9.13).

Box 9.13: Types of committees

Type of committee	Role of committee
Boards of directors Management committees	• Provide direction • Responsible for projects or organisations • Management of staff and budgets
Advisory boards Policy committees	• Feedback and advice • No responsibility for management • Discuss issues; develop proposals • Present findings
Task forces Working groups Action forums Subgroups	• Short term projects with a specific purpose • Report to another body
Youth councils Youth forums	• Network to discuss issues • Disseminate information • Make representation to other bodies

An understanding of the specific roles and responsibilities that members undertake when joining a committee can provide clarity for both young people and the committee. A youth worker can suggest different options (see the table in Box 9.14) to enhance the decision.

Enabling young people to participate fully

Young people who feel involved in decisions and are able to contribute to the process and outcomes of decision-making can be a great asset to any

Box 9.14: Roles for young people on committees

Roles	Rights
Chair, Secretary, Treasurer Full member Appointed member Worker or volunteer Representative from subgroups or other groups	Voting and speaking rights
Chair, Secretary, Treasurer Worker or volunteer Representative of subgroup or other group Contributing member	Speaking rights but no voting rights
Representative of subgroup or other group Invitee to discuss specific topics or make presentations Consultant Advisor	No voting rights and restricted speaking rights
Observer Representative of network or forum Shadowing member or officer	Right to attend only. No voting rights and no speaking rights
On mailing list	Receive minutes and/or reports; no voting rights, no speaking rights, no right to attend

organisation that works with young people. Certain circumstances can encourage or enable individuals to participate fully, such as an understanding of the topic, the potential choices being made and the implications of the decision. Young people also need information about the decision-making process and how they fit in (see the table in Box 9.15 for some examples). Simply adding young people as members to an existing adult committee without any thought to how they might be received or how either party might feel about the culture and procedures is not usually a very successful way to enable participation. Usually both the existing committee membership and the new younger members need some induction and training as to how to proceed.

Honest and open discussion about participation and answers to questions (such as those outlined in Box 9.15) are important. If a youth worker is unsure about whether a young person will be listened to when attending an adult committee meeting, this needs to be honestly communicated. Encouraging a young person to go to a committee meeting without knowing what to expect could lead to disappointment at a lack of tangible outcomes. At the very least, a discussion of possible scenarios is advisable. Preferably, young people attending meetings should be prepared with clear explanations of their roles and the procedures of the meeting.

Box 9.15: Factors relating to participation in decision-making

Factor	Questions raised
Relevance	• *Do I understand the topic, the discussion, the decision and its impact?* • *Am I interested in this topic or the decision? Do I care?* • *Will the decision make any difference?* • *Will my participation affect anything?*
Purpose	• *What is the purpose of the decision? Is there another agenda?* • *Is a decision being made? What is it? What are the choices? What are the implications of the different choices?* • *What are the potential impacts of this decision? Will this decision have effects other than those intended?* • *Do I want this responsibility? Do I have concerns about being involved in this decision (e.g. reputation, comeback, confidence)?*
Process	• *Do I have sufficient information on which to base a decision?* • *Can I ask about this? Will my questions be answered? Will the options be discussed?* • *Is there too much information? Are too many decisions being made?* • *Do the others making the decision with me understand me or my perspective?*
Power	• *Will my opinion or decision be listened to? Respected? Implemented?* • *Do the mechanics of the process or culture of the organisation enable me to agree or disagree with what is being decided?* • *How will my involvement be perceived by others?*

Essential skills for developing participation

- Defining participation
- Understanding the aims of participation
- Recognising young people's experience of participation
- Understanding the benefits of involving young people
- Recognising participation as self-development
- Improving services through participation
- Promoting anti-ageist attitudes through participation
- Recognising own approach to change
- Involving young people in organisations
- Monitoring and evaluating a project.

Further reading about participation

Arnstein (1969); Driskell (2002); Hart (1992); Wates (1999).

CHAPTER 10: Using research

Research involving young people can inform the development of relevant and accessible activities and practice that can make a real impact on young people's lives. This chapter outlines the skills involved in identifying appropriate research methods and sources of information in a staged and participative approach. The chapter focuses on more formal or structured research for the purposes of identifying need for youth work rather than the informal methods of research, such as networking, which have been explored in previous chapters.

Understanding how research could make an impact

Finding out about young people's interests and potential resources sets in motion a planned approach to youth work practice. Informal and regular interactions with individual and groups of young people in the community constantly inform and affect practice. Issues are brought to the attention of youth workers who are accessible and well known in a community. Through listening, conversations and more formal discussions, a picture can be compiled of individual and group concerns that inform a grounded knowledge of the community and the area. This process and ongoing formative evaluation of youth work provides a context for more formal research (see also Chapter 3 Reaching out).

More structured investigative research, such as a community audit or profile, enables youth workers to make decisions based on analysed data. Reports of research provide a means of communicating this evidence to others. More formal or structured research may be necessary to select or prioritise issues or identify the feasibility of a project. A research project can also be a useful method for involving young people and others in the community in issues that affect them. Instead of simply providing a service, a ready-made and planned programme or solutions to perceived problems, a youth worker involves young people and their communities in emancipatory research where they identify their own issues as well as any ways to address them. Involvement of others in research can generate and promote demands on existing services, provide suggestions for changes and/or ideas for new services to address needs more effectively (see Box 10.1 for an example).

> **Box 10.1: Practice example: Research to identify a need**
>
> A group of young people complained to a youth worker that there was 'nothing to do around here.' The youth worker encouraged them to find out about existing leisure facilities. The research could either corroborate their views about gaps and accessibility or identify under-publicised activities that they could become involved in. The young worker pointed out that in either case, their views could be fed back to service providers. The youth worker provided advice and guidance, use of phone and stationery and took their views seriously. The complaint, in the form of a research report compiled by the young people, was forwarded to leisure services. The area manager invited the young people to make a presentation to their board. Soon the young people were involved in decisions about allocation of resources for young people in their area.

Clarity about the aims of the research is important in developing the design of appropriate and useful research projects. Research can identify barriers that may prevent young people from accessing certain services or changes that could enable or encourage their participation. For example, if young people express an interest in a new facility, research can identify whether the capacity of any planned services relate to the potential take-up. Funding applications or project proposals would be enhanced by this type of supportive information. Research carried out with young people can lead to the discovery of new information, inform learning and develop practice (see the table in Box 10.2 for some examples of the links between different types of research and the aims).

Box 10.2: Types of research

Aims of research	Sample research projects	Sample questions
Exploratory research • to find out about something unknown	A youth worker moves into a new area and carries out research to identify priorities for work.	What's going on? Who is here? What do they want? What services are available to them? Why is this happening? What are they interested in?
Baseline research • to establish a starting point for planning or monitoring purposes	An outreach worker carries out research with a group of young people gathering on a street corner on a particular night to find out whether individuals are involved in certain types of risky behaviour. Subsequent actions undertaken to address the issues will be able to monitor changes by comparing the findings with a re-run of the research in three years' time.	How will we know when or if the project is working? What is going on now so that in the future we can identify what changes are taking place?

Continued

Box 10.2 - *Cont'd*

Feasibility study research • to identify whether a project will work or what is necessary to make it work	Research put together a detailed project or business plan, to be discussed with others (e.g., potential funders, users, managers, workers) who may become involved to make sure that sufficient resources are in place.	Is this project possible? What resources would we need to make it work? If we did this, who would be interested or involved? What are the necessary steps to make this happen? What are the consequences?
Evaluation research • to identify ways to improve its effectiveness or appropriacy	Research to identify the outcomes, quality and effectiveness of a project or piece of work	What was the impact of this work? On whom? How do the results compare to our aims and objectives?
Experimental research • to try out something new, analyse its effects and evaluate its use	Consultation during or after a project. The same idea could be attempted in two areas for comparison or two different ideas could be tried out in the same area to see what works best.	What happens when we do this? How does it compare with when we do that?

Designing ethical and appropriate youth work research

The aims of the research, the type of research, the type of data required, the data collection methods, the research instruments and the sources require attention to ethical and professional practice (see Box 10.3 for some suggestions about the attributes of ethical youth work research). Participation by young people and the community as well as accountability are important issues to consider when planning a research project. The involvement of young people can assist youth workers in retaining a youth work perspective when identifying how the research findings might be used and carrying out the research.

Youth work research generally has a clear relationship between theory and practice. The research needs to be based on youth work values and practice and carried out within an ethical framework. Research that involves young people, including peer-led research or peer researchers, supports a participative approach to appreciative enquiry that builds on strengths. The research tends to be empirical in

---

Box 10.3: Attributes of ethical youth work research

- is for the benefit of young people whether directly or indirectly
- is based on positive, participatory and anti-oppressive practice
- involves voluntary and informed consent
- incorporates the right to withdraw
- includes an assessment of risk
- avoids unnecessary physical or mental suffering, such as embarrassment, publicity, invasiveness
- is clear about what happens to the results
- involves young people in design, management, steering and/or researcher roles
- includes participatory evaluation.

---

that reality is studied through experience or observation. Observations are carried out to develop new theories to put into positive anti-oppressive practice rather than having a deficit model of young people or their communities. Theory is either applied or tested to gain useful knowledge or data for evidence-based practice to promote continuous development and application of practice. Box 10.4 provides a practice example of how youth work values can inform the identification of an appropriate approach.

Box 10.4: Practice example: Identifying appropriate aims

We were concerned about young people's involvement in gangs but didn't want to sensationalise what was going on – it didn't seem like that would be helpful. Obviously there are problems with violence and drugs in the area and related gang activity goes on. Our research wasn't about highlighting this. We wanted to hear from young people about their experiences. We wanted to see if we could understand and identify what pressures, if any, led to their participation or membership of gangs. Maybe what they gained from being involved in a gang. We wanted to avoid negative labels and we didn't want to demonise their actions. We didn't want to deduce from certain evidence that they belonged to a gang. We used their definitions and their perceptions and used their language. We didn't even want to use the word 'gang' ourselves unless a group was clearly involved in illegal behaviour. As street-based workers, we also wanted to make sure that the information we collected did not lead to the arrest of individual young people. That wasn't the point of our research. We just wanted to hear what the young people thought so that we could work together to address their real situations.

A street-based youth worker

Involving young people in research

Rather than simply 'using' young people as subjects or sources, good research practice involves young people as researchers, managers and directors. (Some examples are listed in Box 10.5.) The reasons for the research should be communicated to the young people and/or interested communities so that false expectations do not develop. The time-scale for the project also needs to be publicly known with a turnaround that is appropriate for the specific aims of the research. Research that takes too long to address the issues raised could be counterproductive. For example, identifying and addressing the interests of a group of young people means that the investigation needs to be carried out fairly quickly. Young people who are consulted through research may move on or change their minds before any plans to address their needs are completed. The results of any recommendations may not be ready until the next

Box 10.5: Involving young people in research

Type of research	Young peoples' role	Methodology
Peer-led research	Young people are managers of the project	• Young people carry out a quantitative survey of other young people to identify their interests to support their application for funding to develop the facilities in the park
Peer research	Young people who are or who could be from the 'target group' are the researchers	• Young people facilitate a discussion with other young people who use drugs to find out about the consequences of drug use.
Participatory or emancipatory research	Young people affected by the issues are managers and researchers	• Young people design and carry out a research project making their own analysis of findings and evaluation of ways forward.
Action research	Young people carry out research alongside youth workers	• A group of young people identify, implement and evaluate a project with a youth worker. • Young people from a different area or organisation work with a local group to provide feedback and guidance on their project.
Reflective practice	Young people involved in youth work activities identify their learning from the experience	• A youth worker provides a range of methods for young people to monitor and evaluate their projects. • The young people network and discuss their projects with other groups of young people through forums, exchange visits and conferences. • The young people compile written, oral and multi-media displays and reports for evaluation and discussion with others.

'generation' of young people – who may prefer quite different facilities or activities. Instead of addressing the issues, this research only raises false hopes. The researcher needs to be clear about the implications of possible outcomes and to communicate with the young people about relevant issues, as well as budgets, time-scales and long-term sustainability.

Ensuring participants' informed consent

When people are the subjects or sources of information for research, ethical and often legal constraints require their informed consent. Individuals or groups who are observed, interviewed, involved in discussions or asked to fill in a questionnaire need to know about the researchers' aims, methods and plans for disseminating the results. This information enables participants to make informed choices about whether they wish to be involved. An ethical approach involves taking steps to address the safety, rights, dignity and well-being of the individuals whose circumstances or views are included in research findings, particularly when participants are young or potentially vulnerable. Participants should be told what will happen with their personal data, both in the short and longer term. Questions about anonymity, whether individual details are linked to responses and findings, as well as how and whether their contribution will be recorded and published are key issues to be resolved and communicated clearly.

Reasonable steps need to be taken to make sure that individuals are able to give informed consent. The methods of gathering information need to take into account issues such as the participants' ability to understand the implications and consequences of participation, their rights to refuse to contribute and to withdraw – and at what stages this is still possible. A researcher needs to be able to prove that steps were taken to ensure that participants understood the implications of participation. Relevant issues can include the level of the respondents' control and understanding of any resulting publicity or dissemination. A researcher needs to check whether the age, abilities or circumstances of an individual means that others, such as a legal guardian, should be responsible. A legal minor, someone who may not be deemed competent or someone who is dependent on the researcher may be perceived as too 'vulnerable' to provide their own consent. Recording the procedures undertaken to verify consent is good practice as is providing backup information in writing for respondents about how to withdraw (see Box 10.6 for some suggestions about protecting informed consent).

Having a planned approach to research

A planned and staged approach to a project can assist a youth worker attempting to keep young people informed and involved. The tasks,

---

Box 10.6: Practice examples: Ways to protect informed consent

1. **Discuss the research procedures** with young people, parents/guardians and other professionals prior to starting the research.
2. **Provide a clear outline of research procedures:**
   - what will happen with their data
   - how to withdraw from the research and any timing constraints on this
   - the commitment required, for example, the timing and schedule for participants and for the project
   - potential risks, consequences and outcomes
3. **Check out consent** whether an individual:
   - is being or feeling pressured to participate
   - has any questions about the research
   - is able to take responsibility for a decision to participate
   - needs an adult's consent
   - understands the information being provided
   - has any objections
   - wants to participate and agrees with the procedures
4. **Record the procedures used for informed consent** *(as above)*
   - The explanation of the project used by all researchers
   - The training provided for interviewers
   - The questions that are used to ensure that participants fully understand the content, methods and what consent covers
5. **Keep a record of participant agreements**
   - signed consent forms
   - recordings of any verbal consent
   - notes as to the circumstances surrounding consent.

---

responsibilities and purpose behind them can be communicated clearly. Individuals will be able to see the different roles and understand how and where they might be able to contribute. The following sections illustrate some stages in first, designing and then undertaking a participative research project.

1. Deciding to carry out a research project

Defining the brief for a project can involve identifying the general topic area and aims or purpose with a time-frame. For example, *a three-month project to engage with young people congregating in particular areas to determine interests and needs or a month-long survey to identify any barriers to take-up of services and whether there is a need for more targeted services or support.*

This first stage is an ideal time in which to involve young people. Young people who are concerned or involved can work with a youth worker to provide clarity and purpose for the brief. A project may be a useful, interesting and necessary piece of work or simply a diversion from addressing an issue that is already clearly defined and recognised. The level of young people's interest and the relevance to youth work practice can assist decisions about whether a specific funding application or research topic is an appropriate way forward.

At this stage, a core group of interested stakeholders could look at previous work on an identified topic to make sure that the project will provide new and required information. Learning from previous approaches and methods is also useful at this point in the process. The ideas and purpose of the research could be discussed with individuals who are in a position to help or give advice about the area, topic or work involved. Other young people, members of the community, colleagues and professionals may be able to share relevant experience or information about research design, possible resource requirements and sources for these. Networking can help to identify stakeholders or other supporters who may be interested in participating as contributors or subjects, researchers, steering or advisory group members, funders and/or disseminators.

2. Setting up support and direction

The second stage of a project involves the establishment of structures for support and direction with a timetable. Critical feedback and support could come from various individuals and groups on an informal or formal basis. Young people should be involved as their perspectives in the direction of the project and monitoring and evaluation is essential. If appropriate, more informal sub-groups for young people could be formed to ensure that their views are heard. The core research group could be expanded unless more structured support is required. (See Box 10.7 for some more examples of structures to support young people's participation in research.)

Box 10.7: Practice examples of support structures for research

- *Peer review:* Young people who had carried out previous surveys or a detached youth worker from another area could provide critical perspectives.
- *A steering group*, with 50% membership from young people in the area, could meet regularly to monitor and evaluate the project.
- An *advisory group* made up of young parents, colleagues, other researchers, potential subjects, members of the community, management, funders, academics and other agencies, could meet regularly to discuss the issues raised by the research project.
- *Supervision or consultancy* for the research coordinator or the researchers could provide a regular sounding board for ongoing practice and discussion of professional issues arising.

3. Establishing a research question or key topics

At this stage, a specific research question, *hypothesis* and/or target group is decided upon so the research can have focus. The key areas are those that are to be clarified through the research and the question or sets of questions that will be answered. (For example, see Box 10.8) Some projects will be quite specific in relation to scope and targets, such as a particular geographic area, age range, set of circumstances or issues. The support groups and resource providers need to agree that questions are interesting and relevant. The topic, scope, targets and the questions need to tally with the aims and purpose of the research.

Box 10.8: Practice example: Establishing key topics

- Focusing on four groups of detached street-based young people: what do the young people say are the reasons why they congregate on the streets?
- Surveying lesbian, gay, bi-sexual and transgendered young people: What drugs area they using? What information do they need? What educational materials would be useful for them?
- To identify service needs for young parents: What facilities do the parents using this baby clinic want? What do they say is lacking in current provision?
- An arts feasibility study: What types of arts projects do young people in this are prefer, for example, is there a need for performance space, short-term projects or full-time schools? How much would such projects cost?

---

4. Identifying resource requirements

Identifying resource requirements influences decisions about project limitations or whether there are sufficient resources to support a project. The resources required for carrying out a research project may come from additional funding or existing resources that could be allocated to the project. Youth workers may be able to carry out the work as part of their usual job description. Resources may be made available from a multi-agency steering group. Multi-sourcing can make projects more viable. One agency could co-ordinate a project, while another provides supervision, a third provides expenses and the fourth has access to the interested young people.

Funding applications to external bodies may be appropriate, particularly for running costs and expenses such as office supplies, telephone, postage and printing, recording equipment, administration, volunteers' expenses or external evaluation, publication of findings and a dissemination conference or event. If external resources are required, involving young people in putting together applications or proposals can develop their understanding of the constraints or possibilities of a research project (see also the next chapter on Managing a Project).

5. Identifying how the research will be carried out

The methodology of the research, or rationale for selecting particular methods, relates to the type of research and the information required. Decisions need to be made about the methods of data collection and the sources that will be useful. Some projects require more statistical information, whilst others seek out opinions or observable facts. Background, history and context can inform the analysis of findings. Surveys, observation, structured, semi-structured or unstructured interviews can be used singly or combined to enhance the project. Clarity about the reasons for selecting different methods is important. Discussions about their efficacy and feasibility also need to refer to positive, participative and anti-oppressive practice.

Most research projects contain elements of quantitative as well as qualitative research. Quantitative research provides the statistics possible from responses to closed questions or numerical data whilst more descriptive information can be gathered from the qualitative research that seeks out views and opinions or observes experiences and actions. Statistical analysis of 'hard' information, such as numbers of individuals indicating preferences for a particular activity, and evidence of young people's points of view, such as direct quotes, can be a powerful combination. (See the table in Box 10.9 for some examples.)

6. Further defining focus of the research

Further reflection on the focus of the research usually leads to a number of subsidiary questions that can be used to design the information collection. Continued discussions about feasibility and practicalities may lead to a redefinition of the question. The research group needs to consider the time-scale in reference to the selected methods and potential sources, particularly in relation to ensuring access to the information. Sub-questions are identified to assist the development of research instruments.

7. Identifying the sources

The range of sources, access to them and interpretation of their meaning will determine the quality of the information and validity of the research. Most research includes information from individuals, groups and organisations as well as text-based or web-based sources. Identifying the relative significance of recorded research findings, first-hand

---

Box 10.9: Practice examples: Redefining the research question

Research topic	Sample research questions
A: Causes of young people being street based	Could the reasons for young people congregating be related to a lack of alternative activities? We need to know more about their hopes and aspirations. Do the young people need more information about how to pursue their interests or what are the barriers to takeup?
B: Educational needs in relation to drug use	What type of drugs are the young people using? For example, are they legal or illegal, expensive or inexpensive, inhaled, swallowed or intravenous? Do they know about safe use or consequences of use? What would deter young people from misusing these substances?
C: Gaps in services for young parents	What ideas do local young parents have about their needs? Are they interested in meeting other parents, money advice, parenting advice, educational development?
D: Arts project feasibility study	Where are young people currently involved in dance, drama, participative arts? What are some of the common factors in the success of other projects? How do these relate to the young people, services and support for a project in this area? How did other projects get off the ground?

---

observation and anecdotes or stories from individuals and groups will benefit from grounded knowledge and stakeholder participation.

First-hand information from primary sources through direct contact, observation or involvement of those experiencing an issue is powerful evidence. In general, the strength of youth work research relates to 'privileged access' to relevant primary sources. Many young people and youth workers have existing relationships with individuals and groups facing the issues concerned. In addition, youth workers tend to have a wide range of contacts and networks within an area that can be called upon for suggestions and advice about relevant primary and secondary sources.

Additional sources can provide different types of data to enhance the research. A literature search could help to provide background and context for the research, such as previously compiled statistical information, while theoretical frameworks could be gained from books and articles about detached young people or causes of exclusion. Other secondary sources, such as individuals or groups knowledgeable about drug use and education, could provide relevant information. Interviews with residents, school records and health services would provide different types of data.

8. Planning the time-table

The research group will need to plan a timetable for the research that includes making contact with participants and carrying out the remaining stages of the research. Information about relevant sources and existing relationships can affect the time-scale and depth of the research. Identifying who will carry out each step of the data collection, allocating other tasks and establishing deadlines can enhance participation and organisation. Examining the following stages of the research and estimating requirements with the researchers involved could help to plan a realistic time-frame.

9. Designing the information collection

The research group needs to think about how the required and relevant information can be collected, including considerations about what is worth investigating as well as what is not. The particular methods, research instruments, such as questionnaires or recording sheets, and time-scales need to be discussed with colleagues. (See some examples of data collection methods in Box 10.10.) In evaluating the feasibility of the instruments, their viability and effectiveness in gathering the necessary information needs to be considered realistically. For example, the language used in any questions has to be understood clearly and the recording and collection of the information has to be practical. A pilot can help in the design of any new instruments prior to the 'rolling out' of the project.

The analysis of the data depends on consistency in relation to the types of question and instruments used. A standardised method of distribution or collection is usually required to provide a basis for compiling and analysing findings. Clarity about the relationship between the researcher and respondent, how the contributors were selected and the level of honesty that can be assumed are all necessary to be able to understand the significance of responses. In quantitative research, only answers from the same question can be added together for true comparison or meaning. When planning the collection of information, the steering group may need to consider the training needs of potential researchers or interviewers to ensure this consistency.

Box 10.10: Practice examples of data collection

- Informal interviews can be recorded by ticking possible responses on a record sheet and scribbling down occasional key sentences. Research can be carried out in pairs, one engaging the respondent in conversation while the other takes notes.
- Games and fun quizzes can be used to identify levels of knowledge at the same time as piloting potential educational materials.
- A short mixture of open and closed question questionnaires can be distributed, with a relevant shopping voucher offered as a prize draw to motivate completion.
- Service providers and potential participants could be invited to a relevant workshop, performance or other event to provide information about levels of interest.

Carrying out the research

1. Collecting the data

Adequate records will need to be kept of the information that is collected and how it was collected. The data then needs to be organised and filed in an appropriately confidential manner.

2. Analysing and interpreting the findings

Once the questions have been asked and answered, the researchers need to make sense of the data. The data is reviewed in order to identify emerging patterns and draw conclusions about their meaning and significance. The background and contextual knowledge that young people bring to the research is crucial at this stage. Analysing the results of a survey is more than counting up the numbers of people that answered 'yes' to a question. Interpreting whether the numbers are significant, indicate a trend or are affected by particular circumstances requires a deeper understanding of the context. The issues raised by those directly affected by the findings can provide a very relevant perspective while a range of perspectives generally enhances data analysis. Even statistical data about age, ethnicity, health, income, housing or educational achievements can be conflicting and reveal bias or error. Making sense of the collected data requires recognition of the strengths as well as limitations of different sources.

   Analysis entails considering whether the findings from one set of questions can be usefully compared with another. For example, the number of young people could be usefully compared with take-up of services to determine a percentage of use. Analysis could also determine whether an apparent relationship between different elements is coincidence or cause and effect. For example, findings may indicate an increase in number of young people who are victims of crime at the same time as an increase in school exclusions. Other information or types of evidence would be needed to determine whether the two statistics are linked.

3. Making recommendations

The analysis of findings may identify further issues and point to areas that need action. Making recommendations to address the findings is generally a key feature of action research, participatory research and youth work practice. Putting together a list of recommended actions or a detailed strategy is a very useful outcome from research (see Box 11.6 in Chapter 11 for a possible format for an action plan). The findings need to be framed in such a way that connections can be seen between the issues raised and any recommendations. Reference to youth work values and principles as well as job descriptions can help to prioritise issues and devise methods to address them. The involvement of stakeholders in this process means that they can help to make and implement any recommendations and plans that result.

4. Evaluating the research and the findings

At the end of the project, evaluation could consider the degree to which the research addressed the aims as well as how useful the findings were in planning future work. Reflection can assist participants to recognise and implement their learning in future projects. A range of criteria can be used to review the information collection and the analysis of findings. For example, the criteria in the table in Box 10.11 could be used to evaluate the limitations or strengths of a research project. Involving young people in applying the evaluation criteria can be a powerful method of enabling participation and learning. Young people can often identify the reasons for any difficulties or unexpected outcomes from a different perspective. The experience will also assist participants to anticipate consequences in future research or related actions.

Box 10.11: Some criteria for research evaluation

young people's involvement	the level of participation, the degree to which they controlled decisions about the research and whether their perspectives, wishes or interests were sufficiently considered
the methods	the validity, transferability and relevance of the research, the consistency provided by the instruments
the sources	the accuracy, sufficiency and usefulness of the data and the sources' knowledge, opinions or experience
the findings	the significance, conclusiveness, contradictory nature or importance of the information collected.

---

5. Disseminating the findings

A dissemination plan can be used to target the specific stakeholders who need to be informed about the findings and recommendations from the research. Some projects have a policy of ensuring 'equality of dissemination' between those directly affected by the issues raised by the research and those with the power and resources to effect the recommendations. In the example provided in Box 10.12, the resources made available for dissemination are equally divided between the

Box 10.12: An 'equality of dissemination' plan

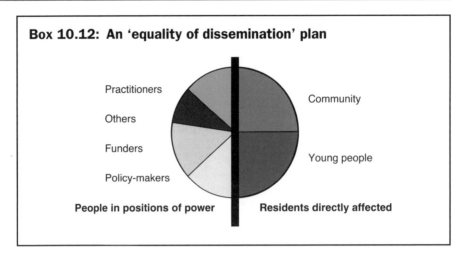

residents in the area and non-residents and between older and younger residents. The targeting of resources for dissemination means that proper attention is paid to the needs and interests of those affected by an issue as well as to ensuring that those in power have the information necessary to effect changes.

Various formats for dissemination could be considered in relation to their relevance for the target audience, the purpose of dissemination and available resources. A celebration at the end of a peer-led research project could include dramatic, visual and participative activities to raise awareness of the issues with other young people and relevant agencies. The launch of a report at a meeting or conference enables everyone involved to celebrate the end of an often demanding project. Face-to-face discussions of the issues raised with an element of training can be useful. A presentation to individuals with resources to take action on the issues raised could incorporate an action plan and budgetary implications. Deciding on an appropriate method of dissemination requires an understanding of the audience, what information they need or would be interested in and some interesting ways in which it could be passed on to them.

Different versions of a report may be appropriate for different audiences: a full report for funders, summaries for young people or the public and alternative media used for specific groups. A research report for a manager might be a brief abstract with recommendations; a presentation to a community might involve a newsletter article, web-page or display; a funding bid might include a feasibility study. In each case, the general headings could be similar, but the level of detail and the terminology would vary greatly. A research report could be compiled by circulating drafts to anyone who has been named or consulted in compiling the research to allow corrections or amendments to be made.

Checking out language and information can be an important aspect of practice.

Different methods of distribution can be used to widen dissemination of research findings. Flyers, which summarise the findings and include a report order form, can be distributed at community events or door-to-door. Copies of reports can be made available to anyone who requests them. Others can be distributed to mailing lists, conferences and members. A website can link with other useful sources and limits paper wastage. A multi-method approach can assist dissemination to individuals whose access to computers, literacy or networks is limited.

Essential skills for using research

- Understanding how research could make an impact
- Designing ethical and appropriate youth work research
- Involving young people in research
- Ensuring participants' informed consent
- Having a planned approach to research design
- Deciding to carry out a research project
- Setting up support and direction
- Establishing the research questions
- Identifying resource requirements
- Identifying how the research will be carried out
- Further defining the focus of the research
- Identifying the sources
- Planning the timetable
- Collecting the data
- Analysing and interpreting the findings
- Making recommendations
- Evaluating the research and the findings
- Disseminating the findings.

Further reading about using research

Bell (1999); Burton (1993); Grieg and Taylor (1999); Hawtin *et al.* (1994); Holdsworth (2002).

CHAPTER 11: Managing a project

Youth workers are often called upon to manage discrete activities or projects; some are also managers of a whole organisation. This chapter provides an overview of some of the skills required to manage a project within a short-term scheme or an established organisation. Relevant skills include defining the purpose of the project, managing financial matters and working with staff in ways that are transparent and practicable. The positive impact of applying youth work values and principles, particularly participation and anti-oppressive practice, is examined with examples.

Applying youth work principles to project management

Managing a project often highlights the differences between the theory and practice of youth work. Ethical decision-making to prioritise resources and facilitate operations requires an analysis of the reality and the consequences of decisions. Having the 'grace and wisdom' (Niebuhr, 1987, see Box 11.1) to make appropriate decisions does not come easily to all managers. Some experience conflicts between their idealism and their organisation's often pragmatic requirements. Some find it difficult to come up with solutions that are based on principles as well as realism. Managers attempting to promote positive change need to develop confidence and clarity when dealing with the conflicts that can occur between their professional principles and individual, organisational or societal expectations and assumptions.

> **Box 11.1: Niebuhr's (1987) 'Serenity Prayer'**
>
> 'God give us grace to accept with serenity the things that cannot be changed, courage to change the things that should be changed, and the wisdom to distinguish the one from the other.' (Niebuhr, 1987: 251)

Youth work managers can maintain focus by promoting participation by young people and staff. For example, a decision to accept certain constraints in order to secure resources can be difficult. One manager may decide to have nothing to do with a project that appears to control or contain young people. Another, recognising possible benefits, may negotiate a compromise to address some of the concerns. Whilst either decision could be defensible, most youth work managers would choose to involve others affected by the consequences of the decision in the decision-making process. Participation aims to share power rather than to gain compliance.

Decision-making that takes into account the power relationships within organisations can result in effective and strategic resolutions. Analysis of the assumptions that can govern beliefs and contexts for choices and behaviours (Hammond, 1998) may also help to illuminate a way forward. An authoritarian and task-oriented 'Theory X' manager (McGregor, 1960) assumes that 'the average human being has an inherent dislike of work and will avoid it if he can'. A participative, process-oriented 'Theory 'Y' manager believes that individuals are capable of creativity and naturally accept work and responsibility. According to McGregor, managers need to be able to identify their own and others' standpoints on these theories (see Box 11.2).

Box 11.2: McGregor (1960) on management theory and practice

'Every managerial act rests on assumptions, generalizations, and hypotheses – that is to say, on theory. Our assumptions are frequently implicit, sometimes quite unconscious, often conflicting; nevertheless, they determine our predictions that if we do **a**, **b** will occur. Theory and practice are inseparable. There is, in fact, no prediction without theory; all managerial decisions and actions rest on assumptions about behaviour.' (1960:8)

Organisational culture and experience may limit change and development. Individual staff members who are accustomed to working with a manager who regularly takes responsibility for issues that arise may not know how to change; others may see no need. Teams may be reluctant to raise or discuss issues through fear of exposure or blame. Hierarchical systems may exclude the majority of staff from participating in decision-making. Established practice may deter certain groups from accessing resources so that individuals may not trust a manager to be non-discriminatory. Encouraging the examination of assumptions and allowing them to be discussed and understood provides opportunities for them to be addressed (Hammond, 1998).

The job title of 'manager' generally indicates that an individual is responsible for some direction and control of operations and resources. The level of responsibility can depend on whether an organisation has established lines of accountability and codes of practice. In following set procedures, both the organisation and the manager are protected from problems resulting from unsanctioned decisions. Moreover, the development of appropriate policies, procedures and codes of practice can help to provide a positive environment for practice for youth work, young people and youth workers. Involving staff and young people in this process can help to create a 'learning organisation' (Senge, 1990), which could benefit all concerned.

Balancing interests

A participative approach to management may require balancing a number of different interests and influences. Young people, members of the community, workers, employers and funding bodies can each have particular needs, demands or opinions about a project. Effective management usually requires consideration of the needs of these key players or issues; deciding which take priority can be more difficult. Giving equal weight to each or finding general consensus is not always possible. Managers may need to negotiate a creative compromise or settlement that balances various influences including the young people's, the communities', the funder's and the organisation's interests. In addition, finding an approach that is feasible with in any resource constraints may require further compromise.

Some youth workers attempt to prioritise projects based on young people's expressed interests or self-identified needs only to find that the employing organisation's aims, objectives or targets conflict with what young people would like. At other times, a manager may find a community's priorities are expected to take precedence over young people's needs. A project may require staff to work on schedules they are unwilling to adopt. Finding solutions that satisfy many interests often requires imaginative approaches, some of which may be found through discussions between participants. Carrying out relevant research can also assist decision-making. (See also Chapter 10 on using research as a basis for practice.)

A 'successful' project could be one in which all of the interested players are equally satisfied or involved in managing or designing a project. An example could be that the young people want a skateboard facility; their parents think that's a wonderful idea and the community is happy to have the facility erected in local waste ground; the youth work organisation says that the tidied up area fits with their priorities to be involved in environmental projects; the funding and expertise are available and so the project works well. Many youth work projects do not naturally emerge with such congruence. Some require considerable attention to conflicting needs to avoid running into difficulties that can affect future work.

Managing short-term projects

Youth work often involves structured projects with young people that culminate in a celebration or event, such as an artistic production, exchange visit or achievement award. Distinct projects can provide tangible outcomes attractive to both young people and funders. Many organisations structure their youth work in a continuous programme of short-term projects, which provide flexibility and fresh ideas to retain the interests of ongoing participants and/or reach new target groups.

Some organisations depend on the funding linked to specific positive project outcomes. The pressure for results and related evidence that follow can often be overly restrictive. The actual completion of certain targets and tasks may become more important than the process of participation. Insufficient or unreliable funding may lead to less of a long-term commitment to young people or staff, a lack of development work or sustainable practice. Having clarity about the aims of short-term projects and the development of management skills and knowledge can help youth workers to maintain youth work principles in their practice and avoid the pitfalls of such projects.

1. Defining the purpose of the project

A useful method of involving others in a project is to develop a mission statement or definition of the core purpose of the project. Individuals and groups of young people, other local community members, staff within the organisation and from other agencies can work together to identify the nature and purpose of the project, what it does, how this relates to any underlying principles and how it may differ from other services, provision or work with young people. A mission statement for a project should be quite short, easily communicated and motivate or inspire. See Box 11.3 for some practice examples of mission statements. Full participation can promote the use of appropriate language and maintain relevance. Putting together a mission statement is also a useful exercise for establishing agreement.

Box 11.3: Practice examples: Mission statements

The 'XYZ organisation' is committed to involving young people in the organisation of enjoyable, educational and inspirational community projects that will assist their transition into mature, caring and committed adults.

The 'ABC youth group' promotes the development, well-being, rights and participation of young people by ensuring that they are able to enjoy themselves while making meaningful contributions to planning and organising activities and making informed choices about their futures.

The '123 Project' creates opportunities for change in the lives of young people and their communities through projects that involve them in improving their own environments and creating sustainable intergenerational relationship.

2. Defining aims and objectives

Defining specific aims and objectives assists in project planning, participation and positive outcomes. The identification of goals conveys the changes that a project hopes to achieve whilst the objectives outline the activities that will be undertaken or the services that will be offered to bring about the changes. See Box 11.4 for a practice example of some aims and objectives. A project with clear aims and objectives that have been designed and discussed by participants should generate or support feelings of involvement and ownership. Negotiation should lead to agreed understanding of the changes needed and the work that will take place to reach those aims. Discussions about ideas for activities,

---

Box 11.4: Practice example: Project aims and objectives

The Transitions to Independence Project
Overall purpose
To improve the life chances of 'looked after young people' through specific projects carried out during their transition from living in 'care' to independent living
Specific aims
- *To increase life skills and knowledge*
- *To provide appropriate support structures*
- *To enable them to find suitable housing and employment*
- *To develop financial literacy and household management skills*
Objectives
- *To make contact with looked after young people who are about to leave care*
- *To develop appropriate relationships with them as individuals*
- *To bring them together and facilitate a support group*
- *To discuss issues arising during their transition from care to independence*
- *To provide information and advice on housing, financial and household management and job-seeking*

---

task allocation and specific targets will enable participants to get to know each other and understand each others' responsibilities. A project then becomes more than a series of unrelated tasks. Those involved can begin to develop a shared identity as a team.

3. Planning the project

A definition of aims and objectives can lead to a more detailed plan of action that can be used to identify resource requirements, define tasks and allocate responsibilities. The design of a viable project involves identifying the activities, reasonable time-frames and resource requirements for each stage of the project plan as outlined in the previous section. A viable project can depend on whether the motivation, resources and need are available. Involving participants in project planning can enhance this aspect of project design. Estimating the time, staffing, equipment and expenses required is much easier when the individuals who are going to carry out the work have some input. For example, plans could identify the number and destinations of journeys that will be required, the length and number of reports to be printed, or the number and size of rooms and the facilities that will be needed. Greater detail in the plan allows for more accurate budgeting (see the next stage). Plans will require flexibility to allow for necessary changes or unforeseen expenses. The table in Box 11.5 contains a possible format for such a plan whilst Box 11.6 provides a rough example.

Box 11.5: A format for project planning

Aims	Objectives	Stages and time-frame	Resource implications	Milestones
Overall aims	The steps that will enable the aims to be reached	The programme that will enable the aims and objectives to be reached with specific dates and/or time requirements	Personnel, equipment and funding requirements	Points at which plans can be monitored

Box 11.6: An example of a project plan

Aims	Objectives	Stages and time-scales	Resource implications	Milestones
To provide some alternative activities	1. Research to identify issues 2. Making contact with target group 3. Identifying potential members 4. Identifying their interests 5. Forming a group 6. Working with them to develop enjoyable activities 7. Involving them in promoting the group to others	**Jan to Feb** • Identifying key staff • Discussions with existing groups of young people • Planning outreach and detached work • Discussions with colleagues • Networking with agencies **March to April** • Making contact with at least 12 potential members • Engaging in conversations about interests **May to July** • Talking about options for activities	• Two members of staff on .5 posts • Two mobile phones • Printing of information material • Travel costs • Notional costs for journey to city/ amusement park/ sporting activity	• Quaterly budget updates • Monthly steering group meeting • Supervision every fortnight • Weekly team meetings

4. Organising a programme of activities

Managing a project often requires a considerable amount of administrative work. Liaising with external organisations to make bookings, scheduling appointments by telephone and e-mail, double-checking arrangements requires communication skills as well as organisation. Maintaining accurate records and files demands either a good structure or a good memory. Acknowledging correspondence, confirming details and circulating information widely can help to create a programme that fits together.

Work styles vary enormously in this area of practice. A system that the individual manager is able to follow is fairly essential for smooth running. However, some managers using random notes on scraps of paper surrounded by piles of files seem able to make sense of a complex array of arrangements. A system that others cannot understand can make their participation or any delegation difficult. On the other hand, colleagues may not see that any assistance is needed when an organised manager appears to have everything under control.

Managing finance

Once the aims and objectives of a suitable project have been identified, the activities that will be carried out need to be planned in terms of resource allocation or procurement. Project planning and financial management should be closely linked. Managing the finance of a project has several stages that provide a framework for this section of the chapter. Clarity about the management of finances will assist a project to involve all participants in efficient and transparent systems. The financial literacy skills that can be gained through such involvement will be useful in many arenas.

1. Designing a budget

Designing a budget or plan for use of financial resources requires costs to be estimated for the different elements of a project. Identifying a project's resource requirements as well as which are new or additional allows funding applications or partnerships to be made to realise the plans. Discussion of possible extra costs or potential problems in balancing income and expenditure or keeping to a budget are useful at this stage.

Differentiating between different types of costs can help with planning and funding applications (see next section). For example, identifying capital expenditure, which covers the purchase of new items such as buildings or equipment, and running costs, such as postage, stationery, rent, heat and electricity and revenue or income, can distinguish 'one-off' and ongoing costs. Fully costing a project, that is identifying all of the costs for a particular project including a percentage of the ongoing overheads, can provide a better picture of requirements for sustainability. Distinguishing core costs from optional activities can also lead to more informed choices about resource allocation. The figure in Box 11.7 provides a tool for analysis. Identifying those resources required for maintaining an organisation's core programme provides an opportunity to review whether the status quo is affordable or desirable. For example, a sizeable proportion of resources may be allocated to the upkeep of an expensive building. Recognising that this is the case could lead to the consideration of alternatives, such as charging a percentage of the costs to specific projects (the shaded areas of the diagram).

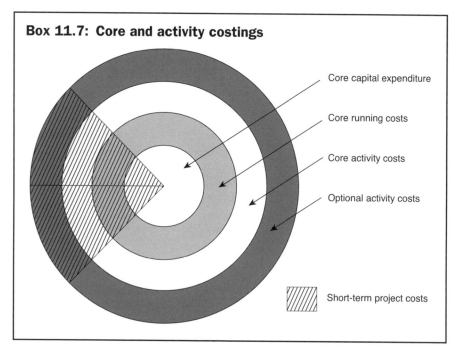

Box 11.7: Core and activity costings

Core capital expenditure

Core running costs

Core activity costs

Optional activity costs

Short-term project costs

A full understanding of financial commitments is particularly important when planning a project. A project budget can be used both to plan and disseminate information about resources. (For some suggested headings, see the table in Box 11.8.) Filling in the headings requires estimates of requirements and research to establish actual costs. Attention to detail will lead to more accurate entries. Capital expenditure, such as the purchase of computers, vans, office or sports equipment, can often lead to further costs, for example, insurance and maintenance or replacement. Participant contribution to budget planning can enhance the detailed nature of the plans as well as more general understanding of budgetary constraints, effective use of resources and adherence to any financial control and record-keeping requirements.

Box 11.8: Typical budget headings

Income

Membership fees	Number of entrances × fees
Grants	Received, committed, pending, to be submitted
Donations	Received, committed, goals
Fundraising	Goals
In kind contributions	Volunteers' time, pro bono (donated) work, goods or services or at a reduced price.

Outgoings *(expenditure)*

General operating costs *(overheads)*

Staffing (such as managers, project workers, administrative and ancillary staff)	Number of staff × rate × time (hours/days or % of salary). Core staff costs may be overhead costs. *The sessional, temporary or % of core staff time utilised by a project may be listed under a separate heading (see below).*
Management overheads	Staff and volunteer management and support may be estimated at a percentage (such as 4%) or separately costed at hourly rates.
Other staffing costs	Staff time and costs for recruitment and selection, tax, insurance, benefits, such as pensions, auditors.
Staff training	Training costs or allowance for conferences, courses + related travel costs
Premises	Rent/mortgage, upkeep, maintenance and safety checks, insurance
Equipment (capital expenditure)	Photocopier, computers – include purchase price + depreciation, maintenance, insurance.

Consumables

Telephone	Identify options for payment schemes or include office running costs as a percentage of budget as (usually 5–10%)
Office supplies	Stationery Numbers of photocopies × cost
Postage/delivery	Estimate the number of letters per week or month
Utilities	Heating/lighting: electricity, gas, water *(check previous bills or research).*

Project or activity costs

Travel	Mileage, train/taxi/bus fares × number of journeys × travellers or coach/mini-bus hire
Expenses	Meals on excursions, fuel
Volunteers expenses	Number of volunteers × donation to expenses
Volunteers benefits	Number of volunteers × equipment/training provided
Overheads	A % of organisational costs (see above)
Equipment	Purchase price, depreciation, maintenance and insurance or hire costs.
Additional consumables	

2. Applying for funding

A critical aspect of management is being able to secure financial support for activities and operating costs. Applications for funding are often part of a manager's responsibility, whether applying internally for resource allocation within the organisation or externally, for support from larger charitable or government bodies. Successful applications generally require an understanding of a project's financial requirements, gained through designing a budget (see the previous section), careful research to know what a potential funder is looking for and a well argued and evidenced match between the two.

Making a successful application may mean recognising gaps as well as overlap between the resource requirements and any potential sources of funding. An individual source may only provide funding for project running costs rather than core organisational overheads. Decisions need to be made about whether such an application is worthwhile; Box 11.9 has a practice example of how inappropriate funding can impact on practice. Access to certain sources may only be available to certain types of organisations. Putting together an application could mean developing a partnership with an organisation that meets the criteria. Discussions about whether sources of funding are suitable can assist the development of an appropriate funding plan.

Box 11.9: Practice example: The 'wrong kind' of funding

We applied for funding for a project because we thought it would enhance the work we were doing with young people in the area. The funding was for projects with a very specific brief to reduce conceptions amongst 11–16 year olds. We were aware that the number of conceptions in this age group was high and it seemed like a project on this topic would be relevant and useful. However, the funder's monitoring requirements really restricted our work. In order to receive condoms or sexual health information, the young people had to give their names, ages and addresses, which created difficulties for some. Any work utilising the funding had to be directly linked to the project outcomes. Activities became specifically target related while other useful activities that did not label young people as 'at risk' were under-funded. We found that we could not 'justify' work with younger children, who often came to the sessions because they were being looked after by their older siblings. Interactions with young people on non-sexual health issues were not recognised or valued by the management team.

---

3. Managing budget controls

Managing finance requires allocating responsibilities and methods for controlling the income and expenditure in relation to the planned budget and then checking that the procedures are being followed. Even a project with a small amount of funding needs a method for making payments for items such as expenses and equipment. Maintaining some control can avoid problems such as unexplained debts or withdrawals. Systems for requesting and authorising expenditure can range from simple measures such as using cheques that require two signatures to more complex tracking systems for invoice requests and purchase orders. The system should provide an opportunity to confirm that a payment is coming out of the correct budget and is allowable under the terms of the budget. Spending according to the budget is more likely to happen when all concerned are aware of the procedures.

4. Keeping accounts

Accurate records of payments both in and out of accounts assist a project to maintain budget controls and to keep track of progress. An understanding and awareness of spending and its relationship to the planned budget means that appropriate responses can be made to any changes in plans. Accounts should enable a record to be kept of how much funding is left under each heading and how much money needs to be kept aside to address planned expenditure.

5. Managing cash flow

Keeping track of what happens to cash, cheque books, credit and debit cards is necessary to manage a project's cash flow. Having a clear account of the movement of money helps to avoid temptation, missing cash or unexplained losses. Ensuring that all participants collect receipts and that there is a system for submitting and organising receipts provides evidence for payments and a record of transactions.

6. Monitoring expenditure

Checking the project accounts against the planned budget can identify under or overspending. Inflation may have an effect, changes of plan or other differences may arise. In some instances, transfers of costs to different headings (known as virement) may be permitted to manage over- and under-spends. A manager will need to consider when funders should be informed about any questions, discrepancies or major difficulties. Sufficient time may be needed to implement alternative strategies.

   The involvement of young people in budget design has a range of benefits. Not only will they gain an awareness of the resources available and any constraints, they can develop associated skills and contribute useful ideas about additional resources and spending requirements.

In addition, a project can gain a better understanding of resource requirements. For example, a project planning an international exchange may not have considered that some young people may be financially excluded from participation unless a budget allocation is made to provide them with the necessary resources to purchase a passport, suitcase and/or suitable clothing for an alternative climate.

Managing people

The management of a project includes a range of duties and responsibilities for ensuring that appropriate individuals are able and motivated to carry out required tasks with sufficient resources. Staff could include paid professionals, volunteer activists and trainee young people. Members of a group may carry out the project themselves. Whether the individuals are paid or unpaid, young people (members) or staff, the responsibilities can be similar. Good working relationships and communication are obviously important in relation to participants' experiences. The success of a project can depend as much on goodwill and individual energy as structured job descriptions and task allocation. Clearly both are essential when working with either volunteers or paid staff.

The management of paid and unpaid youth work staff can start or significantly change at any of a number of points in a cycle of work and responsibilities. (The figure in Box 11.10 illustrates some of the responsibilities that can be incurred when managing people). The definition of a job or task could be seen as an ideal starting point for this cycle although new projects often develop or emerge through ongoing work rather than having a clear beginning. Reviewing previous experiences can inform the development of an appropriate plan for a new task description.

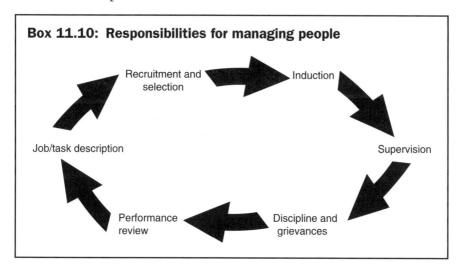

Box 11.10: Responsibilities for managing people

Recruitment and selection → Induction → Supervision → Discipline and grievances → Performance review → Job/task description →

1. Designing a job or task description

A critical part of managing a project is defining and communicating the work that needs to be carried out. A job description can be a useful vehicle for defining work objectives whether the individual is an employee, volunteer or young person. Any difficulties in carrying out the work can be more easily addressed through managerial supervision when clear job and task descriptions provide an organised and defensible basis for performance review. The table in Box 11.11 includes some suggestions for key elements in a job description. Using a job description as a basis for discussion can provide valuable opportunities for input as well as guidance and feedback on specific duties and responsibilities.

2. Recruitment and selection

A job description can provide the focus for communication with prospective applicants during recruitment and selection. Accurate information about

Box 11.11: Components of a job description

Job description	For employees or volunteers
Job title	• Rank or job title.
Task title	• Name of the project or piece of work.
Setting	• The department, base and organisation. • The base or area of work.
Level of the post	• Payment or salary scale. • Whether full-time or part-time (and how that relates to the pay, such as pro rata or hours worked). • Whether the job is permanent or temporary. • Whether job shares are welcomed or possible. • Probationary period.
Aims of the post/ position	• A short summary of the main purpose of the job and why the position has been set up. • If applicable, relevant information about the history of the post, such as whether the position is new, to cover temporary leave, why the position is vacant.
Responsible to	• Reporting relationships and to whom the postholder is accountable. • The individuals or groups responsible for providing overall direction, line management and/or day-to-day support.
Main duties and responsibilities	• The main duties listed first from the essential to the non-essential, from most important to least important or from the most time consuming to the least time spent. • The specific tasks or required outcomes. • Highlight any physical or mental demands. • Be sure to include 'Other duties as required by the project.' *(see also the disclaimer below).*
Working conditions	• Describe the general physical environment or surroundings and any potential conditions related to physical or mental health or access.

Person specification	• The minimum requirements for an individual to do the job competently, the *essential* criteria, and the *desirable* points • Practice or educational experience • Qualifications or certification • Skills • Knowledge • Personal attributes or qualities • The ways in which the points can be evidenced and/or assessed in the selection procedures *Note: A project may wish to prioritise the involvement of individuals with experience of living in the community or awareness of certain issues over others with more 'professional' skills to promote community involvement and development.*
Disclaimer	• This job description is not exhaustive and may be added to in the future depending on the needs of the project, or • The list of job elements, responsibilities, skills, duties, requirements, or conditions is not intended to be comprehensive, or • The project reserves the right to revise the job description or require that other tasks be performed when the circumstances of the job change (for example, emergencies, funding issues, changes in personnel, workload or technical development), or • Other duties as assigned (one of the favourites in the US).
Date	• A record of the date of preparation or approval of this version of the job description.

the position, including management and support structures as well as duties and responsibilities, can help potential applicants to decide whether the job is for them. Information about the criteria that will be used in selection, which provide a structure for the questions during selection, may also help to narrow the field to appropriately qualified candidates. Ideally a panel trained in equal opportunity policies and practice would be involved to reduce unfair discrimination and questioning. The panel would be responsible for ensuring that the job is advertised appropriately and the procedure is carried out fairly.

3. Providing support and direction

Providing support and direction for project participants means making sure that individuals are clear about what the work entails and where support is available. There needs to be a balance between direction that is spoon-fed or is so laissez-faire as to leave participants feeling stranded. Regular discussions about progress, showing an interest and project team meetings can assist with project monitoring and planning that results from ongoing evaluation. Engendering a sense of co-operative working can start with the induction, where participants are introduced to each other and roles are clarified.

Individual managers and projects exercise widely varying levels of control and monitoring of projects and project workers. Relationships with and between staff, working with colleagues, team working and leadership are all issues that can arise and are handled differently by individuals. Some project managers place a high value on conflict avoidance, meet regularly with each member of staff and provide precise directions for handling issues as they arise. Others leave the project workers to address issues in their own way and make their own mistakes – only dealing with conflicts that impinge on their horizon. Clearly there are a number of approaches in between.

Preparing an outline of a task can be a useful basis for a discussion about expectations of participants, such as anticipated outcomes, ways of working, roles and allocation of responsibilities. Box 11.12 provides an outline for specific work that needs to take place. The list could be used with young people, staff members, volunteers or a project management group. Discussions of the outline can elicit suggestions as well as agreement with what needs to take place.

Box 11.12: Components of a specific task

Components

Task title	• An appropriate name for the task or project could be identified by those planning the task and redefined by those carrying it out
Summary	• A short summary of the project/task • Aims and objectives • Relevant background information
Those responsible	• Include names and roles, such as members of project management team, project workers • Contact details
Time-scale	• Start and finish dates • Any scheduling information, such as estimated or planned stages • Approximate number of hours
Setting	• Base for operations, contact details, access issues • Resources available, for example, desk, phone, photocopier
Benefits	• Whether any educational award or certificate of participation will be made • Any expenses that can be claimed
Responsible to	• Reporting relationships, for example, to the project management group, the youth worker • Who provides overall direction and day-to-day support and contact details.
Main duties and responsibilities	• Specific tasks or required outcomes
Requirements	• Criteria for participation and/or selection, for example, availability on the required dates • For young people: parental permission if necessary, plus any criteria dictated by the organisation or funder for targeting purposes, such as gender, age range, situation.
Disclaimer	• *Details may be subject to change*
Date	• A record of the date of preparation of this version.

4. Handling disciplinary matters

A project establishes what is expected of individuals involved through discussions to gain clarity about what constitutes unacceptable actions or activities. Where staff are involved, task or job descriptions, recruitment and selection procedures, ongoing training, guidelines or codes of practice, supervision and project meetings form part of project management. When young people manage a project, ground rules may be a better tool (see also Chapter 12 on Supervision). Managing a project includes defining which actions are considered to be misconduct and what, if any, penalties can be expected for differing levels of misconduct. Generally, an organisation is responsible for providing clear guidance on disciplinary matters, on which a manager should be able to advise staff. For example, a well designed disciplinary scheme will include a clear definition of what constitutes misconduct, appropriate penalties, opportunities to present responses to 'charges' and opportunities for fair and impartial grievance resolution (see the table in Box 11.13. for some examples of staff misconduct).

Box 11.13: Examples of staff misconduct

Misconduct, incompetence or negligence	Gross misconduct, incompetence or negligence
• Poor timekeeping • Absenteeism • Not following procedures, such as health and safety, dress code, publicity approval • Unauthorised use of facilities or equipment, such as vehicles, computers, telephone, post • Poor performance of duties • Acceptance of gifts or bribes • Conduct outside work that affects the organisation's reputation in a fairly minor way	• Theft, fraud or deliberate falsification of records • Physical violence, serious bullying or harassment, particularly in work, but often outside of work as well • Deliberate damage to property • Serious insubordination or failure to maintain work responsibilities • Misuse of an organisation's property or name • Bringing the organisation into disrepute • Serious incapability whilst at work through use of alcohol or illegal drugs • Serious negligence which causes or might cause unacceptable loss, damage or injury • Serious infringement of health and safety or other policies and procedures such as confidentiality.

Any disciplinary and grievance procedures that are developed as part of the management of a project will need to comply with legislation protecting the rights of employees and young people. Providing opportunities for due process and accurate reporting and recording structures are important when dealing with matters related to complaints or disciplinary matters. Having a named individual with whom employees, volunteers or young people can discuss grievances or appeals is generally considered to be good practice. An individual's wish to be represented or supported by a peer, colleague or union official should also be respected.

5. Training and staff development

A project can often offer participants a new experience. Identifying and addressing areas of learning or professional development needs before, during and after the project can be a useful exercise for all concerned. This type of summative and formative evaluation can inform the project management and future project planning. The next chapter looks at supervision, which is a useful tool for professional development.

Essential skills for managing a project

- Applying youth work principles to project management
- Balancing interests
- Managing short-term projects
- Defining the purpose of the project
- Defining aims and objectives
- Planning the project
- Managing finance
- Designing a budget
- Applying for funding
- Managing budget controls
- Keeping accounts
- Managing cash flow
- Monitoring expenditure
- Managing people
- Providing ongoing support and direction
- Recruitment, selection
- Providing support and direction
- Handling disciplinary matters
- Training and staff development.

Further reading about managing a project

Butler (1990); Drucker (1990); Gann (1996); Senge (1990); Wylie (2004).

CHAPTER 12: Using supervision

Supervision is a process of critical reflection in which youth workers discuss ongoing work and professional development issues with a more experienced youth worker, whether a manager or a peer. Professional supervision focuses on the core values of youth work in order to support good practice and learning from experience. Sometimes supervision is part of student's or volunteer's training. This chapter explores the process of supervision and looks at the essential skills required for providing and using supervision effectively.

Understanding the aims of supervision

Regular discussions about practice with supervisors allow supervisees to develop clarity about their role and the relationships between goals, values, ongoing work and development plans. Youth work supervision, like youth work, is based on dialogue and problem-posing. Freire (1972) describes this approach that deepens understanding and praxis through mutual respect and learning and working together (see Box 12.1). Supervision can be a developmental process for both supervisor and supervisees as they learn from each others' perspectives and identify ways forward.

Supervision provides a structure for professional youth work practice, where supervisees can reflect on recent practice and plan future

---

Box 12.1: Freire (1972) on liberating education

'Liberating education consists in acts of cognition, not transferals of information... . Through dialogue, the teacher-of-the-students and the students-of-the-teacher cease to exist .... The teacher is no longer merely the-one-who-teaches, but one who is himself taught in dialogue with the students, who in turn while being taught also teach. They become jointly responsible for a process in which all grow. In this process, arguments based on 'authority' are no longer valid; in order to function authority must be on the side of freedom, not against it. Here, no one teaches another, nor is anyone self-taught. People teach each other ....'
(Freire, 1972, Chapter 2)

developments that are consistent with youth work principles. A core focus for supervision is the identification of the changes and development of individual young people, groups and communities. Youth workers use supervision sessions to identify needs and strategies for changes to their practice and their understanding or professional development. Supervision also includes the consideration of ways to implement organisational changes, particularly if development is impeded or prevented by structures or practices within the workplace. Reflection on issues arising from practice is carried out in an environment that is both supportive and challenging.

Having a planned approach to supervision

A planned approach to supervision requires attention to the periods before, during and after the supervision relationship (see the table in Box 12.2 for a suggested plan). Prior to starting supervision sessions, both supervisor and supervisee seek clarification about the type of supervision and what they bring to the relationship. The relationship and meetings are established with agreements about structure and any recording. Once the focus of the sessions is on practice, supervision includes reviews of ongoing work and discussion of relevant issues. Plans to address the issues through work and professional development are made and then reviewed in subsequent sessions. Exiting from a supervision arrangement can include a number of methods for ensuring ongoing professional practice.

Box 12.2: A planned approach to supervision

Preparing for supervision	• Understanding the type of supervision required • Locating self in relation to identity, skills and experience
Establishing the supervision relationship	• Exchanging information about the above • Making practical arrangements to meet • Structuring the sessions • Record-keeping
Examining practice	• Listening and valuing experience • Providing critical feedback • Reviewing practice • Identifying issues
Moving on	• Action planning • Reviewing what has been achieved • Identifying learning outcomes • Allowing the relationship to end.

Understanding the type of supervision required

Supervision can take place within a series of regular and structured two-way meetings to ensure that professional values are maintained through continuous critical reflection. Some supervision arrangements have additional functions, including management, quality assurance or consultancy (see the table in Box 12.3 for some examples of different types of supervision). Internal supervision, provided by a peer or manager who works within the same organisation as the supervisee, usually means that the supervisor is familiar with available resources and organisational aims, culture and procedures. External supervision, arranged with someone who is unconnected with the supervisee's organisation, can provide a new perspective unconstrained by organisational culture. Supervision may be provided by a line manager, peer, co-supervisee or consultant. Managerial supervision usually involves staff appraisal and discipline alongside responsibilities for co-ordinating, administering, monitoring and/or evaluating the development of programmes of youth work. Student supervision usually includes the assessment of specific learning outcomes. Peer supervision is arranged with an individual who can provide feedback from a shared perspective of the position and level of work. In co-supervision, each party takes turns to provide the other with supervision in an equal relationship without hierarchy. Consultancies in this context are generally short- and fixed- term external supervisory arrangements to access particular knowledge or experience.

Box 12.3: Types of supervision

	Managerial supervision	Non-managerial supervision
Internal supervision	• Line management or management from a member of staff further up a hierarchical structure • Co-supervision within a team • For a student undertaking a project or placement within the organisation.	• Peer or co-supervision with a colleague • A consultancy from within an organisation • A cross-disciplinary forum or internal support network within an organisation.
External supervision	• From another agency within a multi-agency structure • From a contracted manager/consultant	• A freelance supervisor or consultant • Peer or co-supervision from outside the organisation • A tutor or peer from a student's learning programme • A multi-agency forum or network

Youth workers may need to network or seek external supervision to experience appropriate support for the development of youth work practice. Many youth workers are unsupervised or experience poor supervision. Rather than facilitating development, some supervision focuses on control and containment within an overly rigid organisational or educational structure, such as the vocational 'education' defined by Field (in Thorpe, 1993) in Box 12.4, which is not appropriate for professional youth work supervision. Challenging discussions about practical and ethical dilemmas are required for professional supervision that assists a youth worker to maintain focus for participative and anti-oppressive practice. Otherwise both youth workers and youth work can become forces for domestication rather than liberation (for further reading, see Freire, 1972).

Box 12.4: A definition of vocational education

'The aims of vocational education are) ... to socialise our consent to the maintenance of the status quo, to contribute to employee recruitment through the development of qualifications, and to generate forms of knowledge and behaviour appropriate from the employer's point of view.' (Thorpe, 1993:2)

Supervision arrangements do not have to be exclusive. Whilst organisational policy often dictates managerial structures and personnel, additional arrangements for suitable professional supervision are not uncommon. An individual youth worker could receive managerial supervision from a line manager; internal non-managerial supervision for a specific project; external supervision from a friend in another organisation and if undertaking training, student supervision from the educational agency.

Locating self

Before the process of supervision begins, taking time to 'locate self' can assist participants to identify potential strengths as well as any limitations that may arise within a supervisory relationship. Location of self involves analysing and evaluating skills, knowledge, attitudes and values acquired through personal, political and work experiences. Reflection on experience can enable supervisors to be clear and open about what they can offer supervisees. Similarly, supervisees who are clear about their needs can take a more active role in setting the agenda for supervision that addresses them. (See Box 12.5 for a practice example illustrating 'location of self.')

> **Box 12.5: Practice example: 'Location of self'**
>
> An experienced practitioner was asked to supervise a recently qualified youth worker who was starting a group aiming to raise young women's educational and career aspirations. Before meeting the supervisee, the supervisor reflected on her own experience to 'locate' her perspective and identify relevant strengths as well as gaps. The supervisor had not worked with a young women's group before, but had a good understanding of starting and developing mixed gender projects and some of the issues faced by young women. For example, she was aware that homeless young women in the area were exchanging sex for a place to stay and personal experience of sexism enabled her to make links between societal attitudes and the young women's perceived and genuine options.
>
> To address the identified gaps, the supervisor visited a couple of young women's projects proactively involved in specific anti-sexist activities and staff training, carried out some reading about challenging sexism and discussed methods of promoting positive images of women and girls with colleagues. She focussed on her own current practice and involved young women in developing some peer education materials and activities on sex working to build their confidence, assertiveness and enquiry skills. These various forms of professional development enhanced the direction and feedback she could provide for the new youth worker and enabled her to suggest up-to-date reading material and contacts.

Identifying boundaries

The identification of boundaries in relation to practical arrangements for supervision could also be seen as part of the location of self. Whilst some supervisory situations have less flexibility, arrangements to suit the individuals concerned can often be accommodated. Communication and establishing a common understanding about practicalities, expectations and ways of working can assist the supervisory relationship to flourish (see Box 12.6 for some relevant boundaries to consider). Discussion of these key points could provide an opportunity for participants to get to know each other, clarify arrangements and reach agreement on the function and nature of the relationship.

Box 12.6: Identifying boundaries for supervision

Arrangements

Contact points and times **Dates/times**	When and where do I not wish to be contacted? Where can messages be unreliable? What arrangements for contacts between us would I prefer? What time do I have available for supervision sessions? Can I allocate an interruption-free time slot on a specific day and time? How long do I think the meetings should be and how frequent? Would it be better to set up a regular programme? Can we arrange (and diary) several meetings in advance?

Box 12.6 - *Cont'd*

Venue	Can I travel to meetings or do I need them to be held at my workplace? Where can we meet undisturbed? Is the venue appropriate in relation to privacy, safety, atmosphere and comfort?
Date of review or end	How long can I commit myself for? When do I think I would like to review the arrangements? Would I prefer an open-ended or fixed term agreement?
Approach to supervision	Do I prefer or need formally recorded and structured sessions or free-flowing and unstructured? Will this be a more discussion-based approach or a reporting style question and answer session? Do I have flexible approaches to practice or do I like to establish clear groundrules and boundaries?
Records	What records will be kept and who will have access to them? Do I need my own records of the sessions? What records does the organisation require and what is their purpose? Who is responsible for the records? Do I have any control over them?
Ethical boundaries	What issues would raise ethical questions for me? What issues would I report to a manager, a training agency, the social services or the police? What personal, political or professional information do I consider to be relevant or irrelevant for these sessions?
Cancellations	How much notice do I need for cancellations? How have I responded to previous cancellations? How would I prefer cancellations to be handled?
Punctuality agreement	How strongly do I feel about punctuality? How have I responded to late arrivals in the past? What arrangements would I like to establish in relation to time-keeping?
Own development needs	What do I expect from the other participant in relation to experience, issues or areas of work? What support, information or learning do I need to make this arrangement useful or work well?
Other issues to consider	What problems have I encountered previously in relation to supervision? What issues have been raised in feedback? How have I reacted to challenges or advice?

Keeping appropriate records

Records of sessions reflecting the supervisees' language and ideas can show that a supervisor values the supervisee's experience and perspective. A record can remind both parties of the issues discussed to provide continuity between sessions, monitor development, identify patterns in issues arising and, in student supervision, assist in the completion of assessment forms. Going through a record of a session together to check accuracy can establish mutual understanding of key issues and any action for subsequent sessions. Sometimes minimal records are sufficient. Summarising the points at the end of a session can preclude the need for taking extensive and intrusive notes during the sessions.

Reaching agreement on the purpose and content of the records is essential. Clarity about any monitoring or reporting requirements and whether these could be used as evidence in appraisal or promotion, disciplinary matters or assessment must be established prior to recording. A manager may be required to follow established procedures for quality assurance. Student supervision may have particular forms for assessment purposes. Shared understanding about what happens to records could help to reduce problems arising from unexpected demands made at a later date. See Box 12.7 for a practice example that illustrates the significance of having clarity about supervisory roles and records.

Box 12.7: Practice example: Conflicting roles and records

A youth worker, who was also a part-time student, asked her manager for suggestions about how to extend her experience of supervision. The manager arranged for her to provide *internal non-managerial supervision* for an individual from another team. A series of sessions was negotiated for the purposes of mutual learning. The supervisee used the sessions to raise and discuss some difficulties he was experiencing with his manager.

After a while, the supervisees' manager contacted the student to make enquiries about her opinion of the supervisee's practice and what information she had about why the supervisee had missed a particular work session. As the student and supervisee had agreed previously that the records would only be used to provide a reminder of issues raised, the student said that the information was confidential. The manager stated that it was the organisation's usual practice to use supervision recordings as evidence in disciplinary matters.

The student had not been provided with the policies, procedures or authority within the organisation to carry through issues raised within the supervision and had not understood that she would be taking on a formal supervisory role. She had initiated and negotiated a more supportive type of peer supervision, which she felt was being compromised by demands for records for formal disciplinary procedures. She had learned a useful lesson about the importance of clarity about roles and records.

Structuring the sessions

Supervision carried out at regular intervals and within a format that is suitably structured to ensure that sufficient time is allocated for key issues and planning can be particularly effective. Whilst a formal agenda is not essential, the establishment of a pattern for the supervision sessions can encourage focussed and useful discussion. Agreements about the structure of the sessions and other protocols can clarify the power relationship and responsibility for the issues raised and their prioritisation can be shared. Supervisees can become involved in planning the session and actively addressing their own learning needs by raising any topics of concern. The agenda in Box 12.8, for example, encourages the supervisor to take responsibility for moving the session on and the supervisee to be responsible for identifying relevant issues. The supervisee can be asked to prioritise points within the time constraints of a particular session. This dialogical approach encourages the development of plans that are realistic and practical.

Box 12.8: An agenda for a supervision session

Agenda items	Supervisor's prompts	Supervisee's actions
1. News	• Tell me what's going on … • Any good or positive developments at work since we last met?	Reflects on recent practice prior to the session to identify positive as well as negative practice issues for discussion.
2. Set the agenda	• What do we need to talk about during this session? • Is there anything left over from the last session? • Can we make a list?	Brings along any records of work, such as a diary, notes from the last session. Reviews these prior to the session and identifies any matters arising.
3. Review ongoing work	• Let's look at how your work is going with the 'xyz' project. • How have your work plans with 'abc' been progressing?	Raises any issues that have caused concern or second thoughts. Passes on sufficient information for the supervisor to understand the context.
4. Problems	• Let's focus on the issues/items on the list in more detail.	Attempts to recall accurate details of the circumstances surrounding events, such as exact words used, emotions felt and expressed, relevant contributory factors.
5. Plans	• What plans can we make to address the issues arising? • What new plans do you have for the 'abc' and 'xyz' projects?	Makes sure to raise any issues that would make plans unrealistic
6. Confirm next meeting	• When should we meet again?	Confirms satisfactory arrangements. Rases any concerns.
7. Record of session	• Can we agree that these notes are an accurate record of the important points raised?	Checks for accuracy.

Both parties are responsible for ensuring that the sessions address relevant youth work issues and practice – although a supervisor who is supervising a student takes ultimate responsibility for this. The purpose of supervision is to challenge and develop practice rather than resolve personal issues. Whilst some individuals need time to settle into a session through greetings and chat about family, health or holidays, both need to make sure that this does not take up much time in the session. If someone appears to need extra time to discuss domestic arrangements or emotional responses to situations or if an individual appears overly distressed or depressed, the supervision session should be brought to an end. Communicating continued interest in providing support for a supervisee's professional development through supervision can be separated from signposting the individual to useful alternative means of support for their emotional health.

Listening

Supervisors strive to provide an appropriate balance between stimulating reflection, listening and feedback. Attentive listening can enable a full exploration of issues and feedback should assist progression towards understanding of how they can be addressed. Initially, supervisees are encouraged to outline their recent work experiences and a supervisor listens attentively to hear the supervisees' perspective on what has taken place. As supervisees recall and articulate their experience, they begin to explore their roles and responsibilities, the consequences of their actions and other influences on situations. Paying attention to the detail in what supervisees are saying, both verbally and non-verbally, about particular circumstances and feelings generated can assist a supervisor to gain a full picture and understanding of a supervisee's experiences. Careful listening also allows a supervisor to recall information later in the session or in subsequent sessions and to focus on the supervisee's account and agenda.

Box 12.9: Egan (1986) on the role of listening

Good attending enables the 'helper to listen carefully to what clients are saying, both verbally and nonverbally. Total or complete listening involves three things: (1) observing and reading the client's nonverbal behaviour – posture, facial expression, movement, tone of voice and the like; (2) listening to and understanding the client's verbal messages; and (3) listening in an integrated way to the person in the context of both the helping process and everyday life.' (Egan, 1986: 79)

Responses that convey interest and demonstrate that information has been heard can encourage further exploration of an issue. Active listening techniques (Rogers, 1969 and Egan, 1986: Box 12.9), such as 'paraphrasing the feelings and content' and 'clarifying and summarising', can convey understanding. Attempting empathy or 'thinking in someone else's terms' such as in the active listening approach described by Rogers and Farson (Box 12.10) are likely to be beyond the remit or possibility of supervision. Using relevant open questions rather than probing or interpretative statements allows the supervisee to explore issues and incidents on their own terms, provide their own emphasis and identify meaning that is significant to them.

Providing feedback

A supervisor responds to what supervisees say about their practice with positive and critical feedback as well as suggestions for further thought.

Box 12.10: A definition of active listening

'Active listening carries a strong element of personal risk. If we manage to accomplish what we are describing here – to sense deeply the feeling of another person, to understand the meaning his experiences have for him, to see the world as he sees it – we risk being changed ourselves. For example, if we permit ourselves to listen our way into the psychological life of a labor leader or agitator – to get the meaning which life has for him – we risk coming to see the world as he sees it. It is threatening to give up, even momentarily, what we believe and start thinking in someone else's terms. It takes a great deal of inner security and courage to be able to risk one's self in understanding another.' (Rogers & Farson, 1987: 327)

A supervisor highlights a supervisee's description of good practice to affirm and confirm positive developments as well as to identify and value the skills and the knowledge underpinning their actions. Positive feedback will ensure that supervisees are aware of how to continue this approach. Building on good practice and making further plans to extend young people's involvement or participation can further enhance supervisees' professional development.

Supervisors are also required to provide an alternative perspective and more challenging or critical feedback in relation to professional values and practice. A supervisor should not ignore or collude with poor practice. If a supervisee describes inappropriate, dangerous or oppressive practice, a clear professional perspective is required. Critical feedback may be necessary when supervisees use inappropriate language, express oppressive attitudes or tell the supervisor about situations where mistakes have been made and appear to have no intention of doing anything about them. A supervisor is responsible for ensuring that supervisees recognise bad practice, learn from their mistakes and develop ways to address them.

In order to stimulate supervisees to look at their practice in new ways, feedback can provide new frames of reference to alter a supervisee's way of looking at a situation (see Box 12.11 for some 'framing techniques'). Using metaphors or a contrasting situation, for example, can assist a change of perspective. Supervisors need to monitor their responses to make sure that a relevant tool provides insight rather than gets in the way. If a framing technique is over-used, the method can lose meaning or if mis-used or mis-applied, the frame is only confusing. For example, a supervisor may identify a tradition or pattern of behaviour within an organisation that in her mind illuminates the organisational culture. Partial evidence could lead to an inaccurate analysis and continuous reference to 'organisational culture' as a catch-all explanation for issues arising could become unhelpful.

Box 12.11: A definition of 'framing techniques'

Metaphor: using a parallel example or symbol to highlight themes that may be similar to the current topic.

Jargon and catchphrases: using familiar language or slogans that relate to a subject.

Contrast: providing a definition of a situation in terms of what it is not.

Spin: talking about various aspects of a subject, such as the positive or negative implications.

Stories: using as an anecdote, myth or legend, to engage attention and emotion.

(Adapted from Fairhurst and Sarr, 1996:101)

The provision of appropriate feedback requires a supervisor to be able to assess and understand supervisees' responsibilities and roles. A supervisor needs clarity about the level of control or power that a supervisee can exert in the context of the work setting. An awareness of available resources, potential for change and a clear view of the type of work that a supervisee should be carrying out also enhances appropriate feedback or direction. Effective supervisors are able to provide positive, constructive and informative reactions and suggestions. When thinking is stimulated and debates are carried out on a level that is understood, supervisees can be encouraged to continue to develop their awareness and practice. This 'conversational learning', as described by Baker *et al.* (see Box 12.12), can enable learners to construct meaning and transform experiences into new knowledge. The reference to 'ontological resource' highlights the value of dialogue in developing a deep understanding of self and others, which supervision can provides.

Box 12.12: Baker *et al.* (2005) on conversational learning

'Taking the time to hear other perspectives through the telling of each other's stories can often provide a path for returning to the questions or decisions at hand in ways that are easier to hear. In storytelling and in recursive conversations, new ways of framing can be grasped – apprehended – and the ontological recourse informs the learning.' (Baker *et al.*, 2005:420)

Reviewing the supervisee's practice

Reviewing practice and applying principles to practice are the essential ingredients in professional supervision. A supervisor assists youth workers to focus on different aspects of practice. A review could include looking at the overall programme of work, a particular work responsibility or session, any developments since the last supervision session, recent events or issues arising. The process can involve reviews of work records and other relevant documents for problem-solving, planning and/or evaluation. Recording forms, diaries and evaluation sheets can be useful bases for discussion. The review can then relate to whether the practice meets the requirements of the post or placement, addresses professional values and principles, makes practical sense in relation to the time and resources available and involves sufficient variation, change and development for both the young people involved and the youth worker.

Supervision can assist youth workers to make sense of organisational or managerial targets. The process of an overall review of a programme of work can start with an analysis of how supervisees actually spend their time in comparison with the needs of the young people and their communities, the job description, project brief or student placement requirements. The needs of the young people may be contradictory. An organisation's expectations may not be feasible or fall within professional boundaries. Supervision can assist supervisees to identify ways to negotiate feasible ways of moving forward. Supervisees can explore methods of asserting themselves, raising issues or challenging rules or requirements. Alternatively, supervisees may need to find a way to work within the constraints in a method that is compatible with the profession and resources.

Evaluating youth work practice

A review of a specific piece of work can evaluate practice in relation to youth work aims and values. A supervisor can provide questions that supervisees apply to a project, event or provision to identify whether good youth work practice has been carried out. Box 12.13. provides some examples of how to stimulate a professional analysis of participation. Through analysis, supervisees begin to identify issues and problems.

Box 12.13: Suggested ways to analyse participation

A supervisor could invite supervisees to review a piece of work through asking:
- How do members participate in decisions made about the design, management and evaluation of this provision?
- Who would feel unwelcome or excluded from this group?
- How was this piece of work inclusive?
- How would the current members react to new members?
- How would [a specific group, such as wheelchair users, younger members, non-readers] participate in this activity?
- What are the reasons for targeting this specific group? Does this relate to issues of exclusion or oppression from other activities?
- How does this work fit into the organisational priorities, your job description, anti-oppressive practice?

A supervisor encourages a supervisee to examine issues from the perspectives of groups and individuals in the community, the agency and the profession. Planning and prioritising will need to balance various considerations or needs, such as young people's needs, organisational priorities and youth work values. Organisational priorities will often impact on planning. Whether the priorities have been formally set, evolved through habit or discussed with managers, the process of identifying problem areas and making plans may challenge existing ways of working. Supervisees need to think about the impact of the changes that they plan and how to involve others in change.

Role clarity is an important outcome from supervision. Evaluation is based on an understanding of youth work roles and practice. A supervisor assists supervisees to come to an understanding of how the aims of the profession relate to their work practice. Supervisees examine underlying principles as well as the overall aims of their job, project or placement. The evaluation identifies practice that conforms to the aims as well as practice that conflicts.

Addressing professional development and practice needs arising

Whether issues are identified by supervisees or the supervisor, reflection on practice can assist supervisees to find ways forward. Developing methods to avoid or address difficult situations in the future forms part of the learning. A supervisor may use suggestions or invite further analysis to assist supervisees to work on issues. Supervisees can be asked to reflect on discrepancies within their accounts or behaviour. A supervisor may provide factual information, positive suggestions or 'handy hints' from experience or an area of expertise. Supervisors may confront supervises with an alternative frame of reference or ask the supervisee to look at a situation from another point of view. A supervisee might be engaged in a discussion of the moral or professional questions raised by a situation or be provided with a parallel scenario for analysis and discussion. Assisting supervisees to 'unpack' or analyse issues and situations is often a useful method of developing practice. Provision of a framework for analysing the circumstances or contributory factors in the situation could assist the development of requisite skills or strategies to develop a more professional approach.

Supervision can be used to plan specific steps to address barriers and progress work towards long-term goals. The practice example in Box 12.14 provides an illustration of how supervision can be used to identify an issue and naturally lead on to relevant planning. Supervisees can be encouraged to identify the strengths of a situation to build a

---

Box 12.14: Practice example: Using supervision to address development needs

A deaf youth worker brought up complaints about her workplace during *external supervision*. She felt unsupported; her hearing manager was prejudiced; she had insufficient assistance to produce reports to schedule. She was on the point of taking out grievance procedures due to what she saw as bullying and oppressive behaviour.

The supervisor listened carefully and then encouraged the supervisee to consider the situation from the manager's perspective. As her written reports were sufficiently coherent for the organisation's requirements and she presented herself confidently and articulately, how was the manager to know that she was having difficulty?. The supervisee began to recognise that perhaps she had not sufficiently communicated her needs or her career and professional development aspirations to her manager.

The supervisor was able to assist the supervisee to put together a sensible and costed development plan, which would enable her to access available resources for English language support and further career development. The shared perspective of the external supervisor in relation to the importance of enabling deaf people's participation as well as some ideas about related practice provided an understanding of the barriers as well as some suggestions about ways forward.

---

solution based on reality, what can be achieved within a specific period with indicators of achievement, and what resources can be used. Establishing clearly communicable aims can assist the supervisee to see how others might be involved in taking the plans forward. A supervisor expresses interest in supervisees' opinions and takes care not to provide all the answers. Supervisees are encouraged to come up with their own solutions to problems and analyses of situations, taking into consideration their personal power, as defined by Rogers (1978, see Box 12.15). This affirmative approach allows supervisees to acknowledge mistakes, present their practice honestly and make practicable plans to address them.

Box 12.15: Carl Rogers (1978) on personal power

'One of our greatest difficulties in any dispute is to recognize or, even more difficult, to accept that the certitude we feel about our own rightness and goodness is equaled by the certitude of the opposing individual or group about their rightness and goodness. If tension is to be reduced, it is this pattern that must somehow be dissolved.' (1978: 123)

Identifying learning

Encouraging supervisees to recognise their learning in relation to specific pieces of work or recognising what they have achieved is part of the ongoing process of supervision. A supervisor may create opportunities for reflection on specific areas of practice or draw out learning from issues arising. A formal or thorough review at certain key points can assist recognition of the journey taken and help to identify learning from the process. Acknowledgement of what has been achieved could include going back to the original agreement, contract or ground rules and reviewing progress. Carrying out regular evaluation of professional development assists the identification of learning and progression.

Student supervision has a clear educative and assessment function. Learning outcomes are generally specified and set by the training and/or professional agency. Part of each supervision session could focus on these outcomes and both supervisees and the supervisor can identify areas of development which are relevant to youth work practice. The evaluation process at the end of a time-specified placement could also focus on what a student has learned and how certain competencies or learning outcomes have been addressed. Additional and related learning outside of the specified outcomes can highlight current issues based on actual practice and enhance ongoing reflective practice.

Reviewing arrangements

A supervisor should encourage supervisees to provide feedback about supervisory practice and address the relevant issues. Reviewing whether a supervisory arrangement has been useful and whether the sessions should continue, change or end (see Box 12.16 for some suggestions). Regularly scheduled communication about the arrangements can include formative evaluation to ensure that supervision continues to meet supervisees' needs. Such reviews can also highlight whether issues of power are negatively affecting the supervision. Summative evaluation at the end of an arrangement could include more formal evaluation forms or appraisals of progress if necessary.

Box 12.16: Ways to evaluate supervision

A supervisor could:
- ask how the supervisee is feeling about the supervision at the end of each session
- check whether the suggestions, information and advice discussed during supervision have been followed up
- notice whether the work plans are have been implemented

Box 12.16 - *Cont'd*

- designate a time for review of the sessions and the supervision records, such as the middle and/or end of a work placement or after the completion of a specific piece of work or project
- invite the supervisee to comment on whether the supervision has covered relevant issues of concern
- use open questions to find out whether the sessions are meeting the supervisee's needs
- review the arrangements for suitability to both parties at regular intervals
- provide opportunities for supervisees to indicate their level of satisfaction with the approach to supervision being used
- review the agenda points that supervisees bring to the session to assess whether they have been fully addressed.

A supervisee could reflect on whether:
- the timing and venue for sessions were convenient
- sessions were uninterrupted
- copies of supervision records were provided, accurate or useful
- enough information was provided
- confidentiality was discussed
- issues could be raised and discussed
- sufficient support was felt
- sufficient challenge or stretch was felt
- plans made in supervision were implemented and practicable
- feedback about the sessions was invited and received well.

Allowing the relationship to end

Either party may wish to end a supervisory relationship. A decision to end a supervisory arrangement may arise due to external changes or readiness for a change expressed during a discussion and review of the relationship. A supervisee may require a supervisor with a different perspective or understanding of issues or who is accessible at different times or venues. The type of supervision, the level of agreement or understanding between the supervisor and supervisee and any of the issues arising may affect whether such changes are possible. Negotiating a change within a large organisation might be agreed and ending an arrangement with an external supervisor is usually straightforward.

A supervisor may end a supervisory relationship because the supervision is not proving to be effective or feasible. As a supervisor is responsible for supervisees' professional approach to practice, continuing supervision may not be possible with a supervisee who refuses to address concerns raised. If a range of approaches have been attempted and a supervisee remains unresponsive, a supervisor may need to end the arrangement. In internal, particularly managerial supervision arrangements, additional procedures may be required, such as disciplinary procedures. Supervisors of students usually need to alert the training agency about such issues.

The ending of a supervisory relationship generally includes an exit strategy, particularly when the ending is expected, agreed and/or otherwise accepted. Highlighting the positive aspects of the supervision, the learning that has been achieved on both sides and options for future supervision is an important aspect of an exit strategy. Supervisees should be clear about ways to move forward and be provided with contacts and methods to promote their continued professional development.

Essential skills for using supervision

- Understanding the aims of supervision
- Having a planned approach to supervision
- Understanding and clarifying the type of supervision required
- Locating self
- Identifying boundaries
- Keeping appropriate records
- Structuring the sessions
- Listening and responding
- Providing feedback
- Reviewing the supervisee's practice
- Evaluating youth work practice
- Addressing professional development and practice needs arising
- Planning ways forward
- Reviewing what has been achieved
- Identifying learning
- Reviewing arrangements
- Allowing the relationship to end

Further reading about using supervision

Brown and Bourne (1996); Carroll and Holloway (1999); Carroll and Tholstrop (2001); Hawkins and Shohet (1989); Kadushin (1992); Pritchard (1995).

Sources and suggestions for further reading

Aire Cadet organisation website: http://www.aircadets.org/.

Arnold, J. *et al.* (1981) *The Management of Detached Work: How and Why*, Leicester: National Association of Youth Clubs.

Arnstein, S. R. 'A (1969) Ladder of citizen participation,' *Journal of the American Institute of Planners*, 35; 4: 216–224.

Baker, A. C., Jensen, P. J. and Kolb, D. A. (2005) 'Conversation as experiential learning' in *Management Learning*, Vol. 36, No.4. London: Sage Publications, 411–427.

Banks, S. (ed) (1999) *Ethical Issues in Youth Work*, London: Routledge.

Banks, S. (2006) *Ethics and Values in Social Work* (3rd ed). Basingstoke: Palgrave Macmillan.

Belenky, M. *et al.* (1986) *Women's Ways of Knowing: The Development of Self. Voice and Mind*, New York: Basic Books.

Bell, J. (1999) *Doing Your Research Project: A Guide for First-time Researchers in Education and Social Science* (3rd ed). Maidenhead: Open University Press.

Benetello, D. (1996) *Invisible Women: Detached Youth Work with Girls and Young Women*. Leicester: Youth Work Press.

Best, J. (2000) "To Whom is Accreditation Acceptable as a Qualification in Community Work?" (unpublished PhD) Youth and Community Studies, Manchester Metropolitan University.

Boreham, N. C. (1988) 'Models of diagnosis and their implications for adult professional education', *Studies in the Higher Education of Adults*, 20; 2: 95–108.

Brown, A. and Bourne, A. (1996) *The Social Work Supervisor*, Buckingham, Milton Keynes: Oxford University Press.

Burton, P. (1993) *Community Profiling: A Guide to Identifying Local Needs*, Bristol: SAUS Publications.

Butler, R. J. (1990) *Managing Voluntary and Non-profit Organisations: Strategy and Structure*, London: Routledge.

Carroll, M. and Holloway, E. (eds) (1999) *Counselling Supervision in Context*. London: Sage Publications Ltd.

Carroll, M. and Tholstrop, M. (2001) *Integrative Approaches to Supervision*. London: Jessica Kingsley.

Cleaver, E. (1969) *Eldridge Cleaver: Post Prison Writings and Speeches*, New York: Random House/Ramparts.

Conger, J. A. *et al.* (2007) *The Practice of Leadership: Developing the Next Generation of Leaders*, San Francisco: Jossey-Bass Inc.

Crimmens, D. *et al.* (2004) 'The role of street-based youth work in linking socially excluded young people into education, training and work', Joseph Rowntree Foundation Ref. 654, June 2004, National Youth Agency.

Davies, B. (2005) 'Youth Work: A Manifesto for Our Times', *Youth & Policy: A Special Feature, No 88,* Leicester: The National Youth Agency.

Development Education Association website, London, UK: http://www.dea.org.uk/

Driskell, D. (2002) *Creating Better Cities with Children and Youth: A Manual for Participation,* London: Earthscan.

Drucker, P. F. (1990) *Managing the Non-Profit Organization, Practices and Principles,* London: Butterworth-Heinemann.

Egan, G. (1986) *A Systematic Approach to Effective Helping,* 3rd edn, Belmont, CA: Brooks/Cole, Wadsworth.

Fairhurst, G. T. and Sarr, R. A. (1996) *The Art of Framing: Managing the Language of Leadership,* San Francisco, CA: Jossy-Bass Inc.

Faulkner, A., Roberts-DeGennaro, M. and Weil, M. (eds) (1994) *Diversity and Development in Community Practice,* New York: Haworth Press.

Federation of Community Development Learning website, Sheffield: http://www.fcdl.org.uk/

Federation of Detached Youth Workers Website: http://www.detachedyouth work.info

FreeChild Project website: http://www.freechild.org/index.htm

Freire, P. (1972) *Pedagogy of the Oppressed,* (translated from the Portuguese ms. by Myra Bergman Ramos), New York: Herder and Herder.

Gandhi, M. (1931) 'Young India, Bombay, India' in Prabhu, R.K. and Rao, U.R. (eds), *The Mind of Mahatma Gandhi: Encyclopedia of Gandhi's Thoughts.* Ahmedabad, India: Navjeevan Trust, http://www.mkgandhi.org/main.htm

Gann, N. (1996) *Managing Change in Voluntary Organisations: A Guide to Practice,* Buckingham: Open University Press.

Goldstein, J. H. (ed) (1994) *Toys, Play, and Child Development,* Cambridge: Cambridge University Press.

Grieg, A. and Taylor, J. (1999) *Doing Research with Children,* London: Sage.

Hammond, S. A. (1998) *The Thin Book of Appreciative Inquiry* (2nd ed.), Bond, Oregon: Thin Book Publishing Co.

Handy, C. (1995) *Understanding Organisations,* Penguin: London.

Hart, R. (1992) *Children's Participation: The Theory and Practice of Involving Young Citizens in Community Development and Environmental Care,* London: Earthscan Publications Ltd.

Hawkins, P. and Shohet, R. (1989) *Supervision in the Helping Professions,* Buckingham Open University Press.

Hawtin, M. *et al.* (1994) *Community Profiling: Auditing Social Needs,* Buckingham: Open University Press.

Hill, R. J. (2007) *Challenging Homophobia and Heterosexism: Lesbian, Gay, Bisexual, Transgender and Queer Issues,* New Directions for Adult and Continuing Education No 112: Winter 2006, Jossey-Bass.

Holdsworth, P. (2002) *DIY Community Street Audit Pack,* London: Living Streets.

Holt, J. (1983) *How Children Learn* (revised edn), London: Penguin.

Hooks, B. (1996) *Killing Rage, Ending Racism,* London: Penguin.

Hope, A. and Timmel, S. (1995) *Training for Transformation: Handbook for Community Workers,* Gweru, Zimbabwe: Mambo Press.

Hunter, D. *et al.* (1995) *How to Create Group Synergy: The Art of Facilitation,* Cambridge, MA: Da Capo Books.

Informal Education website: London: http://www.infed.org.uk/

Joseph, J. *et al.* (2002) *Towards Global Democracy: An Exploration of Black Perspectives in Global Youth Work,* London: Development Education Association.

Kadushin, A. (1992) *Supervision in Social Work,* New York: Columbia University Press.

Kolb, D. A. and Fry, R. (1975) 'Toward an applied theory of experiential learning' in Cooper, C. L. (ed.) *Theories of Group Process,* London: John Wiley, 27–56.

Lee (2003) *Plato: The Republic* (revised edn), London: Penguin Books.

Le Fevre, D. N. (2007) *The Spirit of Play: Cooperative Games for All Ages, Sizes and Abilities.* Findhorn, Scotland: Findhorn Press.

Lewin, K. (1946) Action research and minority problems (original chapter), now in Lewin, K. (1997) *Resolving Social Conflicts and Field Theory in Social Science.* Washington, DC, US: American Psychological Association, vol. 422: 143–152.

Luft, J. (1982) 'The Johari Window: A Graphic Model of Awareness in Interpersonal Relations,' NTL Reading Book for Human Relations Training, NTL Institute.

MacBeth, N. and Fine, N. (1995) *Playing With Fire: Creative Conflict Resolution for Young Adults,* British Columbia, Canada: New Society Publishers.

Macpherson of Cluny, Sir W. (1999) *The Stephen Lawrence Inquiry. Report of an Inquiry.* HMSO.

Maslow, A. H. (1943) 'A theory of human motivation' in *Psychological Review,* American Psychological Association, 50: 370–396, Accessed via OVID.

Max-Neef, M. A. (1991) *Human Scale Development: Conception, Application and Further Reflections.* New York: Apex Press.

McGregor, D. (1960) *The Human Side of Enterprise.* London: McGraw Hill.

Mullaly, R. P. (2002) *Challenging Oppression: A Critical Social Work Approach.* Ontario: Oxford University Press.

Mullender, A. and Ward, D. (1991) *Self-directed Group Work: Users Take Action for Empowerment,* London: Whiting & Birch.

National Youth Agency, Leicester, website: http://www.nya.org.uk/

National Youth Agency (2004) *Ethical Conduct in Youth Work: A Statement of Values and Principles from the National Youth Agency,* Leicester: National Youth Agency, Summer 2000 reprinted December 2004.

NCVYS (2007) *Keeping it Safe: A Young Person-Centred Approach to Safety and Child Protection* (2nd ed). London: National Council for Voluntary Youth Services. (1986)

Neibuhr, R. (1987) *The Essential Reinhold Niebuhr: Selected Essays and Addresses,* New Haven: Yale University Press.

Nyerere, J. K. (1976) 'Declaration of *Dar es Salaam*: Liberated man – the purpose of development' in Hall, B.L. and Kidd, J.R. (eds) (1978) *Adult Education: A Design for Action,* Oxford: Pergamon.

Oliver, M. (1996) *Understanding Disability: From Theory to Practice*, Basingstoke: Macmillan.

PAULO NTO (2002) *National Occupational Standards for Youth Work*, January 2002, http://www.lifelonglearninguk.org/

Poole, M.S. (1981) 'Decision development in small groups: A comparison of two models', *Communication Monographs*, 48: 1–24.

Popular Education for Environmental Action website: http://webpub.allegheny. edu/dept/envisci/

Pringle, M. K. (1986) *The Needs of Children*, (3rd ed). London: Routledge.

Pritchard, J. (ed) (1995) *Good Practice in Supervision*, London: Jessica Kingsley.

Pruitt, B. and Thomas, P. (2007) *Democratic Dialogue: A Handbook for Practitioners*, International IDEA, United Nations Development Programme, Organization of American States and Canadian International Development Agency.

Putnam, R. D. (1995) 'Bowling alone: America's declining social capital', *Journal of Democacy* 6; 1: 65–78.

Rogers, C. R. (1969) *Freedom to Learn*, Columbus OH: Charles E. Merrill Publishing Co.

Rogers, C. R. (1978) *Carl Rogers on Personal Power: Inner Strength and Its Revolutionary Impact*, London: Constable and Company Ltd.

Rogers, C. R. and Farson, R. E. (1987) 'Active Listening', Ferguson, S.D. and Ferguson, S. (eds), *Organizational Communication* (2nd ed). New Brunswick, NJ: Transaction Publishers.

Sapin, K. and Watter G. (1990) *Learning From Each Other: A Handbook for Participative Learning and Community Work Learning Programmes*. Manchester: The William Temple Foundation.

Sapin, K. (ed) (1998) 'Supervision of Practice and Professional Development – Keeping Track of Community and Youth Work – 1', Community Work Unit, University of Manchester.

Sapin, K., ed. (2005) A Black Perspective in Community and Youth Work 2005: A Community Work Unit Conference report, University of Manchester.

Scarman, L. G., Baron (1981) 'The Brixton disorders 10–12 April 1981: report of an inquiry by the Rt. Hon. the Lord Scarman; presented to Parliament by the Secretary of State for the Home Department'. London: HMSO. Sea Cadets, The, Website http://seacadets.ms-sc.org/Home

Seeds for Change website: http://seedsforchange.org.uk

Senge, P. M. (1990) *The Fifth Discipline: The Art and Practice of the Learning Organization*, London: Doubleday.

Shier, H. (2001) 'Pathways to participation: Openings, opportunities and obligations, in line with article 12.1 of the United Nations Convention on the Rights of the Child' in *Children & Society*, Vol. 15, No 2. John Wiley & Sons.

Smith, M. (1988) *Developing Youth Work: Informal Education, Mutual Aid and Popular Practice*, Milton Keynes: Open University Press (also available as e-text).

Smith, M. K. (1994) *Local Education: Community, Conversation, Praxis*, Buckingham: Open University Press.

Street Games, Street Talk website: http://www.myrecollection.com/christianog/games.html

Thompson, N. (1993) *Anti-discriminatory Practice* (4th edn in 2006). Practical Social Work Series, Basingstoke: Palgrave Macmillan.

Thompson, N. (2006) *People Problems*, Basingstoke: Palgrave Macmillan.

Thorpe, M. *et al.* (1993) *Culture and Processes of Adult Learning*, London: Routledge/Open University Press.

Tuckman, B. W. (1965) 'Developmental sequence in small groups', *Psychological Bulletin*, 63: 384–399.

Unks, G. (ed) (1995) *The Gay Teen: Educational Practice and Theory for Lesbian, Gay and Bisexual Adolescents*, New York: Routledge.

US Scouting Service Project website: http://usscouts.org/games.asp

Wates, N. (1999) *The Community Planning Handbook: How People Can Shape their Cities, Towns and Villages in any Part of the World*. London: Earthscan.

Weil, M. (ed) (2005) *The Handbook of Community Practice*, Thousand Oaks, CA: Sage Publications.

Wylie, T. (2004) *Costing Street-Based Youth Work*, NewYork: Joseph Rowntree Foundation.

Youth Work Central website, Boston, MA: http://www.youthworkcentral.org/

Youth work definitions

This section suggests some definitions of terms in relation to their application to youth work practice. Cross references appear in italics.

Ableism – A belief in the superiority of individuals who conform to an assumed physical or mental norm and discrimination against individuals with different learning, mental or physical abilities, appearance, impairment or illness. Includes personal or individual *prejudice* as well as *societal, institutional* and internalised *oppression* (see also a *social model of disability*).

Accountability – Communicating to *stakeholders* about work, financial records or plans so that they can be involved in decisions.

Activist – An unpaid individual whose own perspective or beliefs provide the motivation to improve provision or services for young people and is usually unconstrained or governed by external standards.

Advocate – Arguing for something or supporting a cause that usually does not directly affect oneself; interceding or speaking up for an individual or group – often defensively.

Ageism – Generalised and negative assumptions about individuals who appear to be of a specific age group that can lead to the denial of equality of opportunity or treatment. Often directed at younger or older people with derogatory language or references to lack of abilities to understand or make their own decisions.

Aims – Definitions of purpose, direction or goals – of an organisation, group or project – that often identify the changes that need be made.

Animator or animateur – An individual whose goal is to transform individuals and groups through their participation in social, educational and creative activities and projects that enhance self-expression.

Anti-oppressive practice – Addressing or countering the effects of *oppression* through proactive work that raises awareness of *prejudice*, illuminates different experiences and challenges discriminatory practice or attitudes.

Appreciative enquiry – A participative approach to research and management that explores possibilities for change by first establishing what the individuals concerned consider to be the strengths of their situations.

Area youth worker – Works with young people within a designated geographic area, which may be defined by political, natural or built boundaries and may be larger than a particular neighbourhood.

Audit – A check or review to make sure that standards are being met and that system controls are in place, such as financial records, health and safety systems, organisational policies. A social audit checks and reports on an organisation's impact on society and ethical behaviour.

Autonomy – Self-government, independence and the capacity to make and act on decisions. Young people develop their capacity to make decisions through their involvement in self-governing organisations.

Black perspective – A recognition of the collective capacity of black people to define, develop and advance their own political, economic, social, cultural and educational interests. (Best, as quoted in Sapin, 2005) Youth work practice with a black perspective promotes an understanding of black peoples' cultures and histories as well as challenging the social constructs of 'race' and racism.

Budget – A plan outlining how resources will be obtained (the income) and used (the expenditure) during a period, usually including headings for staffing, equipment and running costs.

Capital – Cash and resources, including the assets of an organisation, such as a building, computers, furniture, equipment, vehicles. Capital expenditure is usually a separate budget heading from running costs or staffing.

Caste – A hereditary system that dictates social position and status. See also class.

Catchment area – An organisation's geographical target area, which may define boundaries for practice and/or address eligibility for membership or participation in a project.

Centre-based youth work – Carried out within a venue or facility that may be purpose-built for young people's activities or owned and used by other groups and purposes, such as a church, sports centre or school.

Challenge – Raising awareness of or addressing unfair, discriminatory or unprofessional *practice*, attitudes or information, including questions to stimulate thinking; pointing out contradictory facts; bringing attention to motivation or procedures; requesting or demanding an explanation, justification or proof.

Class and classism – A social construct that distinguishes economic and social status and is often used as an indicator of an individual's position, status or power in society. Classism is based on prejudiced assumptions about individuals and groups from specific classes that can lead to discrimination and denial of equality of opportunity and access to resources. Related to *caste*, inheritance and heritage through family trees or ancestry.

Closed questions – Can be answered with specific and generally limited responses, – such as 'yes/no', a number or a multiple-choice list, useful in *quantitative research* (see also *open questions*).

Codes of practice – The requirements and expectations of workers and members outlined in relation to organisational standards and how they can be achieved. Issues such as equality, ethics, conflicts of interest, duty of care, respect for young people, *accountability* and *confidentiality,* are addressed and detailed in *policies* and *procedures*, such as those related to fees, contracts, quality assurance or evaluation.

Community work – Work with individuals and groups in a community to bring them together for collective activities and action in relation to issues that affect them.

Community development work – Work as a *facilitator* and *enabler* to improve the capacity of a community to address their physical, economic, political, educational and social needs.

Confidentiality – Agreement on the limited use and protection of information, particularly when related to individuals' personal details, history or circumstances.

Consensus – A widely held understanding of a concept or general agreement within a group or community that could be based on an accurate analysis or a false premise. A full consensus can be reached when participants negotiate and agree a decision. Genuine consensus depends on access to and understanding of accurate evidence, a wide exploration of views and unanimous and voluntary compliance.

Cultural competence – The confidence to interact with the individuals and organisations from another culture or identity that may be enhanced by relevant knowledge, understanding and practice.

Data – Verifiable information collected using research methodology, including statistics, opinions and ideas.

Deficit model – The perception of a community, group or individual as inadequate, lacking something or failing to meet an often ill-defined goal, which assigns blame and responsibility to them rather than examining the circumstances or the 'service' they receive.

Depreciation – A figure or percentage of purchase price used in budgets to indicate the level at which an item decreases in value over time. Enables financial resources to be allocated for replacement of a larger piece of equipment or vehicle when necessary.

Detached youth work – Going out into a community to make contact and build relationships for informal education, signposting and enjoyable activities with young people in their own 'space'. See also *street-based youth work*.

Detached young people – Are not connected to or supported by family, school, employment or other social institutions and services.

Discrimination – Different and unequal treatment of individuals, bodies or groups because of perceived differences.

Dissemination – Distribution and publicity about research *findings* or information.

Diversity – Recognition of the range of different individuals, ethnic groups, groups of interest and identities that supports their rights to *equal opportunities*.

Emancipator – Works with individuals to set them free from oppression, slavery, restricted aspirations or limited opportunities.

Empower – To promote opportunities for other to develop their skills and confidence or self-esteem, which enables them to exercise their power to make decisions or take actions.

Enabler – Provides the resources and opportunities to make something possible or feasible. Applied positively to the role of a community or youth worker or negatively to someone assisting an abuser.

Equal opportunities – Access to basic social justice, employment and services, such as health, education, housing, without negatively discrimination.

Evaluation – Reviewing records to determine the value, success, quality, importance, extent or condition of a group or project, particularly in relation to the original aims, objectives and targets. Can be external or internal, ongoing (formative) or at the end (summative).

Evidence-based practice – Using methods or procedures that have been monitored through research and/or *evaluation* and been found to be successful or effective.

Exclusion – Not being permitted or being able to participate fully so that access to social or economic opportunities that are available to others, such as education, housing, employment, family life, the arts or sports, is denied. Some young people may 'self exclude'. Poverty, prejudice or lack of information, welcome or confidence may prevent participation. Schools may deny young people the opportunity to attend school on a temporary or permanent period for disciplinary reasons. Sometimes referred to as social exclusion. See also *financial exclusion*.

Exit strategy – A planned withdrawal from a commitment that keeps those concerned informed about any resulting changes. For example, when a worker is unable to continue with a particular group of young people or to provide supervision for a colleague, those concerned are informed about any alternative arrangements.

Face-to-face work – Working directly with young people or other members of the community; usually distinguished from responsibilities for management in job descriptions.

Facilitator – Assists a group to find their own ways of addressing tasks or finding solutions to problems by sharing observations and questioning to develop the processes of participation, communication and decision-making.

Feminist – An advocate of political, economic and social equality for women and girls.

Financial exclusion – A lack of access to or ownership of certain financial mechanisms or products, such as pensions, life assurance and savings accounts, which can disadvantage individuals and/or present barriers to full participation in society.

Findings – Information or *data* that is collected and analysed from *primary* and *secondary* sources to identify significant trends or patterns.

Funder – Agencies and individuals that provide resources, particularly financial support, such as national or local governments, charities, community associations or any combination of these.

Goals – The planned changes that an organisation or group wants to make or address, which can be identified clearly as solutions to problems or specific positive developments. (See also *targets*).

Grievance procedures – The steps undertaken by an employee making a complaint against unfair or unreasonable treatment.

Grounded knowledge – Knowledge that is gained from firsthand experience of living or working in an area that, if clearly defined and acknowledged, can provide a valuable context and perspective for practice. See also *location of self*.

Heterosexism – Discrimination, prejudice against or oppression of lesbian, gay, bi-sexual and transgendered people based on assumptions that heterosexuality is the norm and other identities are inferior, an attitude also referred to as heteronormativity.

Hypothesis – A belief or understanding that is to be tested through research.

Idealism – A belief in and pursuit of perfection, particularly in relation to standards and principles (see *pragmatism* as a contrast).

Impact – Long-term and sustainable changes resulting from activities whether positive or negative (see also *outcomes*).

Inclusion – Work to involve diverse individuals and groups in activities and services, particularly those who are usually excluded or not involved.

Induction – Procedures that introduce a new member, volunteer or employee into the resources, policies, procedures and practice of a group or organisation to enable full and safe participation.

Informal educator – Passes on information and skills so that others develop and learn to make positive and informed choices in a responsive rather than curriculum-based approach.

Informed consent – Steps taken to ensure that participants have sufficient information to make a decision about whether they wish to be involved, particularly when participants are young or potentially vulnerable and when issues of confidentiality are at stake, for example, through publicity or research reports.

Institutional oppression – Discrimination and oppression within specific institutions or organisations that *'can thrive in a tightly knit community, so that there can be a collective failure to detect and to outlaw ...'* (MacPherson, 1999: 6.17)

Intervention – A proactive activity, piece of work or plan of action.

Issue-based practice – When the focus of an activity or project is on political or social issues such as *sexism, racism, hetero-sexism, ableism, ageism, class* and poverty (see also *anti-oppressive practice*) or particular areas of concern such as crime, drugs, gangs, sexual health, educational achievement, social relationships, homelessness, the environment.

Literature search – A thorough and often structured examination of information that has already been compiled or written about a topic (see also *secondary sources*).

Location of self – Identification, analysis and evaluation of one's skills, knowledge, attitudes and values as well as their origins, particularly in relation to experience and identity. Often related to the effects of identity on power as well as practice, perspective and understanding.

Marginalised – A group or individual excluded from or ignored by mainstream services. Occurs through *oppression* and *discrimination*.

Misconduct – Inappropriate actions by an employee or volunteer that may warrant a verbal or written warning with a clear explanation of what improvement is needed. Gross misconduct is more serious and can lead to dismissal.

Mission statement – Overall aim(s) condensed into a sentence or paragraph about what an organisation plans to achieve and why. More concrete, 'action-oriented' and clearly related to outcomes than a *vision* statement.

Monitoring – Recording and checking change and development using particular indicators at regular intervals to measure progress, particularly in relation to the group's established *aims, objectives* and *targets*.

Neighbourhood work – *Community work* with residents within a small locality to bring them together to address relevant issues and develop community relationships and *social capital*.

Networking – Developing and establishing links and relationships with individuals and organisations generally through informal exchanges of information. Networks can become forums or partnerships for regular information exchange or sharing of resources.

Objectives – Demonstrate how the *aims* are going to be reached through outlining a programme or set of activities that are required.

Open questions – Prompts used in *qualitative research* to elicit more unique, complex and/or potentially lengthy responses than *closed questions*.

Oppression – Cruel and/or unfair treatment backed up by societal or cultural forces; denial of life, human rights and/or equal opportunities. Examples include *racism, sexism, heterosexism, ageism, class or caste systems, ableism*. Oppression can also be internalised to affect an individual's self-perception and self-esteem. See also *institutional* and *societal oppression*.

Organisational culture – *Policies* and ways of working established through individual and organisational *practice*, such as *institutional oppression* in relation to access, flexibility and discrimination; generally incorporating well-established habits that may include unwritten *procedures* that are difficult to *challenge* or change.

Outcomes – Planned or unexpected changes, benefits and results arising from a group or project. Hard outcomes are measurable and quantifiable, such as specific outputs or targets easily identified through counting. Soft outcomes are qualitative benefits that may be difficult to measure or count. Unplanned outcomes not anticipated in the original plan possibly occur because of unusual circumstances or individuals.

Outreach work – Publicity and recruitment or activities that encourage young people to join activities in mainstream provision centres or facilities. Sometimes refers to external, or satellite or extension programmes.

Overheads – The ongoing expenditure required to maintain an organisation such as core staff, rent/mortgage.

Participation – Taking an active part, for example, in issues and decisions that affect one's life. Young people take an active part in developing youth work activities and organisations.

Participative – Describes activities and approaches that involve participants rather than a passive audience.

Partnership – A formal or informal arrangement and agreement between organisations, groups or individuals to share responsibility for specific work, activities or resources.

Policy – Definitions of boundaries, roles, relationships and responsibilities that are guided by an organisation's *principles* and *values* and provide a basis for consistent decision-making and resource allocation. Generally contained within written documents, but may be understood or part of *organisational culture* (see also *procedures* and *Codes of practice*).

Power – The opportunity and ability to control one's own and others' lives.

Practice – Work that is carried out based on the values and principles of a profession. What a worker or organisation actually does as opposed to their policies or theoretical approach.

Pragmatism – A way of thinking or dealing with decisions or issues, which generally means prioritising the results of an action. *Outcomes* and outputs may be seen as more important than *principles*, *values* or process.

Praxis – Action based on reflection: an examination and analysis of reality in order to understand what is going on and to identify practical ways forward that can transform that reality. (Freire, 1972)

Prejudice – A fixed like or dislike based on ignorance or without any reason that can limit expectations, aspirations and attainment of self-determination, employment, responsibilities, understanding and learning of self and others. See also *oppression*.

Primary sources – Information gathered directly from individuals, groups, observation rather than from others' records or analyse (see also *secondary sources*).

Principles – The *values* and fundamental and often generalised truths or assumptions on which a profession or organisation is based, which may be written down or simply understood. Youth work principles include having respect for young people, establishing voluntary participation, being accountable, maintaining confidentiality and involvement in continuous professional development.

Procedures – Agreed or imposed steps to be followed in particular circumstances that are ment to ensure efficiency, safety, equity or other quality assurance concerns and that implement or maintain organisational policy. Often designed to protect an organisation from litigation through systematic responses and prescribed time-scales for actions (see also Codes of practice).

Qualitative research – Attempts to understand and gain insights which may not be easily measured, such as how individuals relate to each other or their views on issues related in their own words. Typical qualitative methods include interviews, case studies, oral histories or self-descriptions.

Quantitative research – Collecting information that can be counted, quantified or measured, such as statistics. Typical methods include closed questions, such as 'yes/no' questionnaires, selection from options, or using previously defined categories during observations.

Quality assurance – Providing evidence of good practice and effective *procedures* for maintaining good quality of service or organisation, usually through documentation regarding the systems in place, such as *policies* and *codes of practice*.

'Race' – Grouping people according to arbitrary visual physical characteristics or cultural differences, despite the 'human race' referring to the whole of humanity. Often associated with assigning values, such as inferiority or superiority, and prejudices towards particular 'race' categories. See *racism*.

Racism – *Discrimination* on the basis of *'race'* or skin colour, which generally benefits people perceived as 'white'. Racism includes personal or individual *prejudice* as well as institutional and societal *oppression*. 'Unwitting racism' (Scarman, 1981) is based on *prejudice*, ignorance, thoughtlessness and racist *stereotyping*.

Revenue – Income generated by activities, such as fees, sales, sponsorship. See also *capital*.

Risky behaviour – Activities that may cause or are perceived to cause harm to health, self or others, such as drinking, smoking, fighting, carrying out sexual or criminal activity, driving too fast, climbing too high or riding on top of trains. Sometimes also minor infractions of the law, such as graffiti.

Running costs – Expenditure on items that will be used rather than kept, such as insurance, postage, stationery, rent, heat and electricity. Usually a separate budget heading from *capital* expenditure or staffing.

Secondary sources – Previously collected and usually already analysed information found in books, articles or websites or from individuals who do not have direct experience (see also *primary sources*).

Sessional work – Part-time employment for specific weekly time schedules, usually to carry out face-to-face sessions with young people.

Sexism – Discrimination on the basis of gender, which generally, although not exclusively, benefits men. Includes personal or individual prejudice as well as *societal, institutional* and *internalised oppression*.

Sign-posting – Providing contact information about alternative individuals, services or organisations that may be able to address specific needs or interests, such as names, postal/e-mail addresses and/or telephone numbers.

Social capital – The benefits of social interactions and informal organisations that develop a sense of trust and community (see Putnam, 1995, for example).

Social model of disability – A definition of *ableism* that recognises that fear, ignorance and prejudice, barriers and discriminatory practices disable people rather than impairments; and that equality for disabled people lies in restructuring society rather than the disabled person.

Socialisation – Training individuals to function within society and to fit in with what is considered to be normal social behaviour (social norms).

Societal oppression – *Discrimination* and *oppression* sanctioned and upheld by society, through attitudes and practices within, for example, the media, the education system, religions. See also *institutional oppression*.

Stakeholder – An individual or group with a direct interest in a project or who is directly affected by an issue.

Statutory organisation or service – Legally required by a government, for example, a legal statute requiring educational services to be provided. Non-statutory organisations are charities or privately run organisations that may yet receive state support.

Stereotype – A commonly held, limited and standard idea or image of a group, or of individuals who are perceived to be a group.

Strategy – A longer-term plan to reach an *aim* that includes more detail than a *vision* or *mission* statement, more specific *objectives* and a time-scale.

Street-based youth work – The development of youth work activities out-of-doors rather than indoors, which is often literally on the streets or pavements/sidewalks. See also *detached youth work*.

Structured interview – Using scripted questions during research. A semi-structured interview follows a set of headings or subjects. An unstructured interview is carried out as an open discussion.

Supervision – Critical reflection on practice with an experienced practitioner to identify and address professional practice dilemmas and development needs, which may be combined with responsibilities for management or assessment.

Targets – The specific *goals* of an organisation with numbers attached used in planning, monitoring and evaluation, such as the number of planned outputs or outcomes.

Theoretical framework – A set of ideas and principles in a system, concept or theory that underpins practice.

Theory base – Well-tested or researched explanations of cause and effect that provide a foundation for good practice.

Transgendered – Individuals who have undergone surgery and hormone treatment in order to acquire the physical characteristics of the opposite gender or (sometimes) individuals whose identity does not conform to conventional notions or definitions of male and female gender, but combines or moves between these identities or traits (see also *transsexual*).

Third sector – The range of non-governmental organisations, including groups of young people and youth forums, which are non-profit, such as community organisations, charities, faith groups, social enterprises and cooperatives, which may receive partial funding from the public (first) and private profit-making (second) sectors.

Transsexual – Individuals who have changed or who want to change their gender due to feeling that they belong emotionally and psychologically to a different gender than the one whose physical characteristics they possess (see also *transgendered* as the terms are often used interchangeably).

Values – The fundamental beliefs that underpin a profession, such as the belief that an anti-oppressive, positive (warm, fun and welcoming), participative approach to work with young people is of benefit.

Vision – A group or organisation's verbal description of a future ideal often articulated in a brief statement that conveys their beliefs and *principles* in a clear and concise form.

Xenophobia – A prejudiced and intolerant view of other people, customs or cultures perceived as being from a different nation or nationality, which often leads to leading to fear or dislike associated with *racism*.

Young person-centred – Aims and practice that focus on young people's perspectives, interests and decisions.

Youth and community work – Work with different groups in communities to develop relevant activities and enable them to have a say in issues that affect them. See also *community work* and *youth work*.

Youth support worker – A *youth work* position for an individual with basic training and no managerial responsibilities for other staff.

Youth warden – An individual who works with young people in parks or recreational areas using the environment as a setting for activities – often interacting with the environment through specific 'green' or gardening projects.

Youth work – Working with young people to develop enjoyable activities that address their expressed needs and interests in a voluntary relationship based on mutual respect.

Index

Entries in bold indicate boxed diagrams/information